# Chinese Fashion

# Dress, Body, Culture

**Series Editor: Joanne B. Eicher,** *Regents' Professor, University of Minnesota*

Advisory Board

**Ruth Barnes,** *Ashmolean Museum, University of Oxford*
**James Hall,** *University of Illinois at Chicago*
**Ted Polhemus,** *Curator, "Street Style" Exhibition, Victoria and Albert Museum*
**Griselda Pollock,** *University of Leeds*
**Valerie Steele,** *The Museum at the Fashion Institute of Technology*
**Lou Taylor,** *University of Brighton*
**John Wright,** *University of Minnesota*

Books in this provocative series seek to articulate the connections between culture and dress, which is defined here in its broadest possible sense as any modification or supplement to the body. Interdisciplinary in approach, the series highlights the dialogue between identity and dress, cosmetics, coiffure, and body alternations as manifested in practices as varied as plastic surgery, tattooing, and ritual scarification. The series aims, in particular, to analyze the meaning of dress in relation to popular culture and gender issues and will include works grounded in anthropology, sociology, history, art history, literature, and folklore.

### ISSN: 1360–466X

Recently published titles in the series

**Brian J. McVeigh,** *Wearing Ideology: The Uniformity of Self-Presentation in Japan*

**Shaun Cole,** *Don We Now Our Gay Apparel: Gay Men's Dress in the Twentieth Century*

**Kate Ince,** *Orlan: Millennial Female*

**Nicola White and Ian Griffiths,** *The Fashion Business: Theory, Practice, Image*

**Ali Guy, Eileen Green and Maura Banim,** *Through the Wardrobe: Women's Relationships with their Clothes*

**Linda B. Arthur,** *Undressing Religion: Commitment and Conversion from a Cross-Cultural Perspective*

**William J. F. Keenan,** *Dressed to Impress: Looking the Part*

**Joanne Entwistle and Elizabeth Wilson,** *Body Dressing*

**Leigh Summers,** *Bound to Please: A History of the Victorian Corset*

**Paul Hodkinson,** *Goth: Identity, Style and Subculture*

**Michael Carter,** *Fashion Classics from Carlyle to Barthes*

Sandra Niessen, *Ann Marie Leshkowich and Carla Jones, Re-Orienting Fashion: The Globalization of Asian Dress*

Kim K. P. Johnson, *Susan J. Torntore and Joanne B. Eicher, Fashion Foundations: Early Writings on Fashion and Dress*

Helen Bradley Foster and Donald Clay Johnson, *Wedding Dress Across Cultures*

Eugenia Paulicelli, *Fashion under Fascism: Beyond the Black Shirt*

Charlotte Suthrell, *Unzipping Gender: Sex, Cross-Dressing and Culture*

Yuniya Kawamura, *The Japanese Revolution in Paris Fashion*

Ruth Barcan, *Nudity: A Cultural Anatomy*

Samantha Holland, *Alternative Femininities: Body, Age and Identity*

Alexandra Palmer and Hazel Clark, *Old Clothes, New Looks: Second Hand Fashion*

Yuniya Kawamura, *Fashion-ology: An Introduction to Fashion Studies*

Regina A. Root, *The Latin American Fashion Reader*

Linda Welters and Patricia A. Cunningham, *Twentieth-Century American Fashion*

Jennifer Craik, *Uniforms Exposed: From Conformity to Transgression*

Alison L. Goodrum, *The National Fabric: Fashion, Britishness, Globalization*

Annette Lynch and Mitchell D. Strauss, *Changing Fashion: A Critical Introduction to Trend Analysis and Meaning*

Marybeth C. Stalp, *Quilting: The Fabric of Everyday Life*

Jonathan S. Marion, *Ballroom: Culture and Costume in Competitive Dance*

Dunja Brill, *Goth Culture: Gender, Sexuality and Style*

Joanne Entwistle, *The Aesthetic Economy of Fashion: Markets and Value in Clothing and Modelling*

# Chinese Fashion
## From Mao to Now

**Juanjuan Wu**

*Oxford • New York*

First published in 2009 by
**Berg**
Editorial offices:
1st Floor, Angel Court, 81 St Clements Street, Oxford, OX4 1AW, UK
175 Fifth Avenue, New York, NY 10010, USA

Berg is the imprint of Oxford International Publishers Ltd.

**Library of Congress Cataloging-in-Publication Data**

Wu, Juanjuan.
Chinese fashion : from Mao to now / Juanjuan Wu.
p. cm.
Includes bibliographical references and index.
ISBN-13: 978-1-84520-779-3 (pbk.)
ISBN-10: 1-84520-779-3 (pbk.)
ISBN-13: 978-1-84520-778-6 (cloth)
ISBN-10: 1-84520-778-5 (cloth)
1. Clothing and dress—China—History.  2. Fashion—China—History.
3. China—Social life and customs.  I. Title.
GT1555.W79 2009
391.00951—dc22
2009020254

**British Library Cataloguing-in-Publication Data**

A catalogue record for this book is available from the British Library.

ISBN 978 184520 778 6 (Cloth)
ISBN 978 184520 779 3 (Paper)

Typeset by Apex CoVantage, LLC
Printed in Great Britain by the MPG Books Group, Bodmin and King's Lynn

**www.bergpublishers.com**

# Contents

# Acknowledgments

I would like to thank photographers Li Xiaobin and Yong He for permission to reproduce their images here. Sincere thanks also go to fashion designers Zhang Da, Wang Yiyang, Wangwei, Wu Haiyan, Liu Yang, and Wang Xinyuan for providing their design images, as well as to artist Shi Tou for her artwork. Thanks to Professor Bao Mingxin at Donghua University for his generous support and suggestions, as always. Also, thanks to Zhang Rong, Yanjiang Hou, and Wenjuan Guo for allowing me to use photographs from their personal collections, and to Angelica Cheung and Yang Shu for permitting me to reproduce images from *Vogue* and *Shanghai Style* magazines. Thanks also go to Zhang Qi and Chen Hua for helping me collect and sort materials.

I would like to thank Joanne B. Eicher for initiating the idea of a book about post-Mao Chinese fashion and for her support, understanding, and insight. I would also like to thank John Major for his invaluable comments and suggestions in the early stages of my writing. I also want to thank the staff of Berg Publishers and my first and current editors, Hannah Shakespeare and Julia Hall.

A special thank you to William Proulx, Katherine Angell, and my other former colleagues at the State University of New York College at Oneonta for their support. I would also like to thank Marilyn R. Delong, Karen L. LaBat, Gloria M. Williams, Becky L. Yust, and my other colleagues at the University of Minnesota for their help and support.

Finally, this book would not have been possible without the continued support of my family in China and the United States. Most of all, thanks to Todd.

# Preface

On November 15, 2008, an exhibition titled "Christian Dior and Chinese Artists" opened at the Ullens Center for Contemporary Art in Beijing. On display at the exhibit were original couture gowns by Dior and recent Dior creations by John Galliano, along with artistic interpretations of Dior by top Chinese artists. "It is always inspiring to see Dior through someone else's eyes," commented Galliano.[1] East and West have long served as mirrors, one for the other, in which both the Orient and the Occident could view their own images through someone else's eyes. The images these mirrors reflect are slightly distorted and exotic, refracted through another culture, yet still recognizable to the viewer. This process of seeing oneself remade, reconstructed, and redesigned in the eyes of another has produced new inspirations and new creations in art and fashion in both East and West. The hybrid designs that this interplay has given birth to—Chinese-inspired Western fashions and Western-inspired Chinese fashions—have stimulated interest in other cultures themselves, as the viewer peers more deeply into the looking glass that produces such a familiar yet strange reflection.

Long before Western fashion labels directly interacted with Chinese artists and designers in China, Western designers like John Galliano, Yves Saint Laurent, Valentino, and Christian Lacroix created their own chinoiserie collections. These collections enriched haute couture and high fashion, but to Chinese eyes these Chinese-inspired Western creations appeared just as exotic as they did to Western eyes: these fashions contained recognizable Chinese elements, but they were distorted, Westernized, and divorced from their original cultural meanings. But just as Chinese artists surely "distorted" Dior in their interpretations in Beijing in 2008, they nevertheless inspired those like Galliano who know the "real" Dior. Similarly, Chinese designers have been inspired and influenced by the interpretations and distortions of Western chinoiserie. While it is interesting to see how the East and West have mixed and melded their respective fashion elements into creations that are neither wholly Western nor Chinese, Chinese fashion itself—unfiltered through Western eyes—today largely remains a mystery to the West.

Chinese fashion of the post-Mao era in particular is a field left virtually untouched by Western scholars. As such, *Chinese Fashion from Mao to Now* is the first to focus on modern Chinese fashion from 1978 to 2008—and it is the first book in English on the subject written from a Chinese perspective. Born during the Cultural Revolution,

I grew up in post-Mao China, where as a child, teenager, and young adult, I adorned myself in the fashions described in the pages that follow. But not only did I come of age wearing post-Mao fashions, I also created, studied, critiqued, and wrote about them as a clothing design student in college, as a postgraduate in costume history and fashion criticism, and as a fashion journalist and editor in Shanghai in the 1990s.

The changes I have witnessed and experienced over the past three decades in China are beyond the measure of ordinary times. They can, perhaps, be measured only by the vast differences between those scintillatingly modern urban centers like Shanghai, Beijing, and Guangzhou and the multitude of agricultural villages and small towns that still constitute most of China. When I left my small hometown in China's heartland to pursue a fashion career in Shanghai, the largest and most modern city in China, the distance I traveled felt temporal more than spatial: it was as though I had entered a new century. I encountered this sensation again when I came to the United States to pursue my doctorate. The path of my "time travel" also mirrors the trajectory of post-Mao Chinese fashion itself: from the pure, simple, re-stricted, and limited to the hybrid, modern, free, and international.

The post-Mao era witnessed the birth of the Chinese market economy, the reju-venation of Chinese society, and the rebirth of Chinese fashion. Economic reform has turned China into the world's leading manufacturing powerhouse. And the fast-growing Chinese fashion industry is eagerly seeking ways to contribute not only its cheap labor, but also its innovative designs to the world of international fashion. At the same time, the world has discovered China as a significant market for interna-tional fashion and luxury goods. However, understanding modern China, its people as well as its fashions, continues to present challenges, not only for international traders and marketers but also for those in the fields of fashion studies, cultural stud-ies, sociology, and apparel and textiles.

The ways fashion has both mirrored and shaped social and cultural change in modern China is the main focus of this book. I have organized the book thematically with a nod to chronology, highlighting major fashion changes of the period and the significant influences of popular culture, fashion icons, gender issues, Chinese iden-tity, the development of the fashion industry, and imported brand names on modern Chinese fashion.

I was heartened to see that Antonia Finnane's *Changing Clothing in China: Fash-ion, History, Nation,* published in early 2008, covered some of these themes in her chapter on post-Mao fashion. While the structure of my book was set long before *Changing Clothing in China* was published, I am pleased to see that Finnane and I took a similar approach to fashion in the post-Mao period. However, my primary focus is the post-Mao period, while Finnane's book covers Chinese fashions stretch-ing back to the Ming Dynasty (1368 C.E.–1644 C.E.). With a scholarly eye, she inves-tigates Chinese fashions in their evolving political, economic, and cultural contexts from the imperial era to the present.

Valerie Steele and John Major's work, *China Chic: East Meets West,* was published as a supplement to an exhibition of the same name that was held at The Museum at FIT in early 1999. *China Chic* has a topical structure, with chapters highlighting significant dress forms in Chinese history, such as dragon robes and lotus shoes of the imperial era and the *cheongsam* and the Mao suit of the modern period. A fascinating feature of this title is the insight it provides into the interplay of Chinese and Western fashion.

Another book titled *China Chic,* by fashion designer Vivienne Tam, was also published in 2000. Tam's book panoramically surveys the *cheongsam,* weddings, Chinese opera, fashion, religion, food, gardens, interiors, and other aspects of Chinese culture. Tam reflects on her own life as a designer and relates charming personal stories and experiences, which makes her book unique but not scholarly in nature. Tam only briefly touches on the fashion of the People's Republic of China.

For my own book, I relied heavily on periodicals, magazines, newspapers, scholarly books in Chinese and English, and interviews I conducted with Chinese designers as the primary sources of my research. The magazines and newspapers of the day served as especially rich sources of the ideas, debates, styles, tastes, and issues of the post-Mao era. I took a narrative and interpretative approach in my writing, examining fashion in relation to pop culture, gender, national identity, mass media, luxury consumption, and Western influence. For a Western audience, *Chinese Fashion from Mao to Now* offers a Chinese insider's point of view; for a Chinese audience, presenting fashion as a cultural and symbolic product is a relatively new approach to the study of dress, since dress has been studied primarily as a physical object in the Chinese academy. In Chinese scholarship, the materials and construction of the physical dress form have often taken precedence over its social and cultural meanings. In this sense, this book itself is a hybrid of East and West much like post-Mao Chinese fashion itself, as *Chinese Fashion from Mao to Now* examines fashion with Western methodology through Chinese eyes.

I begin with a short overview of the dress regime of the Cultural Revolution during the 1960s and 1970s, followed by a discussion of the transitional period of the late 70s and early 80s, when great controversies surrounded the meaning and practice of dress after China opened up to Western influence. During this transitional period, increasing connections with the West were accompanied by the fear of Western "spiritual pollution." Moreover, dress manifested and contributed to the unsettling feelings about the vast changes that were transforming Chinese society and uncertainties many had regarding governmental policies. Nevertheless, Western fashions leaked into China and left their mark.

A discussion follows in Chapter 2 of the influence of the entertainment industry on fashion in the post-Mao era. Changes in Chinese pop culture accelerated the transition from a rigid uniformity in dress to the adoption of novel styles by the young, with dozens of new styles originating from popular TV dramas and movies. In this period, novel fashions sprang from the seedbed of pop culture and often seemed to have little connection to the Chinese apparel industry.

Chapter 3 charts the history of women's liberation and gender issues relating to dress in China throughout the twentieth century, from the end of the imperial era through the Republican period, the Cultural Revolution, and up through the sexual revolution of the late reform era. This historical background serves to frame the discussion of the progression from asexual to unisex styles that occurred in the 1970s to 1980s.

Chapter 4 provides a detailed discussion of the development of the fashion print media and the history of the fashion magazine and fashion newspaper in the post-Mao period, from the roots of the post-Mao fashion press in women's magazines in the late 70s to the entry of major Western fashion magazine titles in the 2000s.

Next, Chapter 5 covers the importation of fashion icons and the development of pop and rock music in China and their influence on fashion. The pop music industry supplied China's fashion-seeking youth with new "super idols" and fashion icons whose images were first engineered and popularized by the pop music industry. These new fashion icons of the 90s, mainly from Hong Kong and Taiwan, replaced the political leaders and propaganda models of previous eras as cultural ideals. The chapter concludes with a discussion of the Japan and Korea crazes of the late 1990s and early 2000s, in which Chinese youth subcultures began emulating the styles of Japanese and Korean pop icons and pop culture.

One theme running throughout the book is the anxiety over Chinese identity that has permeated modern Chinese history. Chapter 6 discusses these issues in-depth, with a focus on the search for a national sartorial symbol. An overview of the evolving form and meaning of the *qipao* is provided, and the chapter also surveys the various dress forms—including the *Zhongshan* suit or Mao suit, the Tang-style jacket, and the *hanfu* or Han-style dress—adopted by Chinese men in their search for a wearable identity symbol.

Chapter 7 outlines the evolution of the Chinese fashion industry through the lens of fashion education and the changing roles of designers and models, examining the various aspects and components of the modern Chinese fashion system. The chapter details the shift in the role of modern fashion designers from clothing technicians in state-owned garment factories and charts the rise of college-educated fashion designers who glamorized the image of the fashion designer as a charismatic, creative, independent, and well-paid figure. The chapter also includes a discussion of the evolution of the fashion education system in China and the rise and shifting role of the fashion model in the reform era.

Finally, Chapter 8 describes the return of luxury to China and the influx of Western fashion brands that made their way to the mainland from the late 1970s through the 2000s. The vigorous expansion of these luxury brands has had a great impact on Chinese consumption values, behaviors, and lifestyles, with the majority of the current generation embracing Western brand names. The consumption of Western brands has also contributed to the reemergence of a hierarchical, class-conscious social order.

The story of fashion in the post-Mao period is inextricably linked to the larger historical forces that have shaped, and are now shaping, modern China. An understanding of the forms and meanings of fashion and fashion change, whether evolutionary or revolutionary, is always historically situated. With this in mind, it would be impossible to form a culturally and historically appropriate interpretation of Chinese fashion in the post-Mao era without reference to the eras that preceded it. This is especially true of a period that follows such a traumatic, world-historical event like the Cultural Revolution. Thus, the Cultural Revolution is necessarily a recurring theme throughout this book.

*Juanjuan Wu*
*University of Minnesota*
*St. Paul, Minnesota*
*December 2008*

# A Note on Chinese in This Book

Romanized pinyin is used for Chinese names, with the family name first in accordance with Chinese convention. In some cases, when a person is usually known in the West by a different form of romanization (for example, Sun Yat-sen instead of Sun Zhongshan), I have tried to provide these more common spellings in parentheses after the pinyin romanization. Chinese names from English publications are listed in the same format as in the original publication. Unless otherwise indicated, the translations of all quotations from Chinese publications are my own.

# The Post-Mao Fashion Revival

The transitional period from the late 1970s through the early 1980s that followed China's Great Proletarian Cultural Revolution (1966–1976) was a period marked by controversy and unease. Fueled by a series of economic reforms and the easing of political controls, social and cultural change accelerated. However, while "resistance to bourgeois liberalization" remained a prominent theme of the Communist Party, in practice modernization was equated with Westernization in nearly all facets of life except for politics. Chinese people clearly felt the cultural shock as China first exposed itself to Western influence after several decades of self-imposed isolation.

The revolutionary changes that took place in nearly every aspect of Chinese life were accompanied by mass confusion, enthusiasm, rebellion, romanticism, and idealism. Bizarre looks and controversial dress styles exemplified and contributed to the inner turmoil that typified the age. The shocking sight of women in high heels, long hair, and jewelry and men with their long hair, sideburns, and mustaches, along with bell-bottom pants, flowery shirts, jeans, and sunglasses, caused considerable controversy. Many conservatives believed that these strange looks reflected a decadent mind that had likely been corrupted by capitalists. But eventually reformists successfully defended the emergence of new fashions, which ultimately led to the separation of dress from ideology in the mid-1980s.

## Deadly Fashions of the Cultural Revolution

The Cultural Revolution was a period marked by turmoil, repression, and violence in every facet of Chinese life. Answering Mao Zedong's call for a sweeping, revolutionary campaign that would give birth to a new China, millions of young Chinese joined the Red Guard, a mass movement that shattered the existing order in an attempt to stamp out everything that was old, feudal, or foreign. Mao and the Red Guard closed the schools and denounced teachers and intellectuals as impediments to the revolution. They "sent down" millions of city dwellers to the countryside for reeducation through hard labor. They spread the thoughts of Chairman Mao far and wide. But Mao and the Red Guard had little conception of what would replace the old society that they hoped to obliterate. And the revolutionary program that was to give birth to a new China instead quickly degenerated into a power struggle among various factions of the Red Guard itself. Chaos reigned, eclipsed only by fear.

The new China that the Red Guards set out to create was to be above all a place free of the "four olds," namely, old customs, old habits, old culture, and old thinking. All ties to China's feudal and backward past were to be severed; however, "feudalism and backwardness lay in the eye of the beholder."[1] Thus, in the tumult of this revolution, every physical object had the potential to endanger whole families and lead to public humiliation, physical assaults, or even death. Across the country people hid or secretly burned books, paintings, family albums, heirlooms, jewelry, garments, and anything else that might be interpreted as having a connection with China's feudal past or, worse, bourgeois capitalism. Despite these precautions, however, when the Red Guards burst into homes searching for any evidence of the "four olds," they rarely came up empty-handed, and members of the household in question were then often labeled counter-revolutionaries. In this tense political environment, the fear of being labeled reactionary led people to speak, act, and dress like others, since blending into the crowd was certainly safer than standing out.

The concept of fashion did not seem to belong to such a revolutionary, proletarian society. Overt attention to outward appearance was deemed shameful, sinful, and anti-revolutionary, and displays of individuality and eccentricity in dress were merely invitations to danger, and thus a rigid uniformity in dress prevailed. But in reality, the Chinese people were trapped in a paradox of this proletarian ideology: on the one hand, one was not supposed to concern oneself with superficial, outward appearances because of the association of fashion with a bourgeois lifestyle. On the other hand, any deviation from the rigid dress code could result in life-threatening consequences, and in this sense, ironically, one had to be fully aware of dress and appearance to an unprecedented degree. Thus, contrary to what the Red Guards and others believed, fashion was not killed during the Cultural Revolution—it just donned a different mask, one not painted with the vibrant colors or covered in the sparkling sequins of high fashion. In fact, the dire consequences of a fashion faux pas during this period made people aware of prevailing fashions down to the minutest of details with a singular intensity. While fashion flattened visually and stylistically, it deepened in its emotional impact and political implications. The range of fashion choices contracted as creativity was stifled, but this contraction only amplified the importance of subtle differences: the position of a Mao button or the manner in which one wore a scarf were fashion choices with clear and often dangerous implications.

The fashion trends followed and adopted during this period were not, as many suppose, mandated by government decree. Rather, it was the atmosphere of conformity and fear—and also of revolutionary fervor—that led people to adopt different styles of dress, styles markedly different from the pre–Cultural Revolution era and after. Ironically, as in the contemporaneous hippie subculture of the West of the 1960s and 1970s, prevailing *anti*-fashion sentiments gave birth to new looks and new fashions that distinguished themselves from the past, an outcome that was certainly neither intended nor desired on the part of China's revolutionaries.

These new revolutionary looks were marked by the feverish pursuit of frugality, simplicity, and sobriety in dress. "The more plain your clothes, the more revolutionary people considered you to be," was how one contemporary described it.[2] Considering the great number of followers these plain trends had, the prevalence of certain dress styles in this period was greater than that of any single garment form in China's sartorial history. These fashions are today labeled *lao san zhuang* (three old styles) and *lao san se* (three old colors). Along with military attire, these fashions encompass what people wore during the decade preceding the start of China's economic reforms in 1978. The three old colors and styles are not to be confused with the "four olds"; rather, the similarity in naming conventions used during the Cultural Revolution and among contemporary Chinese scholars today describing Cultural Revolution dress styles perhaps reveals a broader style of classification in Chinese scholarship.

The "three old styles" consist of the *Zhongshan zhuang* (Mao suit), the *qingnian zhuang* (youth jacket), and the *jun bianzhuang* (casual army jacket), all of which were worn by most men of the period. The "three old colors" are the subdued blue, white, and gray that were worn by most people and consequently earned the Chinese nicknames in the West like "blue ants" and "gray ants." Usually seen in the military garb worn by the Red Guard, olive green was also an enormously popular color, and military attire was a much coveted dress form of the period. Variations on the "three old styles" worn by men did exist but looked so similar that it is often hard to see the difference at first glance. The ubiquity of these plain, drab dress forms camouflaged differences in people's political backgrounds and views and, in a broader sense, mirrored the country's allegiance to the proletariat and the "revolutionary masses." In addition, the use of practical, simple designs and stain-resistant colors was an economic necessity in an era of scarce resources.

The Mao suit, featuring sober colors and a neat cut, encapsulated the proletarian style and was typically worn with all buttons buttoned up. It has five buttons for the front closure, one button on each of the four frontal patch pocket flaps, and three buttons on each sleeve. It was generally worn with matching loose pants. Its creation is usually accredited to Sun Zhongshan, the "Father of Modern China," commonly known in the West by the Cantonese version of his name, Sun Yat-sen. But the physical form of the Mao suit was slightly modified compared to the original *Zhongshan* suit. When master tailor Tian Atong at the Beijing Hong Du Clothing Company was appointed to customize the *Zhongshan* suit for Mao, he increased the size of the collar fall and sharpened the corner of the collar to match Mao's face.[3] Often made of khaki and fine cotton cloth (with high-quality versions made of woolens), the Mao suit was also less form-fitting than the original style designed in the early Republican era. In the wintertime, it could also be interlined with cotton batting. By the 1990s the Mao suit had been mostly discarded in cities, but it is still worn by the elderly in rural areas even today.

When production halted to give way to revolution, ready-to-wear garments were rare and mostly distributed as a means of promoting the Red Guard. Most garments were produced in individual households, and inevitably many simplified and modified versions of the Mao suit emerged from home sewing machines. The result of one such modification was the youth jacket, a modified form of the Mao suit that was nearly as common as the Mao suit itself during this period. It had one upturned flap chest pocket and two slashed pockets with flaps. In fact, the pockets on the youth jacket resembled those of Western suits. The third of the three old styles, the casual army jacket, was modeled after both the uniform of the People's Liberation Army and the Mao suit. All four of its slashed pockets had flaps with topstitching reinforcing the edges. With the top button sometimes left undone and the cut roomier in the lower section than that of the Mao suit, the casual army jacket was worn as both formal and informal wear.

On the outside, women looked much like men during this period in their similarly loose-fitting outfits and drab colors: femininity had been overruled by the revolutionary spirit. Skirts or dresses were rarely worn, and women usually had either short-cropped hair when married or two braids, short or long, resting on both shoulders when unmarried. The most commonly worn garments by women during the Cultural Revolution were the plain *liangyong shan* (dual-purpose jacket) and the traditional-style jacket. The proletarian dual-purpose jacket resembled the Mao jacket in color and silhouette but had four buttons and two rectangular, flapless front patch pockets. As its name suggests, the dual-purpose jacket was genuinely versatile, with construction materials altering its purpose without altering its cut or style. When constructed of thick materials, it served as a winter coat. When constructed of light materials, it served as a simple summer shirt. Light, summer-weight versions, sometimes decorated with plaid or small-flower patterns, were often worn beneath thicker, winter-weight versions. Featuring a standing mandarin collar, simple frog closures down the middle front, and plain or subdued flower patterns, the traditional-style jacket was particularly favored by young women. An accepted and modest way of being fashionable was to wear the inner shirt's patterned collar on the outside of the plain jacket so that the pattern could be seen. This careful expression of fashion lasted until the end of the 1970s and was also adopted by older women (Figure 1.1). Young women also subtly revealed the edge of a patterned inner collar or scarf worn beneath a plain jacket. These details were minor in their visual effect but significant as a sign of the desire of women to look attractive even in the heyday of the revolution (Fig. 1.2).[4]

This particular trend was carried forward in the use of the *jia ling* (fake collar), a unique by-product of the rationing era. The fake collar was essentially a detachable collar worn underneath a jacket that created the illusion that one was wearing a full shirt beneath the jacket. Economical in its use of materials and easy to wash, the fake collar created a trendy image for those with limited means at a time when both laundry soap and fabrics were rationed. Fake collars were sometimes also matched with traditional-style jackets. Aside from the fake collar, in the wintertime women (and occasionally men) wore scarves, sometimes with plaid patterns, which, given the

**Figure 1.1** All three women are wearing the patterned collar of their inner shirts on the outside of a plain jacket. Note the difference between the closures on the jackets worn by the two younger women and the older woman. Circa 1978. Courtesy of Zhang Rong.

predominance of drab colors in the rather monotonous wardrobe of the day, brightened the otherwise gloomy faces of the young (Fig. 1.3).

In the mid-1970s, Mao's wife, Jiang Qing, a member of the infamous Gang of Four and a key figure in the Cultural Revolution, attempted to break this monotony. She promoted, and in some cases mandated, a dress style now commonly referred to as "Jiang Qing dress." This dress form combined Western construction techniques such as set-in sleeves with elements of traditional Chinese dress (supposedly from the Song dynasty) such as a plunging V-neckline, narrow piping, and wide banding. Other than the unattractive visual effect that this hodgepodge created, its highly restrictive tailored structure and wasteful usage of materials made this dress prohibitively expensive for the average person. Besides, in the hypersensitive political environment of the time, trying out new styles was always risky, no matter how powerful or politically correct the creator of the style might seem. And in this case, a costly, so-called feminine dress that drew inspiration from both the West and China's feudal past made Jiang Qing's creation doubly suspect, impractical, and unpopular.

For both men and women, army attire comprised the trendiest and most revolutionary look in the Cultural Revolution's sartorial system (Fig. 1.4). The high social status of soldiers in this period made the official army uniform as prestigious as the

**Figure 1.2** A young woman in braids and a Chinese-style jacket with mandarin collar and a patterned inner collar, 1976. Courtesy of Li Xiaobin, photographer.

Armani suit of today. Millions and millions of Red Guards donned unofficial army uniforms (devoid of epaulets and insignia) when traveling around the country disseminating Mao's revolutionary thoughts. A brown leather belt and flat green cap were common accessories, but a fully equipped member of the Red Guard would also have had a red armband, Mao's little red book, a Mao button on the chest, a metal canteen, laced canvas shoes, and a green bag worn over the shoulder, sometimes embroidered with Mao's quotation *wei renmin fuwu* (serve the people). While homemade black or gray cloth shoes were popular among the common people, "liberation shoes," canvas shoes with rubber soles, were luxury items worn by relatively few as part of the army attire ensemble. Army attire had a long-lasting effect on Chinese wardrobes. Even today in small villages in China one can often spot men in green military garments, caps, or shoes.

**Figure 1.3** In this wedding picture, taken in 1972, a young couple from Shanghai are wearing scarves as fashionable accessories. Courtesy of Zhang Rong.

**Figure 1.4** Men and women in army attire mourning Prime Minister Zhou Enlai in Tiananmen Square, 1976. Courtesy of Li Xiaobin, photographer.

Apart from the styles deemed suitable for this radical, revolutionary era just reviewed, numerous dress forms were also proscribed during the Cultural Revolution. Prohibitions on dress items were often tacit and implicit and were enforced at the local level or *danwei* (work unit) rather than officially promulgated from above. As visual symbols of the bourgeoisie, both the Western suit and the *qipao*—a one-piece form-fitting dress combining design elements from East and West that was popular from the late 1920s through the 1940s on the mainland—were prohibited. Their matching accessories, such as rings, bracelets, high heels, stockings, bow ties, and top hats, were also shunned. Virtually every aspect of dress had its own sartorial taboos. For example, sleeveless shirts, sheer fabrics, vivid colors, zipper or snap closures, embroidery on men's shirts, and jewelry and cosmetics were not produced or sold during the Cultural Revolution. Exceptions were sometimes made for actresses performing in political plays or variety shows during sporting events and for cadres receiving foreign guests. For instance, a group of young women marched in knee-length skirts with various flowered prints on them at the opening ceremony of the first Asian Table Tennis Championship held in Beijing in 1972.[5] Exceptions were also made for children, who had the privilege of dressing in relatively lively colors and ornamentation. But politics were never far behind. The Research Department of the Shanghai Clothing Product Industrial Company documented a criticism of an embroidery design featuring a cat and a fish on the back of a garment for little girls: one cadre asserted that cats ate fish—and wouldn't putting natural adversaries like cats and fish together in such a playful manner undermine the notion of class struggle between other natural adversaries like the proletariat and the bourgeoisie?[6]

In a political environment in which even depictions of animals on children's garments could be criticized as counterrevolutionary, the dangers involved in deviating from accepted styles in seemingly innocuous and trivial ways become clear. But the lack of any sort of explicit, codified dress code generated uncertainty and forced the people themselves to interpret what was revolutionary and what was counterrevolutionary, with faulty interpretations often having dire consequences. While the people were forced to deal with this ambiguity, a binary outlook prevailed among the authorities: everything was either right or wrong and dress was either revolutionary or reactionary. There was no middle ground. As such, dress was a highly visible and tangible target for political attacks, and dressing often became a high-stakes guessing game. But at the same time, dress was also a powerful tool for protection. In this sense, in the years of the Cultural Revolution, everyone had to be fashion conscious in order to adjust to the nuances and subtle changes in dress and appearance in order to wear the "correct" fashions.

## Bizarre Looks and Unhealthy Thoughts

In the spring of 1980, photographer Li Xiaobin captured a group of fashionable young people disco dancing to pop music at the Summer Palace in the heart of Beijing

**Figure 1.5**   Disco dancing in stylish attire at the Summer Palace in Beijing, 1980. Courtesy of Li Xiaobin, photographer.

(Fig. 1.5). Some of the stylish dancers in the picture are wearing sunglasses, jeans, and T-shirts. A few have long, disheveled hair. One young man is decked out in a short-sleeved shirt with an abstract flower print, while several foreigners and even some middle-aged men in Mao suits dance behind him. Surrounding this stylish group of dancers, a crowd looks on with curiosity and skepticism. Unimaginable only a few short years before, this raucous scene of avant-garde artists, poets, film directors, and their devotees dancing in public was not without controversy or consequence for those pictured. But its very possibility indicates a dramatic break with the preceding decade.

Mao's death in 1976 and the subsequent arrest of the Gang of Four finally brought an end to the Cultural Revolution. With the adoption of the Open Door policy in 1978, China took its first steps on the path of economic reform, a move that signaled the beginning of the post-Mao era and marked a turning point in modern Chinese history. During the transitional period that followed, which lasted until the mid-1980s, fundamental shifts in political ideology and changes in China's economic system led to cultural dislocation and confusion. Controversies bloomed in every corner of the cultural and political landscape.

In 1978, the short-lived Democracy Wall movement in Beijing ignited the enthusiasm of young intellectuals who sought to express their concerns over domestic political affairs after a decade of imposed silence (Fig. 1.6). Banned the next year, big-character posters posted on the Democracy Wall offered Chinese a taste of free

**Figure 1.6** Big-character posters on the "Democracy Wall" in Beijing gave Chinese a taste of free expression. 1978. Courtesy of Li Xiaobin, photographer.

expression but also demonstrated the dangers of being outspoken: some participants in the movement were subsequently arrested or harassed by the security services. However, this narrowing of freedom of expression did not lead to a return of the repression of the past. As Cohen and Cohen noted, during this transitional period "Chinese who never previously dared to speak with foreigners proved willing and eager to do so, and some began to wear more colorful, Western-style clothing. Even disco dancing with foreigners was permissible in certain places."[7] This taste of free expression in the political sphere, while it ultimately proved dangerous, stimulated the desire for other, less overtly political forms of expression. But even these so-called safer forms of expression were fraught with controversy and stirred up debate.

Dress mirrored the drastic changes taking place in Chinese society. And since dress was often the first visible manifestation of change, dress itself once again became a subject of controversy. Dress was also one of the freest forms of expression, relatively speaking, at the time, which only further increased the controversy surrounding it. Chinese intellectuals vigorously debated the proper image the reforming nation should uphold, while the government attempted to formulate its own regulations regarding what people could wear.[8] Nevertheless, fashion made its own choice. As the government loosened the tight grip it had maintained over the preceding decade, copies of Western styles leaked in through the cracks. But while a few bold youth challenged fashion limits by donning Western styles, most people felt uncertain about how to react to new ideas, lifestyles, and fashions. After three long decades of self-imposed isolation, anything new, whether foreign or domestic, seemed unsettling and daring.

New looks that men and women adopted began to unsettle the Mao era's sartorial order and slowly displaced the monotony that prevailed during the years of the Cultural Revolution. For daring young men, bell-bottom pants, plaid shirts, and other changes in grooming and accessories, such as wearing sunglasses and growing sideburns, mustaches, and long hair, combined to form a trendy male image at the end of the 1970s. Meanwhile, women experimented with permed hair, sunglasses, bell-bottoms, high heels, jewelry, and makeup. However, the public response to these novel images was overwhelmingly negative, and the few people who dared to don these bizarre looks were often labeled *liumang* (hoodlums) by the conservative majority. While reformist intellectuals were sympathetic to these new fashions and tried to steer a middle course through the controversial looks, agitated radicals guarded the old sartorial order with scissors and once again took to the streets to shred fashion transgressions just as they had during the Cultural Revolution. In their eyes, the strange appearance of these new fashions reflected a decadent and corrupt mind filled with "unhealthy thoughts."

As the first prominent Western fashion to enter China in the post-Mao era, bell-bottom pants were greeted with shock. Since they tightly hugged the hips and thighs and flared out from the knee, bell-bottoms created a body-hugging silhouette that looked eccentric to most Chinese of the time, who were used to the sight of baggy pants that concealed every line of the body. The extravagantly flared legs, which could "sweep several streets" with the amount of material they used, were also an affront to the frugal Chinese mindset, especially since the rationing system for fabrics was still in place at the time. Only audacious youngsters with a confused mind had the nerve to wear them in public. However, many young people were attracted not only by the novel look of bell-bottoms, but also by the rebellious image they projected. The very fact that they were a fashion from the West that the conservative majority scorned only heightened their appeal. But most young people, although they longed for new fashions, only tried on their new bell-bottoms at home or had the wide legs secretly altered due to social pressure. And those who did not alter them at home risked having them altered on the street by scissors-wielding guardians of public morality. In fact, the act of shredding bell-bottoms has since come to symbolize this transitional period in nostalgic pop songs and movies. For example, in pop star Ai Jing's song "Yanfen jie de gushi" (Story of Yanfen Street) from 1995, she reminisced on this era:

> One day a long-haired big brother
> passed by Yanfen Street
> His bell-bottoms stylish and unique
> That's what he got in trouble for
> The old women in the neighborhood

paraded him in the street
His bell-bottoms shredded
His pride peeled off
His facial expression elusive

However, bell-bottom pants with a moderate width in the hem were seen on main-stream movie stars, who tended to be judged less harshly for their novel appearance than ordinary people. For instance, the popular magazine *Dazhong dianying* (Popular Cinema) featured movie star Shao Huishan wearing noticeable makeup, permed hair, and bell-bottom pants on the cover of the tenth issue of 1980.

Along with bell-bottom pants of various materials, jeans also made their way into China at this time. Controversies surrounding jeans arose not only due to their tight-fitting silhouette and their association with so-called hoodlums, but also for blurring gender distinctions. Both men and women wore jeans with the same front zipper closure, while Chinese women's pants had always had side closures on the right. The older generation was especially bothered by this eccentric look—"neither like a man nor a woman," as they put it. But artists, students, and even some open-minded professors championed this new fashion. The conservative majority hoped to expel jeans from China as part of political campaigns that sought to "repudiate capital-ist liberalization" and "cleanse out spiritual pollution." And no state-owned stores would sell jeans in the early 80s.[9]

In one case, extreme leftist opponents of this new fashion wrote: "In the past, im-perialists called us pigs and now they want us to wear cowboy pants. Next they'll call us sheep and donkeys!"[10] But Yu Qiuyu, then a young professor at the Shanghai The-atrical Institute, countered such criticism by convincing other young, like-minded professors in Shanghai to wear jeans as a sign of protest. Their forceful demon-stration silenced critics and won themselves the nickname *niuzai jiaoshou* (cowboy professors).[11] (The literal translation of "jeans" in Chinese is "cowboy pants.")

Ultimately, both supporters and critics of jeans underestimated just how wide-spread and popular jeans would become in China. Conservatives assumed that this unseemly fashion would quickly lose its novelty and go out of style. And most looked down on small merchants and street peddlers, only recently legitimated and officially sanctioned by the government, for selling petty things like jeans. But jeans did not go out of style, and many of those small merchants made their fortunes in a booming jeans market that is still expanding almost three decades later. Despite the eventual success of jeans, however, fashionable clothing and activities remained dangerous for some time to come.

In 1983, the government launched its first national campaign against crime of the post-Mao era. This severe crackdown on crimes proved wise the circumspect attitude that most Chinese held of new trends and fashions. Some disco dancers, much like the ones pictured at the Beijing Summer Palace in 1980, were accused of sexual promiscuity and sentenced to death.[12] Pop singers from Taiwan and the mainland were either banned or attacked in state-controlled media in order to cleanse out the "spiritual pollution" they had disseminated. Influential newspapers and magazines labeled pop songs "decadent music," "low quality in style and morality," and "valueless."[13] Nevertheless, despite the ban, the spread of pop music gave birth to its own fashion accessory: the boom box completed the trendy, rebellious image that many young people found so appealing at the end of the 1970s and early 1980s. In the home, it served as a high-tech status symbol. On the street, carried in hand with pop songs blaring, the boom box loudly declared one's desire to be fashionable.

Young men wearing their hair long (often shorter than shoulder-length) was another "disturbing" fashion trend of the time. Cartoonists ridiculed the gender confusion long hair supposedly generated by drawing back views of young couples in long hair and jeans, with senior citizens or children invariably mistaking the men for women or the women for men. Since one's appearance was thought to be tightly connected with morality and life attitudes, one widely debated scenario posed this question: Is it possible for a young man in long hair and bell-bottoms to save a drowning child?[14] People were in the habit of equating the pursuit of fashion with ideological backwardness and immorality, and thus this scenario challenged long-held, ingrained beliefs.

A common element of ideological and political education at schools and work units was to call for young males to cut their long hair and shave off their mustaches. In one model example, twenty-three construction workers at Shanghai's Sixth Construction Company made headlines in the *Xinmin Evening News* by cutting their long hair.[15] In the report, four of them confessed, "We never heard any compliments on our long hair, whether we were at work, sitting on the bus, or walking on the street. That showed us that long hair is not a beautiful thing. [We realized] if one has a bad outward appearance, having a beautiful heart is out of the question."[16] Accepting their heartfelt confessions, polite society and the media warmly welcomed these lost lambs back into the fold, holding them up as examples for other so-called backward, fashion-conscious youth to emulate.

Aside from the visual discomfort that "bizarre looks" generated, in the eyes of many Chinese fashion itself was morally questionable. Fashion absorbed time, money, and energy, all of which were in short supply at the time, while it yielded nothing useful or practical. And after a decade of cultural revolution in which most people were denied access to education and other opportunities for advancement, many people sought to make up for lost time. When the government reestablished the national college entrance examination in 1977, eager readers and aspiring students mobbed the recently reopened bookstores with a hunger for knowledge and an eye to the future. English overtook Russian to become the most popular foreign language to study. And although society as a whole was critical of Western materialism and always made a clear distinction between the capitalist West and the socialist East, studying English was viewed in a positive light as a sign of ambition. Thus in the early years of the post-Mao era, the fashionable male, with his long hair, sideburns, mustache, sunglasses, and bell-bottoms, stood in stark contrast to the mainstream ideal: a short-haired, clean-shaven young man in a white shirt and loose pants who immersed himself in the study of English and avoided the "bizarre looks" and "unhealthy thoughts" of fashion rebels.

Criticism of these "bizarre looks" often came from conservative intellectuals who saw themselves as guardians of public morality. They wrote scores of articles criticizing strange dress and eccentric fashion phenomena, while promoting simple, "healthy" styles of dress. In an article published in the *Xinmin Evening News* in 1982, one writer advocated the idea of "natural beauty" by citing the conservative viewpoints American youth held regarding adornment in hopes of educating young Chinese men who "tastelessly" sported long hair, mustaches, sunglasses, and bell-bottoms.[17] Since fashion-hungry Chinese often looked to America for fashion inspiration, this seemed to be an effective argument. A common theme was that "the enthusiasm for fashionable clothing, hairstyles, and shoes distracted one from work and study and encumbered one's financial capacity."[18] Other articles published in the same newspaper in 1982 similarly criticized women's "impractical" high-heeled shoes and "uncivilized" ear-piercing practices.[19]

Firmly in the Maoist tradition, meticulous attention was paid to the use of language in naming new fashions for any possible ideological significance. One article noted that such names as *Xiaojie Shan* (Miss Shirt) and *Shenshi Xue* (Gentleman Boots) used in window advertisements along Huaihai Road in Shanghai sounded both foreign and outmoded: "The name of our merchandise should follow the pace of our socialist production and reflect our healthy and upward spirit."[20] City governments joined this growing chorus of conservative criticism. Some announced in local newspapers that women with loose shoulder-length or longer hair would be barred from entering city hall because of their "offensive" appearance.[21] According to *The New York Times* (October 18, 1983), young municipal employees in Beijing were told to avoid "bizarre dress" and to preserve "habits of simplicity and bitter struggle" in their appearance or they would be fired and sent home. Workers were also told that "men must also cut their hair and shave off sideburns and mustaches, and women may not have hair longer than to their shoulders or wear heavy makeup or earrings or other 'unhealthy ornaments.'" But despite such pervasive criticism and stern warnings, novel styles and previously prohibited dress forms continued to gain popularity.

While fashionable youth were harshly criticized and often accused of "blindly imitating the Western, capitalist lifestyle," these criticisms were relatively mild in light of the violent attacks that took place during the Cultural Revolution. And despite all of the negative press new fashions received in the media, supporters of fashion in China gradually became more visible and their arguments more compelling. Admitting the immorality of capitalist lifestyles, these advocates of new fashions took a new tack by attempting to separate fashion from capitalism and ideology.

Reformist intellectual Guo Siwen published an article in the widely read magazine *China Youth* titled "Discussing Guidance—Starting with Youth Hairstyles and

Trouser Legs" that exemplified this new approach.[22] Without attempting to challenge mainstream hostility to long hair and bell-bottoms, Guo advised the young not to spend too much time on clothing and hairstyles but to concentrate instead on work and studying. However, he made this seemingly innocuous article exceptionally controversial by claiming that society, for its part, should not excessively criticize and interfere with clothing, hairstyles, and other issues relating to the personal lives of the younger generation. To make his argument more persuasive, he quoted Chairman Mao's saying regarding criticism: pay attention to the important aspects of the problem instead of frivolous details. "In terms of one's personal life and preferences, as long as they are not against the law or moral principles, we should allow for small differences while seeking common ground on major issues. There is no need to impose uniformity. It is especially inappropriate to tie preferences in someone's personal life to ideological principles and to criticize them on that basis."[23] Guo concluded that "the length of hair and width of trouser legs are not necessarily connected to a good or a bad mind."[24] This call for the separation of ideology from physical appearance also comported with Deng Xiaoping's theory of emancipating the mind and breaking with old ways of thinking. Nevertheless, it was still risky to argue against mainstream views, especially since resisting the "decadent capitalist lifestyle" to which fashion had been tied remained a major issue in Chinese daily life. Other articles published in the same journal expressed similar views to Guo's.

Other controversies of the day indirectly affected views of dress by challenging traditional notions of the body in general and body exposure in dress in particular. In the decorative and performance arts, controversies surrounding works by artists in these fields illustrate how deep-seated views of the body in Chinese culture influenced mainstream views of many of the recently imported "bizarre looks."

One such controversy erupted over a large wall painting designed by modern artist Yuan Yunsheng in 1979 for the Capital Airport in Beijing. The painting caught the public's attention with its majestic display of the nude female body.[25] Although depicted in a somewhat abstract form, such a public display of nudity was nevertheless sensational and shocking. In the still idealistic and morally pure era of the 1980s, people were generally repulsed by the painting and labeled it an imitation of Western art. Any sort of imitation of the West was both officially and ideologically taboo, and on this score alone many viewed the painting as shocking. The shock, however, had deeper roots.

Nudity had long been depicted in Western paintings and sculptures, dating back to ancient Greece, but this had never been the case in Chinese art. In a Chinese context, the naked body had rarely been viewed as merely natural. From a Confucian point of view, the body is bestowed upon one by one's parents and is thus sacred and private and not to be shared with the public. Historically speaking, if naked bodies ever appeared in any form of visual representation, it was safe to assume that those representations were pornographic. In terms of dress, throughout Chinese sartorial history up until the 1980s, female body curves had always been concealed except in the subtle lines of the *qipao*. Words like "cleavage" and "sexy" were purely Western notions. Even in the Tang dynasty (618 C.E.–907 C.E.), which had a liberal mindset regarding dress unprecedented in Chinese history, only a little bare skin above the breasts was ever revealed. In fact, the long tradition of concealing the shape of the breasts was not abandoned in China until the beginning of the twentieth century when the brassiere made its first appearance there.

Thus, Yuan's painting imparted a real visual and moral shock to the Chinese public in a culture that was sensitive to any "unhealthy thoughts" regarding the body. The political and ideological turmoil generated by this painting was quelled only when reformist leaders of the country personally reassured the public of the political correctness of the painting after seeing it for themselves.

A year later, another controversy erupted when male ballet dancers from the Shanghai Ballet School donned tight-fitting white leotards for a performance in Hunan province. After the performance, one disturbed cadre in the audience angrily shouted: "How does this have anything to do with China?"[26] This cadre spoke for many in the audience who sat silently embarrassed by the outfits of the male dancers, which clearly revealed the contours of the male body. Although fully dressed, the dancers looked naked in the eyes of the audience. The cadres were furious over the eccentric outfits, but the "meaningless spinning" of the dance did not help either. The unfamiliar sight of the movements of the dance and the scandalous costumes of the dancers were not Chinese in nature—and foreignness was rarely regarded as anything but unpleasant to Chinese sensibilities of the time.

Although these newly imported art forms and styles generated discomfort and controversy, they contributed to a gradual shift in mainstream views regarding public displays of the body, nudity, and Western influence in the arts more generally. As time passed, all of these factors would contribute to a greater tolerance for body exposure in dress and ever more radical (and Western-influenced) fashions.

Another area of great controversy, which fully encompassed dress, centered on the question of individualism. As we have already seen, displays of individuality—whether in dress, in art, or in politics—were dangerous during the years of the Cultural Revolution. And although such displays were relatively less dangerous in its aftermath, the notion of individualism still retained a strongly negative taint.

Ideologically, culturally, and historically, China remained a collectivist state that valued the group over the individual and conformity over individuality. But as China began the transformation of its economy and society away from the Marxist confines of its recent past, the role of individualism and its meaning in a socialist society came to the fore. In the economic sphere, individualism was officially promoted in the guise of entrepreneurship. Small merchants came to exemplify Deng's call to "allow some people to get rich first"—an attempt to ease fears of economic inequality and to encourage small enterprise. But no one knew for certain the extent to which individualism could be practiced in other aspects of Chinese cultural life.

A reader's letter published in *China Youth* in 1980 captured this anxiety, along with the confusion and misery shared by a whole generation that had just awoken from the long nightmare of the Cultural Revolution. Written by twenty-three-year old Pan Xiao, the letter was titled "Why Does Life's Road Grow Increasingly Narrower?"[27] The author made a strong impression through her frank expressions of the despair and bewilderment she felt after living through so many revolutionary miseries. She questioned her faith in "unselfishly serving the people" and declared that she had now come to believe in the pursuit of individual interests. She now realized that "to act for oneself subjectively is to act for others objectively."

The letter resonated with people all over the country and provoked nationwide discussions regarding individualism and the meaning and value of life. More than sixty thousand reactions to the letter swamped the desks of *China Youth*'s editors. Even Hu Qiaomu, president of the Secretariat of the Communist Party's Central Committee, took part in this momentous "Pan Xiao discussion." He affirmed the correctness of Pan's proposition: to act for oneself subjectively is to act for others objectively. But to the government, the content of this debate was probably less critical than the fact that the magazine had allowed such a wide-ranging discussion of ideology to take place at all. Sensing this, *China Youth* then penned an editorial in its first issue of 1981, "Echoes of Sixty Thousand Hearts," in which it concluded: "[T]o take an active role in life, we should promote the spirit of putting public interests before self-interest." This politically correct and uninspiring statement, however, failed to shield the editors from the wrath of the authorities. A few years later, in its first issue of 1984, *China Youth* harshly criticized any emphasis on individual interests for its "individualist nature." The boundaries of individualism remained ambiguous. And pushing its limits was left to a bold few.

Like Pan Xiao, fashion could not overcome the official and cultural limitations set on individualism in the early years of the post-Mao era. Overt expressions of individuality in dress still proved risky. To play it safe, most Chinese simply avoided being the first to try a new style, or they chose the safer new looks produced by state-owned factories. But the controversies that raged in nearly all corners of Chinese cultural life partially shifted public attention away from "bizarre dress" and diverted social pressure away from the fashion pioneers who dared to don new looks. The Cultural Revolution had left China severely wounded as a country, and the authorities were anxious to reestablish confidence, among both outsiders and its own people, both in socialism and in China's recently initiated economic reforms. People were encouraged to dress to "reflect the spirit of socialism" and to emancipate their minds to become more creative. They were also cautioned to guard against the "sugar-coated bullets of capitalism" and to continue to oppose "bourgeois liberalization."

Throughout most of the 1980s, this sort of political influence on dress and fashion remained, and political leaders set examples, as well as parameters, as to what was suitable. In an article for the *Shanghai Apparel Yearbook*, Tan Fuyun, vice chairman of the All-China Women's Federation and director of the Shanghai Women's Federation, pointed out the importance of dress in portraying China's new image in the new epoch.[28] She urged "correct guidance" in the refinement of consumers' aesthetic appreciation and exhorted people to lead a "civilized, healthy, and scientific" lifestyle. Tan also argued that strange and "bizarre dress," such as dress that is "too slim, revealing, transparent, or short," should be "corrected." Tan's views on fashion represented the authorities' definition of what was appropriate and permissible.

However, it was never easy for people to draw the line between the appropriate and the inappropriate, the egalitarian and the bourgeois, or healthy and obscene looks. If the color green represented egalitarianism, did red signify the bourgeoisie? If four pockets on a shapeless jacket represented a healthy conformity, did a pocket-less, form-fitting jacket constitute an unhealthy display of individuality? Dress is inherently ambiguous. And thus the answers to these riddles could not be found within fashion itself or through studying dress forms. These were ultimately political questions with political answers. Nevertheless, the evolution of fashion in China continued to push the boundaries of what was officially deemed "too slim, revealing, transparent, or short." And "bizarre looks" only multiplied in the years to come despite any official protestations.

# –2–

# The Spread of Fashion through Mass Media

When China opened up to the outside world at the end of the 1970s, economic reform brought with it the reinvigoration of the mass media. Magazines, journals, and other publications shuttered during the Cultural Revolution reopened to a public hungry for information and entertainment, two commodities in short supply over the preceding decade. But it was the spread of television and film that had the most visible impact on the dissemination of new fashions—and especially youth fashion—in the early years of the reform era. TV and film further influenced post-Mao fashion by facilitating the shift in public attention away from politics to the world of entertainment. Both legal and underground video playhouses, along with karaoke dance clubs, quickly spread throughout China in the early 1980s. As television established itself as a popular medium in China and foreign and domestic films found new audiences on the mainland, new fashions found new avenues and entryways to the mainland.

## The Growth of Television

When the television set first came to China in 1958, locally produced black-and-white TV models were available only to high-ranking government officials. For the next two decades, television remained an expensive luxury item far beyond the meager means of most Chinese. For example, in the mid-1970s an eleven-inch set cost seven hundred *yuan* while the average monthly income in Shanghai was only twenty-seven *yuan*.[1] In addition to their steep price, rationing coupons for televisions were also hard to come by. (Rationing coupons were required for many consumer goods in this period.) But from its introduction in 1958 through the end of the Cultural Revolution in 1976, television was little more than a platform for government propaganda. And coupled with the relative scarcity of television sets, the effect of TV on mass culture was negligible. Since the political and economic climate of the 60s and 70s also impeded the growth of any sort of domestic entertainment media—and with foreign imports strictly forbidden—the quality of Chinese television during these years further limited its appeal.

But as the economic and political climate changed at the beginning of the reform era, the demand for television grew. During the 1970s most Chinese aspired to own three consumer products nicknamed the "big three" (*san da jian*): a wristwatch, a bicycle, and a sewing machine. As the 1980s began, though, a new trio of consumer products came within reach of increasing numbers of Chinese families: a television, a refrigerator, and a washing machine. This change is a clear indication of the rise in the standard of living during the early reform period. Throughout the 1980s the number of television sets skyrocketed, already reaching 27,620,000 by 1982.[2] In 1983, the *Xinmin Evening News* reported that the production of color models that year doubled that of the previous year in Shanghai, but television manufacturers still had trouble keeping up with the growing demand.[3]

Television in this period not only transformed Chinese nightlife but also revolutionized Chinese fashion. Electric power, often only recently acquired in villages and towns, lengthened Chinese nights, and the "magic box" finally brought the outside world into homes across China. TV dramas and other programs first imported into China, mainly from Japan and Hong Kong, were filled with fashion inspirations that provided convenient models for the Chinese to copy, and the styles depicted in TV shows became immediately recognizable symbols of fashion that came to define the trends and fads of the early post-Mao era.

The sweeping influence TV programs would have on fashion to a large extent resulted from the scarcity of information in China about fashion due to decades of isolation from the outside world. With few other entertainment options available, watching television in the 80s quickly became a national pastime, and virtually all Chinese who were fortunate enough to be able to watch TV—and TV dramas in particular—did so. At first, the number of TV dramas that aired on Chinese television was rather small. But the limited number of shows ensured a mass audience for each program, which enabled particular fashions to spread quickly all over China.

Dress and hairstyles in these dramas were recognizable symbols of fashion and thus were often named after the widely adored characters who wore them. With a large pool of fans adopting the same form of dress or hairstyle, a new type of conformity emerged that was apolitical but still informed by the habit of conforming to majority dress styles that had been cultivated during the Cultural Revolution. This habit of conformity remained influential in the spread of these new TV fashions in this era after the ubiquitous, sober forms of dress of Mao's era started to lose their appeal.

## Imported TV Dramas and Fashions

Coeval with Hong Kong's economic golden age, the popularity of Hong Kong TV dramas peaked in the 1980s and maintained its momentum into the 1990s on the mainland. TV dramas made in Hong Kong were mainly set during the Republican and late Qing periods and mixed the timeless themes of love, patriotism, hatred, and revenge. The radiance and charm of the characters in these dramas appealed to viewers widely across Asia. The styling in these TV dramas was not always historically accurate: costumes and hairstyles were either theatrically exaggerated or boldly modernized to suit contemporary tastes. And the modern flair and flavor that the costume designers of Hong Kong TV dramas added to the looks of characters helped to popularize TV show fashions among mainland Chinese.

The Asian entertainment powerhouse Hong Kong Television Broadcasts Limited (TVB) and its main competitor, Asia Television, were perhaps the two largest exporters of Hong Kong's fashion trends and pop culture to all regions of East Asia. While Hong Kong served as both a conduit and filter of Western fashions and values to mainland China, it also reconnected the mainland to China's own traditional past—a connection that had been severed during the Cultural Revolution. Memories of traditional family values, expressions of love, the routines of the business world, the appreciation of fashion—all of which were scarce during the Cultural Revolution—were brought back to life through these TV dramas from Hong Kong.

When the first Hong Kong TV series imported into China, *Huo Yuanjia,* aired in 1983 on China Central Television (CCTV), most people watched it on a black-and-white TV set shared by an entire village, town, or community. The series chronicled the exploits of its eponymous title character, Huo Yuanjia, a historical martial arts figure who gained fame in the first years of the twentieth century by challenging foreign wrestlers, boxers, and martial artists to highly publicized matches. As the TV series gained popularity, children could be heard singing the theme song of the show, "Wanli changcheng yong budao" (The Great Wall will never fall), in schools and on the streets across the nation. Teenagers began parting their bangs down the middle in the style of Huo Yuanjia. Hairstyle seemed to provide the most efficient and economical way for fans to look and feel close to their idols, especially when clothing styles seemed impractical to imitate. Although the story was set at the end of the Qing dynasty (1644–1912), Huo's hair was styled in the fashion of 1970s Hong Kong. Apparently, this deviation from history did not undermine the appeal of the show but only piqued the audience's interest further. Thus began the influence of the TV drama on Chinese conceptions of style.

A year later, the nationwide broadcast of *Shediao yingxiiong zhuan* (The Legend of the Condor Heroes), produced by Hong Kong TVB and based on the popular novel by the bestselling Chinese novelist Jin Yong, further shifted popular attention from the world of politics to the world of entertainment. While the series did not produce a specific fashion trend (since the characters were styled in historical costumes), its great popularity stimulated demand for more Hong Kong dramas, many of which would have a lasting impact on fashion. Nevertheless, *Shediao yingxiiong zhuan* had a lasting effect on the ideal male image of the 80s and 90s. Simple-minded, honest, warm-hearted, and diligent: these were the traits of the leading male character, Guo Jing, that would subsequently become the characteristics of the ideal boyfriend or husband. The ethereal love story of Guo Jing and the beautiful woman who was his lover, Huang Rong, proved so powerful and appealing to audiences that mainland television stations began to import dramas from Hong Kong with increasing regularity after the tremendous success of the series.

The next hit import, *Shanghai tan* (The Bund), first aired on the mainland in 1985. Zhou Runfa (Chow Yun-fat) starred in this twenty-five-episode TV drama that immediately established Zhou as a superstar. The signature look of Zhou's character consisted of a 1930s' well-tailored Western suit, a tie, a trench coat, a fedora, a long white scarf that contrasted strongly with his dark suit, and moussed hair neatly combed back. Soon after the airing of the show, young men throughout China, from city streets to small-town roads, could be seen with slicked-back hair and long white scarves. Trench coats in the style worn by Zhou in the show also came into vogue. *Youth Daily* reported that some high school students went to school dressed exactly like Zhou's character.[4] No one seemed to mind donning these anachronous styles out of the 1930s; Zhou had imbued the style with his romantic and heroic image, and the desire to adopt this image overshadowed any concern on the part of fans about appearing out of time or place. Zhou's fans even copied the refined manners and mannerisms of his character, attempting to match the elegance of a stylized Shanghai underworld of the 30s with the drab reality of the early 80s.

While TV dramas imported from the United States, South America, Singapore, and Taiwan also gained notoriety in this period, only those from Japan came close to matching the predominant role that Hong Kong TV dramas played in the early 80s. Imported Japanese TV dramas centered on themes of perseverance, aspiration, family bonds, and love and were often set in modern times, which made the adoption of fashions from these TV dramas even easier than adopting them from Hong Kong dramas, which were often set in earlier time periods. The influx of Japanese TV dramas also reflected the honeymoon period in Sino-Japanese relations that began after the successful negotiation of the Sino-Japanese Peace and Friendship Treaty in 1978.

The first of the imports from Japan—and the first foreign TV drama aired in China—was *Zi san si lang* (*Sanshiro Sugata,* the name of the main character), broadcast in 1981 by Shanghai Television Station. Based on Akira Kurosawa's Oscar-winning directorial debut of the same name, this drama instantly grabbed the audience's attention and contributed to the popularity of Japanese TV shows in China thereafter. *Zi san si lang* made judo, along with the Gaozi *shan* (Takako shirt), popular fads among Chinese youth, especially in Shanghai. Based on the lead female character Gaozi's shirt, the so-called Gaozi *shan* did not take on a strictly defined form but featured meticulously embellished ruffles, pleats, gathers, and ribbons. It also featured voluminous bishop sleeves, a standing collar decorated with ribbons, and an elongated rectangular section filled with pleats and ruffles inserted in the front closure. Although great variations existed in the use of materials and decorative details, Gaozi *shan* generally resembled a Victorian-era blouse. The mismatch of this overly decorative shirt with the image of Chinese laboring women was noted in the first issue of the magazine *Beautifying Life* in 1983. *Beautifying Life* was sponsored by the Shanghai Textile Bureau Committee and aimed to guide consumption, promote production, and enrich the lives of Chinese women. In short, it served as a governmental spokesman for "new socialist lifestyles." But the incongruous image of the modern, socialist Chinese woman in a Victorian-era blouse proved too much for some:

> The era of Miss Gaozi ended over a hundred years ago. Nowadays, whether in Europe or Japan, the Gaozi *shan* has entirely disappeared. Western women's dress has also gotten more and more succinct, simplified, comfortable, and composed. It seems this is the inevitable trend of history, let alone [the trend] for China's great mass of laboring women. Despite its delicate craftsmanship, [the design of] the Gaozi *shan* is too excessive, which is incompatible with the spirit of the times.[5]

The article urged artists and designers to take on the social responsibility of creating a greater variety of new styles that would reflect the spirit of the era and the characteristics of the nation instead of merely revamping old styles from the West. The critical tone that this article employed regarding imported looks was typical in the early years of the 1980s. Officialdom routinely emphasized the historical and social responsibility that both designers and consumers of fashion had to reflect their own time and place. In other words, anything too foreign was still disfavored in the state-owned media.

In 1983, the popularity of another Japanese import, *Paiqiu nvjiang* (Volleyball Girl; the original Japanese title was *Moero Attack*), did reflect the spirit of the time quite directly. The five consecutive championships (1981–1986) won by China's Women's National Volleyball Team engendered deep and intense feelings of patriotism throughout China that counteracted widespread feelings of self-doubt and dismay in the aftermath of the Cultural Revolution. *Paiqiu nvjiang,* the story of Xiaolu Chunzi (Aka), a girl from Hokkaido hoping to join the Japanese national volleyball team to realize her dream of competing in the 1980 Olympics in Moscow, tapped into (and contributed to) the popularity of volleyball in China at the time. Chunzi's eye-popping volleyball moves, like the "somersault spike" and the "UFO ball attack," captured the imagination of every Chinese teenager. Her straight, long hairdo, which was parted in the middle and pulled up with barrettes, became known as the "Chunzi *tou*" (Chunzi hairdo). Girls could hardly wait to pull their hair up and start practicing Chunzi's volleyball moves in physical education classes at school. This volleyball and "Chunzi" craze brought the sportswear trend to new heights, a trend that is still popular today. Twenty years after the series first aired, when the actress who played Chunzi visited China and gave a special TV interview, many Chunzi fans in the audience were still wearing their hair in the Chunzi *tou*.

Another Japanese TV drama, *Xueyi* (Red Suspicion), which first aired in China in the mid-1980s, popularized a whole collection of garment styles for both men and women, for the young and the middle-aged. Yamaguchi Momoe, a Japanese pop singer and actress who enjoyed tremendous popularity across Asia at the time, starred as the tragic character Xingzi (Sachiko), a girl who is accidentally exposed to radiation and is later diagnosed with leukemia. To make matters worse, Xingzi unwittingly falls in love with a half-brother she never knew she had. Faced with such a bleak future, struggling against her fatal diagnosis and troubled by the mystery surrounding her uncertain parentage, Xingzi's life story was both touching and heart-wrenching. With the success of the show, girls cut their hair in the Xingzi style (neck length with full bangs parted to the side) and longed for pale skin (and some, even leukemia) so that they would look just like Xingzi. Many of Xingzi's dress items, such as her knitted hat with a round dome, belted shirtwaist dresses, puff-sleeved summer dresses, knitted sweaters, grey or black overcoats, and even white socks with a zigzagging header, became popular styles named after the character, such as the Xingzi *mao* (hat) and Xingzi *shan* (tops), and so on. The show became a rich source of fashion for Chinese who were eager to try out new styles. According to the *Shanghai Apparel Yearbook,* 327,000 Xingzi *shan* produced by the Shanghai Fourth Garment Factory quickly sold out in 1984. And over 10,000 Xingzi-style overcoats produced by the Shanghai First Garment Factory sold well also.[6] Because of the overwhelming popularity of these styles, books were also published to teach home sewers how to sew Xingzi's entire wardrobe.

Other characters from the show also generated their own fads. Guangfu, Xingzi's love interest and mysterious half-brother in the series, donned shirts and knitted sweaters, accordingly named Guangfu *shan,* which became popular fashion items for young men. Dressed in a white turtleneck, knitted sweater, and bell-bottom pants, Guangfu came to personify the romantic ideal for many young Chinese women of the day. Xingzi's father, Dadao Mao, and aunt, Lihui, also provided fashion inspiration to the middle-aged: the Dadao Mao *bao* (briefcase), Dadao Mao's windbreaker, and the Lihui *qun* (skirt) are prominent examples.

The popularity of all the fashions inspired by *Xueyi* also had an impact on early fashion marketing in China. Private merchants named their products after these popular TV characters, even if their products had little connection to the original styles. Apparently, this crude marketing strategy, first inspired by *Xueyi,* proved to be effective. In this sense, so-called socialist merchants of the time learned not only how to make money on fashion, but also the value of celebrity marketing.[7]

Although dramas from both Japan and Hong Kong had the greatest impact on fashion in China during the 80s, American TV shows also left their mark. A year after the establishment of diplomatic relations between China and the United States in 1980, *Man from Atlantis* became the first American TV series to air in China. The main character in the series, Mark Harris (played by Patrick Duffy), donned large sunglasses that seemed to cover half his face, which were quickly adopted by young Chinese as a means of adding an exotic touch to their often drab wardrobes (Fig. 2.1). Sunglasses of this sort were nicknamed after the character and dubbed *Maike jing* (Mark sunglasses). This exotic and foreign-sounding name perhaps helped to

**Figure 2.1** Two young women wearing fashionable "Mark" sunglasses in Tiananmen Square celebrating China's National Holiday, October 1984. Courtesy of Li Xiaobin, photographer.

legitimize sunglasses as a fashion item, as sunglasses were previously called *mang jing* (blind glasses) and were mainly worn by the blind in China. "Mark sunglasses" rapidly became an indispensable fashion item among the fashionable youth of the 1980s. The popularity of *Man from Atlantis* led to the airing of another American show, *Garrison's Gorillas*. However, the American TV drama fad did not last long: *Garrison's Gorillas* was withdrawn halfway through its run allegedly for lack of artistic value and its bad societal influence.

Almost every imported TV series in the early 1980s, no matter the country of origin, caused a sensation and inspired millions to imitate and emulate the fashion styles of TV characters. Even cartoons, from both Japan and the United States, contributed substantially to the formation of Chinese pop culture, which was the main source of fashion inspiration at the time. But the national fascination with TV shows, as well as fashions from TV shows, was peculiar to the 1980s; there were numerous popular TV shows in later years, but none was able to spread such a broad range of fashions or to generate such intense emotions as those of the 1980s. This is due in large measure to the advent of a greater number of channels and other media outlets, coupled with the fact that TV had lost its novelty by the end of the decade.

Comparatively speaking, the influence of domestic TV dramas on fashion was negligible. Echoing the emergence of *menglong shi* (misty poetry) and *shanghen wenxue* (scar literature), the so-called *shanghen dianshiju* (scar TV dramas) depicted the scars inflicted on people's psyches and bodies by the Cultural Revolution. *Cuotuo suiyue* (Idle Away Time) of 1982 and *Jinye you baofengxue* (A Snowstorm Is Coming Tonight) of 1984 were typical TV dramas of this genre. From the mid- to late 1980s, more influential, domestically produced TV dramas became classics, such as *Sishi tongtang* (Four Generations under One Roof) of 1985, *Honglou meng* (*Dream of the Red Chamber*) of 1986, and *Xiyou ji* (*Journey to the West*) of 1987, all of which were based on popular novels. Depicting the present-day lives of ordinary people, the early 1990s dramas *Kewang* (Thirst), *Bianji bu de gushi* (A Story from the Editorial Department) and *Guo ba yin* (Satisfy a Craving) also achieved record-breaking TV ratings. Although these popular shows had a great impact on contemporary values and ideals, they rarely had any recognizable influence on fashion since most of their characters wore the ordinary dress of the day.

Mainland TV stations were all state funded and under state control. And despite the relaxation of control taking place in the economic sphere, every aspect of Chinese cultural life was still far from apolitical. In the eyes of the authorities, TV stations were initially created not to entertain but to serve as an effective propaganda tool. However, at the end of the 1970s, TV stations started to diversify their funding by showing commercial advertisements. Although early TV viewers perceived TV advertising negatively, it became the norm in the Chinese TV industry by the end of the 1980s. Still owned by the state but no longer entirely reliant on government funding, Chinese TV stations multiplied in the 1990s.

Despite the initial inability of these new TV stations to produce dramas that had a noticeable influence on fashion in the 1980s, these stations became fashion conscious in other, more direct ways. Serving as a giant classroom, some of them occasionally offered long-distance dressmaking lessons to their fashion-hungry audiences. Starting in the winter of 1981, Shanghai TV Station began airing a popular tailoring program in which famous master tailors gave lessons on pattern making, calculating material usage, and other tailoring techniques. As a reflection of the popularity of the program, over a million copies of the program notes were published and sold.[8] TV stations also held modeling contests to help boost ratings and to promote the domestic fashion industry.

Later on, newly emerging fashion outlets, such as fashion-oriented TV channels and programs, fashion magazines, newspapers, and the internet, replaced TV dramas and movies as major sources of fashion inspiration. Addressing the increasing demand for fashion information, since the late 1980s Chinese TV stations have created fashion channels and programs to provide a broad range of fashion coverage. The earliest television fashion program, *Fashion Galaxy,* hosted by Xiao Shuang, began in 1988 on Guangzhou TV Station. It was later shown on over a hundred TV stations in China, mainly reporting on international fashion trends and events.[9] Because of the success of this program, Xiao Shuang was awarded a cultural scholarship by the French government and gained the opportunity to study at the Institute Français de la Mode (IFM) as a visiting scholar. Upon her return, she created other fashion programs for Shanghai TV Station, Oriental Satellite TV, and Guangzhou TV Station.[10]

Today, fashion programs have become an indispensable part of nearly every national and municipal television station. For example, CCTV features *Oriental Fashion,* a program covering international fashion news, shows, and events, which delves into contemporary Chinese fashion attitudes and ideas. It also provides professional advice on clothing selection, care, makeup, and skin care, as well as topics like interior design, housing, and travel. Another influential fashion program, *The Complete Fashion Manual,* was created in 1997 by Hong Kong's Phoenix TV, broadly covering fashion trends, runway shows, interior design, high-tech electronics, luxury cars, and high-end consumption. Chinese TV stations have also featured imported fashion programs, such as the popular American reality television series *Project Runway,* which went on the air on dozens of TV channels throughout China in 2008.

## Styles from Movies

Besides TV shows, movies at the end of the 1970s and into the early 1980s provided another source of inspiration for fashion-conscious youth. After the Open Door policy was implemented, foreign movies were no longer automatically considered "spiritual pollution," though individual movies might still be banned because of their ideological disposition. Among the first apolitical foreign movies to make it past the censors in the late 70s were edited versions of the Japanese movies *Wang xiang* (Sandakan Brothel No. 8) and *Zhuibu* (Arrest, or *Kimi yo funnu no kawa wo watare*). Both were eye-opening experiences for a Chinese audience who for many years had been watching *yangbanxi* (model plays) and revolutionary movies imported from other communist countries such as the Soviet Union, Albania, North Korea, and countries in Eastern Europe.

Ba Jin, an influential and highly respected Chinese writer, recorded in his later-year retrospective, *Suixiang lu* (Whimsy Collection), the moral struggles Chinese experienced after the release of *Wang xiang* in 1978:

> Recently, the Japanese movie *Wang xiang* played in the capital in Beijing, in Shanghai, and in other big cities and caused intense debates. Some people openly opposed it. Some said, "Won't there be more hoodlums after showing movies like this?" And some even labeled this movie "obscene," which means it has to be banned. In short, the pressure is high. But there are also many people who supported the release of this movie ...[11]

The debates centered on a few scenes involving the exposed upper body of the lead female character in the film, a woman forced into prostitution. Various levels of public nudity continued to challenge the limits of the "emancipation of the mind" that the Chinese government promoted.

Unlike the turmoil surrounding the main character in *Wang xiang,* the main character in the movie *Zhuibu* played by Gao Cangjian (Ken Takakura) had universal appeal. Gao's character idealized masculinity for a generation of Chinese men stuck in the Mao suit and baffled by the displacement of their traditional male role during the Cultural Revolution in which everything revolved around class struggle. The austere, rugged, and masculine looks of Gao's character, dressed in a windbreaker with an upturned collar, matched his bold, aloof personality. Gao's character fascinated women so much that they began seeking "the Gao Cangjian type of man" thereafter. An influential play, *Xunzhao nanzi han* (Looking for Real Men), written by renowned Shanghai playwright Sha Yexin, keenly captured this common desire for powerful male figures. However, the lead female character in the play was disappointed to find such "manly" men in short supply in modern-day China. Chinese actors came to fear the appellation *naiyou xiaosheng* (creamy boy), which was used to describe men with effeminate looks and mannerisms—the opposite of the Gao Cangjian type. Nearly thirty years later when Zhang Yimou, one of the most renowned film directors in China, collaborated with Gao Cangjian on one of his movies, he recalled that at his graduation ceremony from the Beijing Film Academy in 1982 every graduate wanted to model himself after Gao. In fact, since coming into the public eye, Zhang himself has always worn his hair in a style similar to that of Gao Cangjian.

The 1980 debut of the first domestically produced post–Cultural Revolution scenic romance, *Lushan lian* (Love on Mount Lushan), launched a whole collection of inspiring new styles. *Lushan lian* tells a romantic love story between a lively Chinese American young woman visiting Mount Lushan and a local young man who would later enroll in the graduate school of Tsinghua University. What was especially touching to viewers at the time was not only the unusual romance between a local man and a woman from the United States, but also the strong sense of patriotism and optimism of the characters, even after the devastation suffered during the Cultural Revolution. In one scene, while watching the sunrise at the top of Mount Lushan, the young couple overflow with patriotism and shout in English into the valley below, "I love my motherland! I love the morning of my motherland!" This display of patriotic idealism matched the ideal image of the Chinese of the 80s. And it was an image that the government strove to promote: patriotic, optimistic, and idealistic, no matter what had taken place in the past. In later years, some critics lambasted the awkward blend of love and patriotism in the film, but audiences of the time were touched by its direct and passionate expression of youthful idealism.

*Lushan lian* was apparently politically correct, following the general guidelines regarding domestic productions of movies and TV programs: advocate socialist ideology and focus on the positive aspects of society. For the authorities, it was an urgent task to rebuild the trust between the people and the state that had been all but destroyed during the Cultural Revolution. They also hoped to regain the people's confidence and ensure their devotion to the country's future. One of the themes of *Lushan lian* was the importance of building a rapport among all Chinese, no matter what part of the world they hailed from and no matter their political affiliation— Communists of the mainland and the Nationalists of Taiwan in particular. The movie also clearly stressed the correlation between the fate of the nation and the fate of individuals, which, in a sense, further promoted patriotism.

Besides its political and love themes, costume design was another major attraction of this movie: more than forty eye-catching outfits were specifically designed for the lead female role. These outfits were considered the most fashionable and stylish of the day in China. At the time, when most women still wore drab jackets, loose pants, and shoes made of cloth, these colorful new outfits, presumably from America—including boot-cut hip-huggers, flowing skirts, blouses decorated with flounces, one-piece dresses, hats, scarves, high-heeled shoes, and handbags—gave the audience a visual shock. In a way, the political correctness of this movie helped people overcome their habitual fear of being too bourgeois. The outfits were therefore widely copied across China. The one-piece summer dress with a flounce collar and abstract small motifs featured in the film was especially favored and started a trend. And while fashion was used in the film only to indicate that the leading character had an American background, the effect of this cinematic display of fashion on the Chinese was just as influential as any Yves Saint Laurent haute couture collection of the 1970s on the French.

*Lushan lian* entered the *Guinness Book of World Records* in 2002 as the longest consecutively played movie in one movie theater—the theater located at the bottom of Mount Lushan, where the story was set. The theatre has continually screened this single movie ever since its release in 1980 and has since become a tourist attraction for visitors to Mount Lushan who wish to steep themselves in memories of that patriotic and idealistic era.

In 1984, fashion was the focal point of another domestically produced movie, *Jieshang liuxing hong qunzi* (Red Dresses Are in Fashion), the story of female workers in a Shanghai cotton mill. The film revolved around the pursuit of fashion and the different fashion attitudes that influenced the lives of the main characters. Tao Xinger, a pretty "model worker" at the mill, defeats all other fashion contestants at an informal fashion contest in a city park. In her long, sleeveless scarlet dress with a broad scoop neckline, fitted bodice, and voluminous skirt, Tao looked as elegant as a queen in her evening dress. But winning the fashion contest resulted in a sequence of mishaps for Tao and her coworkers who supported her and took part in the contest. The leader of their work unit ultimately disfavored Tao's sleeveless dress for being "too revealing." And the movie ends with these young textile workers learning important lessons about fair competition, work relationships, and attitudes toward fashion.

On the one hand, this movie expressed the universal desire of young women to look pretty and fashionable; on the other hand, it criticized the obsession with fashion as vain and the cause of many troubles in life. This movie clearly revealed the mainstream attitude toward fashion in the early to mid-1980s. People were encouraged to dress properly and appropriately. While moderate attention to fashion was deemed acceptable, bold pioneers of new fashions were stigmatized.

The year 1984 also saw the release of *Hongyi shaonv* (Girl in Red), in which a daring, boyish teenage girl named An Ran finds trouble by wearing an unconventional buttonless red shirt and publicly challenging the authority of her teacher by pointing out a pronunciation mistake. Adapted from a novel titled *Meiyou niukou de hong chenshan* (Red Shirt without Buttons), written by novelist Tie Ning in 1983, this movie viewed social relationships and social reality through the fresh eyes of an honest and fearless teenage girl. The red shirt itself was antitraditional because, unlike most shirts, it did not have buttons. The shirt came to symbolize the rebellious role of the character. In order to make a good student out of An Ran, An's sister forbade her to wear the red shirt. An Ran was puzzled by all she saw and experienced: why would wearing a beautiful red shirt cause trouble? This movie exemplified the struggles between conformity and individuality in both dress and life during the 1980s. These two popular movies both featured red clothes and are often cited as the source of the red clothing fad of the mid-80s that was evident in ski jackets, skirts, dresses, and athletic wear.

In 1987, the Hollywood movie *Breakin'* was imported into China and created a long-lasting break dancing craze among Chinese youngsters, who secretly practiced the dreamlike moonwalk at night. It did not take long for break dancing to emerge on school playgrounds and in public parks. Half-fingered black leather gloves, headbands, black or white Shanghai *Huili* brand sneakers, and baggy pants became the most sought after trendy gear of the time. Baggy pants were called *luobo* (daikon) pants in Chinese because they made the legs look like daikon radishes. They were loose around the hips and thighs and then tapered down, tightly gripping the lower calf and ankle. Break dancing gear gave Chinese youth a sense of fashion power that tapped into the energy of American youth culture.

The influence of movies on fashion continued with the influx of films from Taiwan, many of which were adapted from the works of the legendary romance novelist Qiong Yao. Qiong Yao movies dramatized romances between passionate, devoted lovers who often had to overcome family obstacles due to differences in social backgrounds. These Chinese Cinderella or Romeo and Juliet stories first swept over Hong Kong in the 1970s and made their way to the mainland in the 1980s. The infatuation with Qiong Yao romances was so widespread that they constitute the collective memory of a whole generation. Teenagers hid Qiong Yao's books under their pillows so their parents wouldn't confiscate this "spiritual pollution." A great number of Qiong Yao's readers were also loyal fans of her movies and TV shows. Along with memorable love stories, Qiong Yao movies brought in Taiwan's newest fashions as well as modernized versions of traditional dress forms such as the *qipao*. Hairstyles (such as long straight hair parted down the middle), dresses, shirts, vests, leather jackets, and skirts with novel patterns and colors that were worn by characters in these movies were widely copied by fans. As with TV show fashions, the influence of movies on fashion faded in the 1990s.

# –3–

# From Asexual to Unisex

As the 1980s began, the role of women in modern China and the dress that reflected that role were once again in flux. Throughout the twentieth century, changes in women's fashion reflected the circuitous course of women's liberation in the modern era. As the bonds of the feudal past receded in the Republican period (1912–1949), women gained more freedom to express their femininity, individuality, and modernity in dress. But many obstacles remained. With the founding of the People's Republic in 1949, the liberation of women and sexual equality became official government policy, codified in both the new constitution and the Marriage Law of 1950, which gave women new rights and new opportunities. During the 1950s, millions of women entered the labor force for the first time as a result of government-enforced communal living in which people's communes replaced families as basic societal units. This new way of living was supposed to also liberate women from their traditional subsidiary role in the family.

Throughout the Mao era, however, the push to recast society into a proletarian paradise in which all were equal also recast the impulses of many women: conformity was not only enforced from above, it was the natural outgrowth of an ideology that valued the communal over the individual. Thus the desire to express one's individuality was curtailed not only through external political and social pressure but also through a genuine commitment to revolution and so-called liberation on the part of many women. Ironically, the attempts at liberation through the complete eradication of all remnants of China's feudal past during the Cultural Revolution, including the Confucian subjugation of women, led to a new asexual uniformity in dress that subsumed most gender differences in a sea of revolutionary fervor.

By the end of the Cultural Revolution, women once again found themselves with feet and breasts bound, metaphorically if not literally, by the very ideology that sought to liberate them from such practices of the past. Expressions of femininity and individuality were once again severely restricted, and just as in imperial China (although for vastly different reasons), uniformity of dress reflected the society's notion of the ideal Chinese woman. But with the opening of China to the West in the reform era, women suddenly faced a myriad of fashion choices and found themselves in a similar position in some respects to the women of the early Republican period: what did it mean to be a modern Chinese woman, and how should dress both reflect and construct this meaning? And how could a woman display her femininity while still maintaining the ideological and moral purity that had been inculcated into women over the three previous decades of communism?

At first, these fashion choices remained risky and controversial, but women nevertheless longed to escape the asexual uniformity that was the hallmark of the Cultural Revolution. That they found this escape in unisex styles that gave them room to express their individuality and femininity without overemphasizing gender and sexual distinctions is not surprising: not only were unisex styles at the height of their popularity in the West, but it was also perhaps easier psychologically for society to accept the gradual shift that the move from asexual to unisex styles entailed. As the 1980s began, the women of China inched their way toward new roles, new freedom, and new fashions.

To examine women's new role and fashion in the reform era calls for a good understanding of how women's role was defined in the past and its influence on fashion. Moreover, the comparison between the modern woman at the beginning of the twentieth century, when the imperial rule transitioned into the Republican regime, and the new woman toward the end of the twentieth century in the reform era, when a centrally planned economy transitioned into a market economy, sheds light into women's changing societal role and their dress.

## The Birth of the Modern Woman

Throughout China's imperial history the role of women in society had always been one of distinct subservience to men in accordance with Confucian teachings. In the Confucian system the role of women was defined and governed by the "three submissions" (daughter to father, wife to husband, and widow to son) and the "four virtues" (morality, appearance, speech, and domestic skills). The roles, behaviors, and appearances of women that these encompassed were defined, interpreted, and judged by men. It was not until close to the turn of the twentieth century, when the imperial era finally came to a close, that Chinese women, largely through Western influence, began to embrace the idea of women's liberation and the notion that women should define their own roles in society.

In the early decades of the Republican era in the 1910s and 1920s, the female student came to symbolize the new, modern Chinese woman, as education was viewed as the first step on the path to liberation. Since many women's schools of the time were sponsored by foreign churches, women studied a mix of Western and Chinese subjects such as the Bible, English, Chinese, mathematics, singing, and domestic skills. Such a curriculum trained students to be "Western ladies with Chinese characteristics."[1] Since few women had the privilege of getting an education, either due to economic circumstances or because they came from a more traditional family that saw no need for female schooling, education also differentiated the new women from the old, who were kept at home and were usually illiterate. In this sense, female education of the time was largely a middle- and upper-class fashion. These privileged, educated young women not only exemplified city fashions but created an entirely new lifestyle for the Chinese woman. They served as national trendsetters as their lifestyles and dress were frequently chronicled in popular fashion magazines and newspapers. Even movie stars, opera performers, and prostitutes, who were the socialites and trendsetters of the age, began to dress like these newly fashionable students. Above all, these new women were characterized by "progressive and independent" minds and views. They stood for "civilized careers" and "civilized marriage," and their modern clothes were called "civilized clothing."[2]

This new lifestyle saw the entry of women into new spaces as well. Educated young women stepped out of their home sphere and entered public spaces that they had never ventured into before. They entered new "physical spaces like the school campus, the street demonstration, the public park, the boulevard; and new imaginary spaces, including newspapers and periodicals, calendar posters, new fiction, and cinema."[3] Expanded spaces for women were also reflected in increased outdoor activities such as swimming, horseback riding, cycling, and tennis.[4] The abandonment of foot binding also contributed to a greater sense of mobility and enabled women to pursue various activities in which they had previously been unable to participate. In short, an ever increasing sense of movement marked the process of modernization undertaken by Chinese women. This process was both influenced by and expressed in dress. From a practical standpoint, less-confining garments and accessories were in great demand in order to accommodate the involvement of women in physical activities. Aesthetically speaking, this new modern, mobile image of the Chinese woman called for a new look to match.

The traditional look of women in the imperial era was highly embellished and heavily accessorized. Garments were trimmed with intricate bands, piping, and rich embroideries; ears were pierced; feet and breasts were bound; long hair was carefully oiled and coifed and decorated with intricate ornaments. The new look of the early twentieth century, on the contrary, emphasized simplicity. Fashion magazines of the time, such as *Shanghai Puck,* aimed to introduce Chinese women to the newest Western fashions and called for a new and proper look for the modern woman:

> Let us have a new era in our dresses; not costly but of propriety, not extravagant but pure and neat ... A solution like this is the duty of every Chinese woman, high- or country-living, in order to improve the social outlook into a systematic one, rather than to beautify ourselves as to how men will be interested in us.[5]

A popular version of the "pure and neat" look among female students in the 1920s consisted of bobbed hair, "civilized clothing," and unbound feet in heeled leather shoes. "Civilized clothing" consisted of a light-colored blouse with bell-shaped sleeves and a round hem matched with a dark-colored three-quarter-length skirt. Bracelets, earrings, fans, and hair embellishments were usually avoided. This new look exuded women's liberation from head to toe and sharply departed from the looks of the past and its patriarchal Confucian system.

The traditional look had maintained a clear distinction between men's and women's clothing in order to differentiate the female sex in the highly sex-sensitive social system. Han Chinese women had worn separate tops and bottoms for thousands of years until the modern *qipao* came along in the 1920s. As Zhang Ailing (Eileen Chang) put it, "From time immemorial, women in China have been identified by the phrase, 'hair in three tufts, clothes in two pieces.'"[6] In contrast, male scholars had traditionally worn a one-piece long gown. Thus, the donning of the *qipao*, also a long one-piece gown, by the new women symbolically signified their equality with men. As Zhang explained:

> The difference between one piece or two pieces seems slight, even inconsequential, but women in the 1920s were quite sensitive to differentiation of this sort. They had been immersed in Western cultural influence and were intoxicated by its calls for equality between men and women, but the yawning gap between these ideals and the reality that surrounded them was a constant humiliation. Soured and angry, they sought to discard everything that smacked of femininity, even to the point of rejecting womanhood altogether. This was why the first *qipao* were angular and puritanical.[7]

The early *qipao* resembled the long gown of the male scholar, with a voluminous cut that concealed every line of the female body, but as time went on, the *qipao* became more form-fitting to stay in sync with Western fashion. The hemline of the *qipao* in the 1930s dropped to the ankle with side slit(s) subtly showcasing the shape of the legs. And in metropolitan areas like Shanghai and Beijing, fashionable women even adorned themselves in sleeveless and collarless *qipao*s made of thin gauze that left little to the imagination. However, the feminine fad of the 1930s did not survive the Sino-Japanese and Chinese civil wars of the late 1930s and 1940s. Generally speaking, despite the fashionable few in metropolitan areas, the prominent S-curve of the *qipao* displayed in calendars and movies was a rare sight in everyday life. The display of female body curves was not in favor in mass fashion until well into the 1980s.

Traditional Chinese society had strict social requirements regarding levels of body exposure, especially for females. In a general sense, both Chinese men and women considered their bodies private, sexual, sacred, and somewhat sinful. Chinese culture emphasized the individual's spiritual and moral life, and rarely regarded the human body as an object of beauty, as was the case in the West stretching back to ancient Greece. The Chinese body had disappeared for ages under loose-fitting garments. In the Qing dynasty and earlier, women securely covered their entire bodies except for the head and hands—women were even admonished not to show their teeth when smiling. Only in some periods during the Tang dynasty were women dressed in relatively revealing styles that exposed the neck and upper chest.

Male-defined traditional aesthetics even stressed the appreciation of the so-called *bingtai mei* (sickly beauty), which centered on extremely vulnerable femininity. This idealized pathological woman was slightly ill and looked pale and weak. She walked slowly, talked softly, and would only passively receive care and sympathy from her male protector. Her bound feet and willowy figure only enhanced her "pathological" beauty. Thus the new women tried to reverse this image by appearing as healthy and as strong as men. Imitating the male image, new women in the early twentieth century tried to obscure the female aspects of their bodies as a critical component of women's liberation.

However, complete equality could hardly be established between the imitators and the imitated. Martha Huang has argued that even Xu Dishan, a renowned scholar and essayist who was sympathetic to women's liberation and advocated new forms of dress for women that would erase their secondary sexual characteristics, was caught in this dilemma himself, because "in the end, it was really men who were to be liberated, and women who were practically erased."[8] As Huang observed, men identified women's liberation with their own personal liberation. And it was really men, not women, who defined modern womanhood. Progressive male intellectuals often deserted their more traditional, illiterate, foot-bound wives for liberated, "new women."[9] So while these men promoted women's liberation in their choice of partners, traditional women paid the price for this liberation by being ignored, stigmatized, pitied, and deserted.

In promoting the emancipation of women, radical intellectuals envisioned a new China in which women would give up adornment entirely because "decoration wasted time and money" and "its practices were unhygienic, obscured natural beauty, and made a woman look cheap."[10] This idea was echoed by educated women like Xie Bingying. When she was accepted to the Central Political and Military School in Wuchang in 1926, she was advised, "All your hair should be cut short. If you can shave it all off, like the men, all the better." And one of her girlfriends had a crew cut.[11] Female intellectuals were even called "Mister" as a token of respect for their education and as a sign of equality with men.

But this idealized androgynous image never really became popular among the masses. In fact, under the influence of Western fashion, femininity embodied in the lengthened and tightened *qipao* reached a peak in the 1930s. Some female activists were concerned that the focus on outward appearance was distracting from more important national issues. They also criticized this new feminine fashion as designed solely for the thin. "Fat women can't be liberated?" one activist asked sarcastically.[12] Accordingly, in the eyes of some, the "*qipao* typified the pseudo-modern woman," similar to their male counterparts who dressed in Western attire and carried canes, who some viewed simply as "Chinese aping foreigners."[13]

In 1934, the Republican government launched the New Life Movement, an effort to combat the rising influence of communism, Western individualism, and the moral ills of Chinese society. While modeled after foreign "modern citizens," the movement also called for women to return to their traditional roles according to Confucian values of motherhood and domestic duty. A spokesman from the Nationalist Party lectured young women students in Jiangsu province: "The women's movement in today's society is not a real woman's movement. It is a movement of imitating men."[14] And in Jiangxi province, detailed regulations were promulgated regarding the exact dimensions for hemlines (four inches below the knee), for the slit in the *qipao* (three inches above the knee), and for the length of blouses worn with trousers (three inches below the buttocks). Women were also policed for immodest clothes or flirtatious behavior.[15]

The trajectory of women's liberation in the Republican era seemed to swing like a pendulum. Rejecting the exquisite but confining femininity of the imperial era, women first sought their liberation through the complete erasure of the feminine. But these attempts to create an asexual uniformity in dress could not be sustained. Western influence and the desire of women to express and exhibit their own femininity led to the development of a more feminized look. The *qipao,* which signified gender equality in its early form, also evolved into more feminine styles. But women were never fully able to liberate their bodies. Well-behaved, respectable women still carefully covered their necks, legs, and the female S-curve until the 1980s. And the attempts of intellectuals of the early twentieth century to erase gender distinctions in dress would finally be realized only in the looks of millions of Red Guards several decades later.

## Revolutionary Asexuality

The Mao era saw a continuous reduction in women's adornment, culminating in the asexual dress prevalent during the Cultural Revolution. The attention given to the status of women, and gender issues generally, in the early years of the PRC was swept away as Chinese society became increasingly militarized. The paramount distinction during the Cultural Revolution was between the revolutionary and the counter-revolutionary—all other distinctions were secondary—and even noticing these "secondary" distinctions was viewed as a distraction from the revolutionary cause, if not a sign of insufficient dedication to the class struggle that was the hallmark of the revolution. Thus, organizations like the Women's Federation, which had long worked on the "woman problem" since the founding of the People's Republic, were shuttered during the Cultural Revolution.[16] Gender differences between men and women were consciously ignored as the Red Guard set out to create a revolutionary soldier who was neither male nor female, but first and only a sharp sword of the revolution.

In some respects this gave women a certain freedom from more traditional gender roles: whether they were sent down to the countryside or traveled far and wide as Red Guards spreading the thoughts of Chairman Mao, women were detached from the traditional family structure and its well-defined roles of wife, mother, and daughter. As traditional Confucian social and cultural values came under attack, women were freed in some ways from social judgments based upon traditional standards. Furthermore, the socialist pursuit of sexual equality through gender sameness resulted in the "loss of image, demeanor and perceptions distinctive to women and different from the male other."[17] Women appeared to be copies of men from the inside out. Whereas during the Republican period gender equality had been premised on women becoming like men, during the Mao era the premise of gender equality was the erasure of gender altogether: the male-centered "mister" of the liberated women of the Republican era became the gender-neutral "comrade" during the Mao era.

Matching their new, sexless role, asexual dress prevailed during the Cultural Revolution. As only time and energy spent on the revolutionary movement were deemed worthwhile, both women and men tried to avoid the appearance of vanity. Thus, adornment was generally shunned and was kept to a minimum. Feminine styles like skirts were thought to be bourgeois and were disfavored. Women wore their hair short and straight, wore neither makeup nor perfume, and dressed in plain clothes devoid of almost any form of decoration. This minimalist look deemphasized female characteristics and minimized biological differences in the appearances of men and women. The popular military style worn by both men and women is a prime example of this asexual style.

Compared to previous periods in Chinese sartorial history, during the Cultural Revolution the vast majority of the Chinese dressed themselves in perhaps the greatest uniformity, regardless of gender. In this sense, asexual dress dominated perceptions of Chinese in this era. However, although both men and women wore plain clothes in the same drab colors and the same square, simple cuts, minor details in women's and men's wear did exist that, to some extent, served to differentiate the sexes in Chinese eyes. For instance, to a casual observer a woman's dual-purpose jacket looked very much like a man's Mao-suit jacket, but it differed in the type and number of pockets and in the number of buttons. So while there was a strong impetus to implement an asexual style, subtle gender-based details remained in some garment forms.

## Femininity Returns

Chinese acceptance of new feminine fashions was accompanied by a gradually changing view of sexual relationships and the role of women in society. At the end of the 1970s, however, even mild public displays of affection between the sexes were still controversial. The picture shown in Figure 3.1, for instance, was taken in 1977, a year before the program of economic reform was launched, and was criticized at the time for its "capitalist" mood.[18] Even this seemingly innocent depiction of a young couple sitting together in public pushed the bounds of propriety between the sexes in the immediate aftermath of the Cultural Revolution. Dating itself, much less kissing in public, had long been considered obscene in China.

In the pre-Mao era, when arranged marriages were still the norm, dating was neither common nor seemly. During the Cultural Revolution, dating was still considered a decadent symptom of capitalism, in spite of the fact that communism had historically promoted free love as a way of dissolving feudal bonds and attachments. Passionate love was enveloped in glorious revolutionary friendships in which the only appropriate topic of conversation before marriage was work. Disguised love letters would often begin with revolutionary slogans like: "Respectfully wish Chairman Mao a long life! A long life!" or "Respectfully wish Vice Chairman Lin good health! Good health forever!" Being the more vulnerable sex to conventional rules, the consequences of being seen on dates were usually more severe for women than

**Figure 3.1** This picture of a young couple was criticized for its "capitalist" mood in 1977. Courtesy of Li Xiaobin, photographer.

for men. Also, the social pressure of avoiding becoming an "old maid" did not seem to recede with the heightened status of women during the post-Mao era.

But as China increasingly came under outside influence during the reform era, Western-style displays of public affection slowly became more acceptable. Love songs, movies, and novels from Taiwan and Hong Kong all contributed to shifting Chinese attitudes toward dating and romantic love. By the 1980s, couples could be spotted embracing or holding hands in city parks. While these displays remained shocking to many, milder displays of affection such as men carrying handbags or holding umbrellas for women were viewed positively, for they softened the traditional image of the austere Chinese male (Fig. 3.2). Such chivalrous displays, which were by nature also displays of feminine vulnerability (allowing men to carry their handbags or hold their umbrellas), were not viewed as negatively as in the previous era of "iron women."

After the abrupt end of the Cultural Revolution, women returned to their homes from their revolutionary posts and earned new positions in the reforming society. Accordingly, revolutionary asexuality in dress and societal roles receded. Society now encouraged women to seek beauty. In fact, both women and men gained a limited amount of political and social freedom that allowed them to begin adorning themselves again. But compared to the small number of urban fashion rebels who donned "bizarre looks," most women pursued a new sense of beauty with greater caution and consequently received much less criticism than those in the vanguard of fashion.

**Figure 3.2** Men carrying handbags for women in the Beijing Zoo in 1980, when such mild public displays of affection were in vogue. Courtesy of Li Xiaobin, photographer.

While new styles appealed to their desire for change, the urge to dress in attractive new fashions was tempered by the fear of standing out from the crowd. The new styles the female masses adopted were therefore not "too slim, revealing, transparent, or short," and conformed to the dress standards promoted by the authorities. At first, the revival of pre–Cultural Revolution fashions and the adoption of entirely new styles often took place in small and subtle ways.

As the 1980s began, women in makeup, with their hair curled, and dressed in colorful, form-fitting dresses and skirts appeared on the streets and "transformed China into a land not only of beauty but also of beauties."[19] But designers knew where the line was and were conscious of the need to "protect the virtuous image of women." "Our female comrades hate exposure. They don't want to appear to be frivolous," said women's clothing designer Fan Yongfa to the *Washington Post* in 1984.[20] The word "sexy" did not yet exist in the Chinese fashion lexicon, and for a few years designs from state-owned factories kept a conservative look with careful, minor modifications in collar and pocket shape, button placement, and trims. As a result, mass fashions emerged quietly on city streets without offending those who held negative views of fashion generally. But while sticking to mostly conservative styles, as Chinese women rediscovered feminine beauty they began to mix and match in unusual ways: fur coats with striped athletic pants was only one unique look among many that could be seen on the streets of Shanghai or Beijing in the early years of the reform era (Fig. 3.3).

But what was feminine beauty? Debates and discussions that attempted to address this question began to appear in the mass media as women wondered what to wear. The magazine *Women of China,* sponsored by the All-China Women's Federation (ACWF), featured discussions of women's beauty with articles representing different viewpoints. An article titled "Fragmental Thoughts Regarding Beauty" that appeared in the magazine in 1980 argued:

> Beauty is always objective, not subjective. Thus, the opinions of individuals could hardly count. Beauty reflects the spirit of the times. One cannot judge beauty without considering current historical conditions ... Beauty is something one cannot live without. But we think real beauty lies in the beauty of aspiration, of morality, of painstaking study, and of the spirit of inquiry, which surpasses the beauty of adornment, of the body, and of the happy life of one's own small family.[21]

This idea that women were insignificant as individuals and were significant only as part of a larger whole was still prevalent in 1980. But by the 1990s, at least in the sphere of fashion, a complete reversal had taken place. In the fall of 1991, *Women of China* published a series of articles discussing the beauty of modern women in which one author wrote, "I do not know what the beauty of modern women is, because in my opinion, the beauty of women lies in the eternal quality of the female sex, which has nothing to do with the era. A woman changes her dress frequently,

**Figure 3.3** Fashionable young women dressed in red down jackets, overcoats, and fur coats, matched with striped athletic pants, scarves, and high-heeled shoes or boots, in Beijing's Zhongshan park in January 1985. Courtesy of Li Xiaobin, photographer.

but underneath is always the woman who is a lover, wife, and mother."[22] This view that women were more than mere expressions of the era and that the feminine had an inherent value of its own provided more room for personal preference in fashion, which subsequently encouraged more individual styles.

The first notable feminine fashion appeared in women's hairstyles: no longer considered decadent and sinful, the perm signaled the return of "legitimate" femininity to China. In big cities, hair parlors capable of producing various permanent waves popped up as early as 1977 (Fig. 3.4). Their window displays advertised the newly popular hairstyles to fashion-conscious city girls throughout the country. But even the exploding number of new hair parlors had a hard time keeping up with demand, and long queues formed at the doors of Beijing's hair salons were a common sight at the end of the 1970s. At first the most popular perm style had large waves down to

**Figure 3.4** Window display of women in permed hairstyles for the Silian hair parlor on Beijing's Wangfujing Street, one of the most famous shopping streets in the capital, June 1977. Courtesy of Li Xiaobin, photographer.

the ear or chin-length, but styles of all lengths could soon be seen, with longer waves mainly reserved for young women. Women of all ages tried out perms, from little girls to senior citizens (Fig. 3.5).

Matching the feminine, exotic perm were rejuvenated clothing styles full of patterns and decorative details. Women of the 80s reversed the progressively minimalist trend in adornment that had prevailed over the previous decades and began to add new elements to their appearances. Initially, a wide variety of new styles were created simply by adding new elements to the existing dress forms of the late 1970s. These styles included women's blouses with flowered prints and ruffles, jackets with a slightly cinched waist, pleated skirts, tailored pants with a prominent crease, shirt-waist dresses, vests, and fur coats. Newly popular shirt styles featured embroideries on the chest and at the corners of the collar with peonies, magnolias, grapes, and peacock tails.[23] A variety of embellishments such as puffed sleeves, lace, ribbons, ruffles, cutouts, and floral prints, all of which had previously been shunned, were now used on women's clothing (Fig. 3.6). Plain shirts with bishop sleeves were often worn under vests with matching skirts made of woolens or woolen simulations.

Skirts, dresses, and flowery shirts, which were disfavored during the Cultural Revolution for being overly feminine, also reappeared. Pleated skirts were adopted by female opera performers as daily wear as early as the summer of 1978 and became a widespread fashion in the 80s.[24] *Jiefang Daily* reported in the summer of 1979 that

**Figure 3.5** This family picture shows a six-year-old girl and two young women in permed hair in Jingdezhen, an inland city, in July 1981. Courtesy of Juanjuan Wu.

Shanghai clothing stores located on Nanjing Road displayed "well-pressed, intensely pleated skirts made of filament fibers; light nylon flowery shirts in vivid colors; plain and elegant polyester and cotton-blend dresses, and paisley long pants with a straight cut and beautiful lines."[25] Early skirt styles were knee-length with pleats evenly spaced all around the waistline and were accordingly called "skirts with a hundred pleats." Pleated skirts were not, however, a recent invention: floor-length versions with "one hundred pleats" had been a common style worn by Chinese women in the imperial era. But when neatly adorned with nylon stockings or socks and leather or plastic sandals, the shortened pleated skirt acquired a modern image. The women of China in the 80s, decked out in their shortened skirts and sunglasses, felt just as liberated as their counterparts in the West in their considerably shorter miniskirts of a generation earlier.

Pencil skirts and their mini versions also made their way to China in the mid-80s. They were always worn with high stockings or pantyhose. Matching tops included suit jackets and loosely knit sweaters. Throughout the 80s and well into the 90s, nylon stockings and pantyhose were popular and became indispensable accessories to any form of skirt, dress, or short pants. They depicted the shape of the legs faithfully yet altered their look and feel, which in a way reduced the psychological impact of suddenly baring one's legs. Many women took new pleasure in the liberation of their legs from decades of concealment in baggy pants, but winter months proved challenging until warmer, opaque leggings came along.

**Figure 3.6** Ruffled pastel-colored or patterned dresses with a belted waist were trendy among female workers in the early to mid-1980s in Beijing. Courtesy of Li Xiaobin, photographer.

These opaque stirrup leggings made of nylon-Lycra were popular from the late 1980s to the mid-1990s. The leggings fashion originated from gym and dance clothes, inspired by the fitness craze of the 1980s in the West. At the same time, *jianmei cao* (aerobics) swept across China and stirrup leggings became known as *jianmei ku* (fitness pants). At first, aerobics was seen more as a novel form of entertainment than a form of exercise. Performers in fitness pants put on disco dancing and aerobics shows to a curious public. Later on, as a widespread fashion, these fitness pants lost their connection to aerobics altogether and liberated women's leg lines from baggy pants. As they became more popular, leggings were adopted by women of various body sizes and of nearly all ages, except seniors. The most popular leggings came in black and various shades of gray. They were versatile as they matched with any tops and were often accessorized with high-heeled leather shoes for a dressier look and running shoes for a casual look. Common matching tops for stirrup leggings were shirts with puffed sleeves, patterned sweaters, and sweatshirts with bat sleeves. Some women also wore them with suit jackets. These ensembles created an inverted triangular silhouette that was popular at the time.

However, stirrup leggings were widely criticized in the media for their bold depiction of female body shapes. Pushing the limits of modesty, stirrup leggings worn like skintight trousers, normally without a skirt or a long top, caused a considerable amount of discomfort as a long-lasting and widespread fashion. Not only were the shapes of the wearer's bottom and legs completely exposed, the leggings' shiny texture and the visibility of panty lines only exaggerated the effect. Most unbearable of all to Chinese critics was that women of all body shapes and sizes adopted this fashion without considering whether it suited them individually. Also, the stirrups were visibly exposed when worn with leather shoes. This exposure was equated with the exposure of panties or bra straps and was thought to be an "embarrassing fashion" and made stirrup leggings the most vulgar of all trendy clothes.[26]

Many critics considered stirrup leggings a catastrophe of Chinese femininity. But supporters of the fashion saw it as a signifier of Chinese women's growing confidence in themselves. "To display one's body curves under public scrutiny is not something that can be done by every woman," one supportive author wrote in the *Shanghai Fashion Times* on June 1, 1992. "Feeling good about yourself, this is a kind of confidence. Apparently, the purpose of adornment is to sell oneself to the world in a visual sense, but more important is that pleases you. As long as you like it and think it is good and appropriate you should wear it."[27] This tolerant and encouraging attitude toward new fashions generally marked the fashion scene of the 90s. It seemed what mattered most was not what women wore but how they felt about what they wore.

New fashions continually emerged that redefined the Chinese notion of femininity, decency, and modesty. After surviving the challenge of stirrup leggings, the Chinese were less shocked by the more revealing fashions of the 1990s: bare-midriff tops, clothes made of transparent fabrics, and underwear as outerwear. Although criticism regarding the immoral aspects of fashion never completely vanished in the state-controlled media, most discussions of fashion by the mid-1990s had shifted focus to aesthetics from morality and ideology. And by the 1990s, the liberation of the female body in China was finally "geared to international standards."

Even though Western influence prevailed in hairstyles, cosmetics, and clothing, some insisted that Chinese femininity lie in traditional garments such as the *qipao*. However, neo-modern women did not embrace the *qipao* as a popular fashion, even though many scholars still saw the *qipao* as a sartorial symbol of China's modern history and a symbol of liberated femininity. People who had fond memories of it from the 1950s, or even from the 1930s, anticipated its widespread return in the 1980s. But after taking their old *qipao* out of storage, many found that it looked out of place on the modern streets of Shanghai and Beijing.

## The Unisex Trend

While reclaiming their feminine side, Chinese women also competed with men in every field in the changing Chinese economy. The important role of women in the workforce called for an appropriate wardrobe that would help to establish and express their new economic role, which was supposedly equal to that of men. The congruent influences of international fashion and women entering the workforce contributed to the popularity of unisex looks in the 80s. Some of the shared, unisex styles of the time included bell-bottom pants, patterned shirts, jeans, business suits, safari suits, Dacron shirts, fencing shirts, T-shirts, jackets, oversized knit sweaters, knee-length trench coats, leather jackets or overcoats, nylon ski jackets, *luobo* (daikon) trousers, athletic wear, and various accessories.

Meanwhile, women's liberation continued into the 1980s, reaching an entirely new level. The media aggressively promoted women's liberation and the ability of women to "hold up half of the sky," a slogan coined under Mao. After the initiation of economic reforms in 1978, the idealized "iron women" of Mao's era metamorphosed into the "able women" of the 1980s. The ubiquitous shapeless cuts and drab colors of the asexual dress of the previous era were replaced with a great variety of both feminine and unisex styles in the 1980s. And unlike the sexless role women had previously played, in the reform era women resumed their traditional roles as mothers, wives, and daughters while also taking on new roles as businesswomen, business owners, and workers. Women's dress both reflected and constructed these changing roles. Thus, the unisex trend of the 80s was paired with femininity, whereas the asexual trend of previous eras attempted to subsume or obliterate femininity altogether.

More and more women entering the workforce supplied the booming economy with much-needed labor. Socialists believed that the involvement of women in public industry was of the utmost importance to the emancipation of women and their quest for equality with men.[28] The reforming society thus embraced its working females with great enthusiasm. Families also encouraged and sponsored their female members to acquire education and skills that would help them secure jobs. Becoming a housewife was usually viewed as an option of last resort. Working women were rewarded with heightened social status, increased economic independence, and greater freedom in their personal adornment and life choices in general. Also, since unemployment was often associated with incompetence and questionable morals— displayed in things like "bizarre looks" and dating in public—lacking a job also had social consequences for women. "No jobs, no morals" was one thirty-eight-year-old teacher's comment on a young couple embracing in Beihai Park on one Beijing afternoon in 1981.[29]

But while opening up to Western influence in the 80s, China was still affected by its own feudal past, in which women were treated as sexual objects and commodities, much as in other pre-industrial societies. Some city officials in southern China, for instance, considered prostitution a form of economic stimulus and thought that the local red-light district provided "a soft environment that attracts investment."[30] And the increasing incidence of the abduction of women for sale in some rural areas was also viewed by some as a "useful commercial activity."[31] Although in rural areas women were still seen as the inferior sex, in cities women made substantial progress in education, employment, and politics and on the home front. Traditional prejudices and obstacles still remained to a degree, however. The implementation of the one-child birth-control policy in the 1970s further increased the value families placed on the female sex. Although in most rural areas infant girls were usually greeted with frowns or even abandonment, in urban areas baby girls were often treasured as the family's only offspring.

At the end of the 1970s, for the most part, only a small number of city dwellers had tasted the excitement of new fashions, but by the mid-1980s the entire country took part. Throughout the 1980s both Chinese men and women made great effort to appear fashionable and socially proper, while the political class attempted to shield the society from "total Westernization." Other than the strong influence of the West, the influence of political leaders on fashion was still great, since most Chinese did not want to take political risks solely for the sake of their appearance. Leaders of the reforming nation encouraged people to don new designs as a symbol of their "emancipated minds." Promoting fashion trends would also have the added benefit of spurring domestic consumption. Diverse dress would also show the outside world the remarkable difference the Chinese had made in themselves and their country.

In addition to political leaders, actors, actresses, singers, and others in the entertainment industry were also important trendsetters. Artists, models, college students, and small business owners—especially those who bought and sold fashionable clothes—were fashion trendsetters, too. Ordinary people finally accepted the notion that a legitimate function of dress was to improve one's appearance, a view formerly regarded as decadent and bourgeois. As much as most Chinese may have wanted a new image, the government desired a new image for China even more, as they hoped to reestablish domestic confidence in socialism and market the new China and its "socialism with Chinese characteristics" to the outside world.

This new Chinese image was first constructed in the 1980s as a sort of fashion Frankenstein made up of both contemporary and retro Western fashions from the 1970s and 1960s. The "bigger is better" trend that was popular in contemporary Western fashion was visible in Chinese fashion as well: oversized shirts, T-shirts, sweaters, sweatshirts, jackets, and suits with padded shoulders were in vogue for both men and women. Matching bottoms, such as tight-fitting pants, ankle-hugging baggy pants, riding breeches, and tight leggings, gave the ensemble a V silhouette. The V silhouette eventually overtook the A silhouette that was popular at the end of the 1970s and in the early 1980s.

The Western unisex trend, spurred on by the hippie subculture of the 60s and 70s, typically consisted of long hair, jeans, patterned shirts, caftans, headbands, Indian shawls, and other ethnic accessories. Because hippies of both sexes wore such similar outfits, it was often difficult to tell males and females apart at a distance, which accounts for the notion that such dress forms were unisex. Stripped of their cultural associations, unisex hippie fashions ultimately reached the other side of the Pacific and transformed the look of Chinese youth of the reform era. Hip young men and women on the streets of Beijing and Shanghai of the late 70s and early 80s emulated the hipsters of San Francisco or New York of a decade earlier, with their long hair, jeans, patterned shirts, and sunglasses. But while their counterparts in the counterculture of the West turned on to rock music, urban Chinese youth, clad in pseudo-hippie fashions, danced to a different tune: disco music and Deng Lijun's love songs.

As China strove to catch up with international fashion during the 80s, the shoulder pads of jackets and coats of Chinese women grew thick and large. The Chinese media ran stories on the contemporary designs of Yves Saint Laurent and Valentino, such as suits and overcoats with exaggerated shoulder pads, which gave the Chinese audience a sense of current Western fashions. Suits and coats with wide shoulders, wide lapels, and a square silhouette depicted the "superwoman" image of the 1980s. Thick shoulder pads were even added to blouses, dresses, and sweaters. Meanwhile, many women started to take on management positions and many started their own small businesses; manly business suits reinforced the sense of power Chinese women had recently obtained in the business world, much as they did for Western business-women.

In a sense, Western suits revolutionized the wardrobes of Chinese women more than they did men's. Chinese men had previously donned Western suits during the Republican era, but women hadn't until the 1980s. Women's suit jackets were often worn with a matching skirt and an intricately designed white or pastel shirt. The ensemble of a vest worn over a matching skirt was also fashionable attire, which created the effect of a three-piece suit worn without the jacket. Plaid or solid colors were both popular, with wool suits considered of superior quality. The style of the suit jacket varied widely, with many types of collars and lapels, and was frequently decorated with unusually placed buttons. Since the silhouette remained rather stable, the fashionability of a suit ensemble depended on its details and trim. Chinese designers in state-owned apparel factories showcased their sophisticated construction skills in women's suits by incorporating traditional embellishing, piping, banding, stylish seams, box pleats, inverted pleats, embroideries, and beading. These new details created a new, complex look distinguishable from that of the previous decades. In suits and other fashions, these detailed decorations and embellishments were the hallmark of local designs in the 1980s. The award-winning designs and new fashions of 1984 in Shanghai published in the *Shanghai Apparel Yearbook* featured a variety of suit styles with elaborate details.[32] Skirts were mostly knee-length with one or more pleats. Some were pencil skirts with short slits and some were bell shaped.

Pantsuits seemed to be less popular than the suit-skirt ensemble in the 80s, while variations on the dual-purpose jacket were still worn over nonmatching long pants. The revolutionary associations of women in pants in the West did not apply in a Chinese context. Elizabeth Wilson considered "the advance of the trouser for women" possibly "the most significant fashion change of the twentieth century" because "for centuries, western women's legs had been concealed."[33] Both pants and jeans were, in some sense, symbols of women's liberation in the West. According to Wilson, trousers were respectable wear for women only in specific areas or on specific occasions until well after World War II. And "trousered women were not allowed into the

Royal Enclosure at Ascot until 1970."[34] Compared to the social and psychological struggle Western women had gone through to incorporate pants into their daily wear, wearing pants seemed natural, if not a little boring, to Chinese women. Unlike the skirt-centered sartorial history of Western women's wear, pants, along with skirts, had been a staple of Chinese women's wear for thousands of years. And Chinese women started to wear only pants, instead of with a skirt worn over it, in the late Qing dynasty around the turn of the twentieth century. Also, pants were worn by everyone in China during Mao's era. Thus, when so many other options suddenly became available, Chinese women did not immediately resort to pantsuits in order to appear fashionable or liberated. However, pantsuits did become popular business attire for Chinese women in the 1990s. On the whole, the designs of the suits in the 90s were greatly simplified in their decorative details to emphasize a refined taste that reflected the professionalism of the business world.

While women's suits went largely unnoticed in the media, men's suits made a notable comeback in the 80s. Men's fashion was just as prominent and changed just as much as women's fashion at the time. The domestic men's suit-tailoring business started with orders from abroad, orders from Chinese going abroad, and orders from overseas Chinese visitors. Greater interaction with the outside world created a growing demand for proper Western attire. For example, a picture featured in *Wenhua yu shenghuo* (Culture and Life) magazine showed Chinese film representatives in suits and ties during a visit to Hollywood[35] in the fall of 1978.

New suits were usually handmade by skilled tailors in private tailor shops or by state-owned stores. In Shanghai, master craftsmen who before 1949 had worked for famous store brands like Peiluomeng passed on unique tailoring skills to the younger generation at newly established clothing factories.[36] The earliest Western suit stores were established in Shanghai by Western merchants in the mid-nineteenth century, mainly to serve Westerners living in Shanghai. And Chinese tailors initially learned suit construction techniques by mending Western suits. A few decades later, in 1896, the first Chinese store specializing in tailoring Western suits, Hechang Xifu Dian, was founded.[37] Thereafter, a fine tailoring tradition in Western suits, as well as other Western styles, was established in Shanghai. Famous stores such as Peiluomeng, Pengjie, Hongxiang, and Hengsheng in Republican-era Shanghai—at a time when Western suits were in vogue among the middle and upper classes— resumed business (under different ownership) and reestablished their reputations early in the reform era.

Secondhand suits from Hong Kong, Taiwan, and Japan that came through Guangzhou or Fujian were also popular among image-conscious urban youth with limited financial means. Recycled suits traded on Wenzhou clothing markets for 50 to 60 *yuan*, roughly the equivalent of a month's pay for city workers. Early in the post-Mao era, suits were worn mainly by salesmen and businessmen or were otherwise reserved for special occasions such as weddings. Photo studios began to rent Western-style wedding gowns and suits to couples for the production of wedding albums. But state

employees and cadres generally resisted Western suits and preferred a more orthodox image in the early 80s, adorning themselves in slightly modified styles of the
previous era.

From a political perspective, the readoption of the Western suit was initially a
political act that confirmed China's desire to reform and open to the West. Hu Yaobang, the Party leader at the time, stressed the need to change lifestyles since, historically speaking, social reform had always been linked to changes in lifestyle. He also
stressed that in terms of ideology one should not be bound by old habits and should
not be afraid of reform. The Party's youth paper, *China Youth Daily,* reflecting the
views of Hu, also "defended young people's attraction to beauty as 'correct and positive.'"[38] Besides, Hu said, "Western suits are convenient; why couldn't we promote
them?"[39] He subsequently appeared on national television wearing a Western suit in
1984, becoming the first Chinese political leader to do so. At the time, it was simply
unthinkable for a Party leader to appear in public in anything other than a Mao suit,
and his appearance in a Western suit was shocking to most around the country.[40]
Similarly, Zhao Ziyang, China's prime minister, was in favor of Western suits and
clothing reform. He appeared in a Western suit when he visited the United States
in January of 1984. "When the prime minister of China wears a Western suit," he
said, "then nobody will fear to wear fashionable dress."[41] The persistence of national
leaders in promoting Western suits curtailed debates over whether this unmistakably
Westernized image was suitable for ordinary Chinese.

In China's search for economic advancement in the 1980s, the suit seemed to be
an immediate and effective way to modernize. Just like adopting fast food (Kentucky
Fried Chicken, McDonald's, and Coca-Cola were all present in China by the early
1990s), wearing the Western suit was viewed as a similarly fast and easy way to
modernize. Since modernization was, to a large extent, equated with Westernization
in China, the modern image Western suits offered was exactly what Chinese craved.
It also matched China's rapidly Westernizing physical and social environments. Furthermore, the support of the country's political elite reduced skepticism and silenced
criticism of the associations suits had with the West. The firm endorsement of the
Western suit, and fashion generally, by national political figures finally helped the
masses separate fashion from ideology, although the media remained sensitive to
ideological issues in fashion for another decade.

In addition, responding to calls from political leaders and following influential
trends had become second nature for many people; after all, no one wanted to be
left behind, and many had learned the hard lessons of standing out from the crowd
over the previous decades. The simplicity and symmetry of the Western suit also
matched Chinese preferences for a neat, orderly, and balanced look. Suits featured
subdued colors similar to the "three old colors" that were worn during the Cultural
Revolution, which made them less alien and therefore more appealing to generally
conservative mainstream tastes. In the early years of the reform era, as the Chinese
economy began to expand and as society increasingly centered on material wealth,

wearing a suit also became a display of economic status, as suits were relatively expensive compared to alternative clothing choices. Thus, as more people adopted the suit, a new type of uniformity emerged that in some ways seemed to echo the era of the Mao suit.

Local newspapers in Shanghai in 1984 recorded skyrocketing demand for suits that year. The Party signaled its final endorsement of Western suits in 1987 when all of the members of the Standing Committee of the Political Bureau donned suits and ties at the televised First Plenary Session of the 13th Congress of the Chinese Communist Party. The resulting media frenzy over this political summit with Party leaders in suits sent a clear massage to every corner of China: Western suits were not only politically safe but politically favored. From then on, suits were the tacitly agreed upon uniform for Communist Party meetings.

Following the leaders of the country, people of all occupations throughout China quickly adopted Western suits as daily wear. However, most of the elderly—Deng Xiaoping chief among them—still preferred older styles such as the Mao suit. And modified versions combining elements of both the Mao suit and the Western suit created an aesthetic and political compromise that fit more conservative tastes. Western suit and shirt, often worn without a tie, became a universal fashion by the late 1980s. However, while the physical form of the suit remained largely intact in the course of its migration from the West to China, the formality of the suit and its connotations of professionalism were lost, partially because suits were not reserved for the business world or formal occasions in China. In fact, Western suits were so popular that peasants wore them when harvesting rice and construction workers wore them when operating cranes. Thus, it was not uncommon to see suit jackets and ties worn with jeans and running shoes.

The exploding demand for suits also propelled the transition from hand tailoring to mass production. As prices lowered and supply increased, the spread of the suit accelerated greatly. But the primitive technology and cheap chemical fibers used in mass-produced suits became apparent after the first wash, especially since dry cleaning was not a feasible option for a majority of the people. As a result, the shape of these suits was easily distorted and the fabrics wrinkled easily. These poorly made suits came to distinguish Chinese from other Asians abroad in the early 1980s.[42] Not until the late 80s did domestic suit producers vigorously modernize manufacturing lines due to intensified competition.

Following suits, zippered or buttoned jackets became popular in China in the mid- to late 1980s. Since jackets were not as closely associated with the West as suits, and since the atmosphere of the late 80s was relatively more relaxed in terms of clothing, jackets were received less skeptically than suits had been. Popular jackets were zippered, with a banded or gathered hem on or below the waistline and cuffed sleeves. A jacket matched with sand-washed jeans was a favorite unisex ensemble for both young men and women. Jackets with creased dress pants were also common. Various jacket styles were designed locally to suit different tastes, such as "champagne" jackets (in Chinese "champagne" rhymes with *xiangpin,* which means "two kinds of fabrics sewn together to create a contrasting effect"). Leather jackets with either a controlled or loose hem were chiefly worn by the newly rich, usually private business owners.

In summer, short- or long-sleeved Dacron shirts in virtually the same style came into vogue for both men and women. Since the mid-1960s, shirts made of Dacron polyester had gained favor for their novel characteristics compared to cotton and were popular for several decades up until the late 1980s. These Dacron shirts were dubbed *dique liang* (cool indeed) shirts, stressing their improved air permeability. At a time when fabric shortages were still commonplace, Dacron shirts made urban workers the envy of their rural relatives, and they were clearly a status symbol at the end of the 1970s and in the early 80s. The shirts usually featured a simple cut for a loose fit for both men and women. And educated men never failed to remember to attach a pen to the outside of the front top pocket of these shirts or to their jackets as a sign of education and intelligence. This was in line with Deng Xiaoping's popular maxim that "science and technology are the first productivity," in stark contrast to Mao's Cultural Revolution–era slogan, "The more knowledge, the more reactionary."

Despite fabric shortages and technical obstacles in the mass production of clothing, the pent-up demand for new styles that had built up over the previous decade fueled the revival of mass fashion in the 1980s. Immediately upon the arrival of new merchandise, people flocked to fabric and clothing stores. Large, state-owned garment factories did a booming business, especially those that produced brand-name shirts. Domestic brand names in the 80s enjoyed a golden era in which everything they produced quickly sold, but competition intensified when Western apparel brands poured into China in the 90s.

One domestic brand that achieved national fame in the early 80s was Xiongmao (Panda). Panda produced shirts for men at the Zhujiang Shirt Factory in Guangzhou. Long queues often formed at Panda-shirt sales promotions in which free gifts like calendar posters were given away with each purchase.[43] And almost as soon as commercial advertisements were permitted in China, Panda shirts launched a series of successful advertising campaigns. Panda launched ad campaigns in early 1980 featuring the slogan "*Xiongmao pai chenshan, ni zhuo zui yan*" (Panda brand shirts suit you the best) in a variety of media, including radio, print, TV, and billboards. And Panda shirts soon proved popular with consumers. Another domestic brand, Tiantan, also produced popular men's shirts and won the National Golden Award in 1979. The Tiantan factory (the Beijing Shirt Factory) also produced shirts for such world-famous brands as Yves Saint Laurent, Calvin Klein, and Pierre Cardin, among others.[44] Simaituo (Smart) and Kaikai brands, both made in Shanghai, were major competitors of Xiongmao and Tiantan. Simaituo had been a well-established brand name since the 1930s. At its peak in the 1940s, Smart brand shirts were a popular export item. The brand shone again in the 70s and 80s after restructuring and upgrading its product lines.

Since shirts were a staple item of dress worn by virtually every adult in China at the time, shirt brands cultivated the earliest post-Mao sensitivity to brand names among mass consumers. Early brand names gained their fame mainly through reliable quality instead of novel fashions. With a relatively uniform design, especially for male shirts, consumers were more concerned with functionality. The firmness and smoothness of the collar and cuffs, wrinkle resistance, and shrinkage were keys to satisfaction. Only relatively technologically advanced and specialized factories located in major cities were capable of producing shirts of this quality. Despite the lack of competition, large factories made great efforts to improve the quality of their products and strove to provide decent customer service. The Shanghai producer of Xinyue brand shirts, for example, offered to repair cigarette burns for a small service fee. And consumers could return Xinyue shirts that had quality defects even after they had been worn.[45]

In this era, styles could quickly gain nationwide popularity, but they could fall out of favor just as fast: mass trends and mass changes in fashion were commonplace in China after the mid-1980s. The unisex *wenhua shan* (cultural shirts) fad was one such trend that came as quickly as it went. While it may be true that "clothing messages are expressive in an indirect and allusive way," in the early 1990s, those who wore *wenhuan shan* wanted to express themselves as directly as possible.[46] The usually discreet Chinese suddenly became outspoken through these "cultural" T-shirts. Large Chinese characters printed on these T-shirts shouted out explicit messages of love, frustration, and other views on life: "Only Mom is best in this world," "My future is not a dream," "Heaven has endowed me with talents for eventual use," "A peaceful life for all good people," "Money is not almighty, but without money, nothing is all righty," and "Leave me alone, I am fed up" (Fig. 3.7). Urban teenagers competed to come up with the most creative sayings for their shirts, borrowing from movies, songs, cartoons, poems, and old sayings to give their otherwise plain T-shirts some character. Cultural shirts were worn with dress pants (both tucked and untucked), casual pants, jeans, or patterned shorts by men and tight leggings, shorts, jeans, or skirts by women.

The coolest T-shirts carried messages that were interpreted as signs of rebellion and unhealthy thoughts, such as "Leave me alone, I am fed up," "I only follow my feelings," "Really exhausted," "I don't know how to please people," and "Getting rich is all there is." Older, more conservative Chinese had a hard time discerning whether the youngsters wearing such slogans on their chests had lost merely their way or their minds. Foreigners living in China also used this fad to vent out their frustrations with living in China in Chinese-style humor: "I am a foreigner. Don't ask me to exchange dollars." As this fad began to turn into a national trend, the government finally issued "emergency regulations" and formally banned the manufacture and sale of "unhealthy" cultural shirts in Beijing.[47] "Cultural shirts transmit an ideology incompatible with our society," *China Youth Daily* warned its readers. "The words—shady, negative, cynical—benefit nobody, and bear dispirited and decadent feelings."[48] And the *Beijing Daily* suggested that patriotic and pro-communist

**Figure 3.7**   On the left, the T-shirt reads, "Leave me alone, I am fed up." On the right, it says, "My future is not a dream." Pictures taken in the early 1990s. Courtesy of Li Xiaobin, photographer.

slogans be used on these shirts; for example, "Study hard and make daily progress," and "I must train myself for the construction of the motherland."[49] Needless to say, these slogans failed to make their way onto T-shirts.

Athletic wear, as a major component of the unisex trend, was perhaps the earliest casual wear in the post-Mao period embraced by Chinese youth, especially students. College students were seen as "The Favored Sons of Heaven," and attending college was the dream of every ambitious young man and woman. College students often adorned themselves in athletic attire, which was both visually trendy and spiritually "healthy." Vivacious female college students shown in artist Luo Qun's oil painting *Huangjin shidai* (Golden Age) in 1980 were dressed in polo shirts or athletic pullover tops with a round neckline and matched with skirts or pants. The athletic wear craze was fueled by the five consecutive world championships won by the Chinese Women's National Volleyball Team. Many saw the victories as a sign of China's rise in the world, and the volleyball team therefore became national heroes and models for all Chinese women. Both young women and young men adopted the dark blue uniforms with white stripes on the side of the sleeves and trousers worn by the team. Many school uniforms today resemble this blue-and-white athletic uniform.

Home sewing in the 80s was still popular and supplemented the limited offerings of the newly reconstituted apparel industry. If people could not make new clothes, they could at least alter old styles into new fashions. Women often altered their boy-friends', husbands', or brothers' old clothes to create oversized trendy styles for themselves when women's ready-to-wear clothing failed to meet the demand for large sizes.[50]

Knitting was another widespread domestic skill at the time. Friends and col-leagues traded novel knitting patterns, and those with superior skills created new pat-terns and silhouettes. Turtlenecks, round necks, bat sleeves, large ribs on knits, and large flowery or geometric patterns were widely adored features of knitted sweaters or vests. Women and men donned similar styles in knits. The knit trend was further stimulated by characters in popular TV shows who wore knitted sweaters. Mass-produced brand-name wool sweaters also started to attract the attention of people with financial means. Along with down jackets, leather jackets, fur coats, and wool overcoats, winter fashion was remarkably diversified in the early 80s (Fig. 3.8).

In 1984, the *Economist* noted that "most Chinese resemble stuffed laundry bags in the winter, but smart young things in Peking and Shanghai have forsaken the drab standard issue cotton-padded navy blue and olive overcoats for down parkas of bright red and electric blue."[51] The down parka, called *huaxue shan* (ski jacket) in Chinese, was the winter rage for both sexes throughout the 1980s. The ski jacket fashion in China started almost by accident. According to *Xinmin Evening News*, in 1978 the Xiangqian Clothing Store, an influential state-owned manufacturer and

**Figure 3.8** Leather jackets and down jackets worn by fashion-forward young people in 1986 in Ti-ananmen Square. Courtesy of Li Xiaobin, photographer.

retailer in Shanghai, made use of bundles of nylon materials left over for export by designing a nylon winter jacket interlined with sponge.[52] The first two hundred pieces were put on the local market for approximately twenty *yuan* each (roughly one third to one half of an urban worker's monthly salary) as a test run. To their great surprise, the jacket was an immediate hit. The design was improved in 1979 by replacing sponge with acrylic, which only made the jacket even more popular with consumers in Shanghai. As other store brands began producing the jacket, they varied the design and expanded the filling materials to include polyvinyl chloride fibers, down, and needle-punched nonwovens, among others. By the late 1980s, people from all walks of life—men and women, young and old—were wearing them. And despite high production volumes, supply could not keep up with demand. In 1988, *China Textile News* reported that overzealous patrons of the Wuxi Trade Show destroyed five checkout counters when rushing to buy down ski jackets made in Shanghai.[53] They interviewed a seventy-one-year-old shopper at the show who remarked with enthusiasm: "Wearing down jackets was something you would never think of a few years ago. But this year I've seen many elderly people wearing them, so I chose this light-colored one that will make me look younger."

By the end of the 80s, fashion was no longer the sole privilege of the young. In the pursuit of fashion, people of all ages began discarding their old clothes long before they were worn out. Thus, fashion had become a critical criterion, in addition to function, in the purchase of new clothes. As the economic circumstances of many improved, frugality gave way to fashion. Nan Ni, a popular essayist, recalled that she wore different colored ski jackets each year. Her preference for the ski jacket stemmed in part from her great hatred of the old cotton coats, common in earlier years, which she thought made her look like a silkworm.[54]

## Popular Fashion Accessories

Along with the emergence of unisex clothing, fashion accessories in similar styles for women and men also appeared. Wristwatches became a prominent and highly sought after fashion accessory in the early 80s for both men and women. And because of their high price, they also became a symbol of prestige: when having pictures taken, people always made sure their watches were visible. A medium-grade watch cost no less than 100 *yuan,* or at least a few months' salary, and they were among the few "luxury" items that women desired as wedding gifts from their husbands.[55] Wearing a wristwatch differentiated not only the well-to-do from the poor but also the educated from the uneducated, and state-employed workers from peasants.

Hats were another popular accessory of the 1980s. The sexless flat green cap worn by the Red Guards during the Cultural Revolution was generally displaced in cities in the 80s when gender-specific hats came into vogue. Popular hats for men included straw summer hats, berets (particularly for movie directors and artists), fedoras, and newsboy caps. Women preferred wide-brimmed, white cartwheel hats in summer to block out the sun and hand-knitted, dome-shaped watch caps in winter (Fig. 3.9). Chinese women had always preferred a light skin color, which was an indication of the leisure and class status that most farmers lacked. Thus, large-brimmed hats and umbrellas became essential gear in summer.

Mufflers made of woolens or synthetic fibers and translucent scarves—the few "neon lights" in the colorless era of the Cultural Revolution—remained stylish accessories in the new decade. Men wore wool scarves in the winter, in either a short plaid or long white design. Items such as hats, mufflers, and gloves left over from export were often available on the domestic market. In fact, accessories or garments left over from export became highly desired items for their trendy designs, superior

**Figure 3.9** A calendar girl of 1980 in a turtleneck knit sweater and a matching hat, accessorized with cloisonné bracelet, ring, and earrings. Courtesy of Juanjuan Wu.

quality, and relative rarity: signs that read "Domestic sales of commodities originally produced for export" always ensured quick sales.

As young men began to perm or style their hair, some men used as much hairspray as women in order to achieve a trendy look (Fig. 3.10). Women adorned their hair, permed or not, with a variety of ornaments like pins, ribbons, and hoops. By the early 1990s, chic women had become quite sophisticated in their use of eyebrow pencils, tweezers, eyeliners, eyeshades, face powder, lipstick, nail polish, mascara, and even false eyelashes. Perfume selections were also greatly diversified, and makeup trends became popular topics in fashion magazines and in other media.

Gold earrings, rings, necklaces, and bracelets, all of which had been shunned before the reform era, came into vogue in the 1980s. The limited purchasing power of most people in the 80s, however, hindered the popularity of gold. Thus, jewelry made of less expensive materials like cloisonné and pearl came into vogue. But by the 90s, both the increased offerings of jewelers and the more favorable economic conditions made jewelry increasingly popular. Platinum and jade were highly sought after jewelry materials—jade especially so since it was traditionally viewed as an auspicious ornamental material and was no longer negatively associated with feudalism. Many believed that wearing jade would bring good health and good fortune, and people often had their favorite jade items blessed at Buddhist temples in order to ward off evil and disease.

**Figure 3.10** Students of the high school of the Central Academy of Fine Arts in the summer of 1985. The male student has permed hair and is wearing a T-shirt and jeans. Courtesy of Li Xiaobin, photographer.

## Wearing Sexual Freedom

The unisex trend evolved into more feminine styles in the 1990s after women had established their places both in and out of the home. Not coincidentally, international fashion also exhibited feminine designs in soft cuts with narrow, round shoulders and see-through fabrics. As the 90s began, attitudes toward sexual relationships changed dramatically in China, and this also had an influence on the way women dressed, especially how revealingly.

In the 1990s, bars sprung up in every corner of urban China and one-night stands became increasingly common. The emergence of internet chat rooms facilitated communication between strangers, which made casual sex and extramarital affairs easier to initiate. Young people could be seen hugging and kissing in public as if no one were around. The mass media propelled this change in sexual attitudes and tested the limits of Chinese tolerance for nudity in the mass media. *Cultural Weekend,* a paper financially in the red, instantly became "the coolest paper in Beijing" because it displayed many nude and seminude women in its first issue in January 1993.[56] Women's magazines, fashion magazines, and lifestyle magazines all began incorporating sexual topics to cater to people's growing curiosity about sex and sexual relationships. Jia Pingwa published his racy novel *Feidu* (The Abandoned Capital) in 1993, which "caused a great literary and publishing earthquake" mainly because of its "unbearably vulgar sex scenes" and "despicable male sexual psychology."[57] Young female writer Wei Hui published *Shanghai Baby* in 1994, a semiautobiographical novel that depicted explicit sex scenes. And ten years later in 2003, Muzi Mei shocked even open-minded internet surfers with her *Yiqing shu* (Ashes of Love), an online diary of her sex life. By then, the sexual revolution in China was in full swing, and the government eventually banned these sexually explicit works in an effort to halt the deterioration of the "mental health" of the society. However, in effect, the bans only stimulated more interest in these publications. The pursuit of sexual freedom was often linked with the pursuit of freedom in general in China, and thus gained much sympathy from open-minded intellectuals.

As monogamy went out of style among the young, so did modesty and conformity in dress. Compared to either the unisex style or the feminine fashions of the 80s, new looks in the 90s were more revealing and more varied. Revealing styles such as bare-midriff tops, one-shoulder tops, spaghetti-strap dresses, strapless dresses, see-through materials, and underwear as outerwear were all common on the city streets of the 90s. Dyed hair also came into vogue, along with various other chemical and physical hair treatments. Jeans, T-shirts, jackets, athletic wear, and sweaters, which marked the unisex trend in the 80s, were designed with more gender-specific details and trims in the 90s. And the thick, large shoulder pads of the 80s disappeared altogether. Pantyhose or high stockings were no longer required accessories for shorts and skirts as women became more comfortable baring their legs. They also began

**Figure 3.11** On the streets of Shanghai, a chic woman with dyed hair, wearing a backless top and low-rise jeans, walks by an ESCADA billboard in 2004. Courtesy of Yong He, photographer.

to bare their shoulders, backs, midriffs, and even nipples on the runway (Fig. 3.11). By the 2000s, anything New Yorkers or Londoners dared to wear, Shanghainese or Beijingers would also wear. Chinese women often went to even greater extremes, and the streets of China in the new millennium bore little resemblance to the streets of China of the 1970s.

# –4–

# Fashion in Print

The anti-intellectual climate of the Cultural Revolution, best exemplified in Mao's slogan "the more knowledge, the more reactionary," brought almost all publication to a standstill. The few publications that were permitted were strictly limited to disseminating Mao thoughts and promoting the revolutionary movement. Publications that did survive, like *Renmin huabao* (China Pictorial), depicted women as merely proletarian *tie guniang* (iron women) without a hint of desire for fashion. Those who did show any interest in fashion outside of the narrow parameters of the accepted styles of the Cultural Revolution were ruthlessly ridiculed and scorned in revolutionary literature and theatre, not to mention in everyday life. This anti-fashion sentiment had been common since the establishment of the People's Republic in 1949, except for a brief period in the 1950s when the government made an effort to promote modest fashions. But as the publication of journals, magazines, and newspapers resumed in the early years of the reform era, wide-ranging debates over the nature of fashion and its proper role in a socialist society came to the fore.

The reestablishment of the print media in the post-Mao era had a strong influence on the transition from a rigid uniformity in dress to the adoption of novel styles by young Chinese. Fashion print media blossomed in the 1980s along with a variety of women's, lifestyle, and fashion magazines. Advocates of fashion in the mass media also helped to transform Chinese fashion from a vain and petty lifestyle issue into a legitimate industry. And the advent of a number of hybrid domestic and foreign fashion magazine titles in the 1990s further connected Chinese fashion and the fashion industry with the international fashion world.

## Fashion Comes to Life in Women's Magazines

As early as 1979, *Zhongguo qingnian* (China Youth) published a number of articles that attempted to reconcile the seemingly fundamental conflict between the state's proletarian ideology and the nature of fashion. The articles published in *China Youth* generally adopted a pro-fashion viewpoint, as evinced in "Is Caring for Dress Capitalist?" "Discussing Guidance—Starting From Youth Hairstyles and Trouser Legs," "What Is the Beauty of Dress?" and "To Adorn Oneself More Beautifully" in 1980; "One Should Not Be Reproached for Wearing a Beautiful Dress" in 1984; and "Being the Messenger of Beauty in Life: A Delightful Discussion of the First China Youth Fashion Design Contest" in 1989.[1]

The resumption of the publication of magazines like *China Youth* in September 1978 and the creation of journals like *Dushu* (Reading) in April 1979 are examples of efforts to "emancipate the mind," a concept Deng Xiaoping promoted after the Cultural Revolution. *China Youth* was first founded by the Socialist Youth League of China in 1923 and was discontinued in 1966, only to be revived twelve years later. The resultant resurgence in literature that took place as restrictions were eased made reading itself a newly respectable and fashionable activity, and even underground literature that dealt with sensitive topics began to spread via handwritten copies. Thus reading a magazine like *Qingnian yidai* (The Young Generation) on the streets of Shanghai signaled fashionality. As China began to develop its own consumer culture, intellectuals, eager to recast themselves after becoming objects of derision during the Cultural Revolution, sought out venues to reshape the country's cultural landscape. These magazines provided one such venue. The dress styles that the Chinese should adopt in this new cultural landscape became a prominent issue of the day.

*China Youth* took the lead in presenting and, in most cases, advocating unconventional ideas and fashion phenomena. As a leading journal of ideological emancipation, it attempted to stimulate nationwide reflection on lifestyle issues and generally adopted latitudinarian views on fashion. Characterized by its careful tone in its defense of fashion, *China Youth* acknowledged the proletariat's right to pursue beauty but still cautioned that care should be taken to avoid the corrupting influence of Western capitalism. However, the journal did not approve of spending too much time on adornment, arguing that the program of economic reform under way in China deserved more time and energy than something as mundane as one's physical appearance.

While *China Youth* strove to provide the masses with purely ideological guidance, a few other women's magazines tried to provide concrete fashion examples for the masses to copy. First founded in 1939 and brought back to life in 1978 after suspension during the Cultural Revolution, *Zhongguo funv* (Women of China) was the first women's magazine of the People's Republic of China. Like all other magazines of the time, *Women of China* felt obliged to provide ideological and lifestyle guidance, especially on issues related to the image, social status, and well-being of women. Illustrations and patterns for new garment styles were occasionally published as a direct means of spreading fashionable styles, as in the fourth issue of 1979 and the fifth issue of 1980. The magazine also provided useful tips on garment care, such as recommendations on the storage of garments made of woolens, leather, cotton, nylon, and Dacron polyester.[2]

On the back cover of its fourth issue of 1979, *Women of China* selected styles from the National Exhibit of Student Clothing, which showcased popular styles of the time; these student clothing styles resembled mini versions of adult wear. Boys modeled sport coats, zippered jackets, and tailored suits with two to four pockets that combined elements of the Mao suit and the Western suit. Girls were shown in zippered jackets, double-breasted suits with matching pants or knee-length skirts in red, green, orange, and pastel colors such as pink and light blue. The three summer dress styles on the back cover of its fifth issue in 1980 featured short puff sleeves, flowered embroideries, a cinched waist, gathers, lace, and ruffles. All three female models are pictured in stylishly permed hair and medium-heeled leather shoes. Commercial advertisements for cotton shoes and hairpins also made their way onto the back covers of the second and third issues of *Women of China* in 1980. This cracked the door open to the greater financial independence and relatively relaxed control by the Party that would come to many publications in subsequent years.

Another popular women's magazine, *Nvyou* (Girlfriend), launched in Xi'an in 1988, positioned itself as an advocate of style from the very beginning. *Jiating* (Family) from Guangzhou and *Zhiyin* (Bosom Friend) from Wuhan, launched in 1983 and 1985, respectively, were also leading women's magazines that had widespread influence on perceptions of fashion. Popular lifestyle magazines of the 1980s included *Meihua shenghuo* (Beatifying Life, launched in 1983), *Shenghuo zhoukan* (Life Weekly, launched in 1984), *Zhishi yu shenghuo* (Knowledge and Life, launched in 1980), and *Wenhua yu shenghuo* (Culture and Life, launched in 1979). These were all state-owned publications that the state charged with disseminating new aesthetics and lifestyle ideas and cultivating a sense of fine taste among their readers. Columns and articles in these magazines often discussed and showcased practical mass fashions that opened a window on new fashion ideas and styles.

These magazines effectively communicated to the public reformist attitudes toward lifestyle, family, marriage, consumption, and fashion. With few images, early black-and-white women's and lifestyle magazines were inexpensive to produce, which enabled them to build up a large reader base quickly in an environment in which fashion information was scarce. In their heyday, many of these magazines sold several million copies per issue at a price of thirty to forty cents *renminbi* per copy. The number of fashion columns and articles in these women's and lifestyle magazines, such as in *Bosom Friend* and *Women of China,* began to dwindle, however, after foreign funds poured into the fashion media market in the 1990s.

In addition to the role that women's and lifestyle magazines played in the spread of new fashions in the early years of the 1980s, national newspapers, to which governmental organizations and institutes usually had mandatory subscriptions, also contributed to the dissemination of fashion guidelines and ideas. Since national newspapers were more tightly controlled by the Central Propaganda Department of the Communist Party than niche magazines, they usually espoused more reserved and orthodox attitudes toward fashion at the beginning of the 1980s. They often firmly criticized the "bizarre looks" donned by audacious urban youth. For example, the *Jiefang Daily* consistently guarded against "odd" styles and continually presented conservative viewpoints on controversial looks (see Chapter 1 for examples) in the early 1980s. But by the 1990s, even the *Jiefang Daily* had become an enthusiastic advocate of fashion, as had most other national newspapers. As fashion critic Bao Mingxin noted in his book *Fashion Criticism:*

> At first in China people read in *Wenhui Daily* and *Jiefang Daily* about the debate over "new adornment and socialism." In *Beautifying Life* and *Fashion Colour* and other maga-zines they read discussions of the meaning of so-called "dress and spiritual civilization," "Is fashion indeed good or not?" and other such issues. Then gradually these newspa-pers and magazines shifted to "red dresses are in fashion," "hip youngsters' bell-bottom pants," "A glance into Shanghai window displays," and so on.[3]

Weekend special editions in national newspapers that centered on fashion and fashionable lifestyles also became a popular phenomenon after the implementation of the forty-hour workweek, which coincided with the growth of leisure culture in urban centers. Historically, the Chinese state heavily invested in "defining and mak-ing a national and nationalist popular culture."[4] But the rapidly growing economy called for greater consumption in addition to increases in production, since economic growth could not be sustained purely through production. Thus, "In the 1990s, state sponsorship of 'popular culture' took an intriguing turn: the state collaborated with the print media and the market in producing a new discourse on 'leisure culture' in urban China."[5] In order to promote leisure culture the mass media advocated con-sumerism and encouraged diligent workers to take vacations and to spend more freely. Newspapers like the *Beijing Youth Daily* started publishing weekly special editions (e.g., "Guide to Today's Fashions," "Auto Age," "The Age of Skyscrapers," and "Computer Age") to encourage people to obtain material goods and fashion, as well as to find pleasure in consumption.[6] In Shanghai alone, *Wenhui Daily, Jiefang Daily, Xinmin Evening News,* and *Laodong bao* (Labor Daily) all created these types of weekend specials for which fashion topics were indispensable.[7]

## The Domestic Fashion Press

By the mid-1980s, the wait-and-see attitude that the populace had taken toward eco-nomic reform—and new fashions—turned to hopeful enthusiasm. The younger gen-eration in particular began to pursue fashion with greater fervor. As women's and lifestyle magazines and national newspapers were starting fashion columns, fashion-oriented magazines and newspapers began to proliferate. While TV shows and mov-ies had been the predominant inspirational sources for fashion from the end of the 1970s to the end of the 1980s, the fashion print media eventually overtook this role in the early 1990s.

In response to the growing demand for fashion information, the 1980s witnessed the launch of a number of domestic fashion magazines and newspapers. These in-cluded *Shizhuang* (*Fashion*) in 1980 and *Xiandai fuzhuang* (Modern Dress & Dress Making) in 1981, both based in Beijing; *Liuxing se* (Fashion Colour) in 1982 in

Shanghai, *Shanghai fushi* (Shanghai Style) in 1985 in Shanghai, *Zhongguo fuzhuang* (China Garment) in 1985 in Beijing, *Zhongguo fangzhi bao* (China Textile News) in 1986 in Beijing, *Zhongwai fuzhuang* (International Costume) in 1987 in Dalian, and *Shanghai shizhuang bao* (Shanghai Fashion Times), launched in 1988 in Shanghai. Before hybrid domestic-foreign fashion titles would establish their dominant market position in the 1990s, domestic fashion publications enjoyed nearly a decade of exclusivity on the market during the 1980s. The birth of the fashion press signaled a new age in Chinese fashion in which fashion was promoted instead of repressed. Fashion journalists and editors, along with various fashion writers, slowly usurped the role of government officials as arbiters of taste. And since fashion appeared to be a prominent issue that directly affected the new image of socialist China, officials from the central government repeatedly stressed that the improvement of Chinese appearance was a high priority on the national political agenda.

An early breakthrough for the fashion press came in 1980 with the creation of *Fashion,* initially a quarterly fashion magazine, by the Ministry of Foreign Trade. Cheng Tianbao, then the chief editor of *Fashion,* explained the motive behind creating the first post-Mao fashion magazine as answering the call of human nature to seek beauty "Although at that time [in 1980] what appeared in the eyes of the people was a world of blue and gray, a glimpse of flicking red and yellow could already be caught from the bottom of people's hearts. Seeking beauty is an irrepressible part of human nature."[8]

Besides the fundamental drive for beauty, the reason the "blue ants" of China suddenly dreamed of a colorful world was in fact very practical. As *Fashion* stated in its first issue, the pursuit of fashion and beauty would serve "to strengthen the relationships between fashion design, assembly enterprises, and foreign trade departments; to introduce distinguished domestic clothing products, foreign clothing styles, and to discuss the international clothing market; to increase the competitiveness of domestic clothing for the development of apparel export."[9] Thus *Fashion* featured many styles for export—"cheap, rather unfashionable clothes, by international standards, but new and attractive to Chinese consumers."[10] Under these guidelines, *Fashion* attempted to make its coverage international. For example, *Fashion*'s first issue in 1985 reported on Paris fashions, runway shows, and trade fairs, the favorite cotton-fabric surface designs in the Soviet Union, Turkish clothing, the newest evening dress styles in Europe and the United States, popular handbags in America, Japanese fashion shows in Shanghai and Nanjing, and the collaborative development of women's fashion between China and West European countries. A strong emphasis on international fashion differentiated *Fashion* from many other domestic titles.

But the creation of Chinese fashion print media had a clear socialist goal. The fashion press was intended not to serve as a means for patrician ladies to while away their leisure time, but rather to influence the masses, to serve as a valuable source of information, to promote mass fashions, to facilitate professional communication, and to guide clothing consumption. As Tan Fuyun, director of the Shanghai Women's

Federation and chairman of the Shanghai Garment Trade Association at the time, wrote in the opening issue of *Shanghai Style* in 1985 (Fig. 4.1):

> The birth of *Shanghai Style* brings welcome news to the mass consumer and the national apparel and accessory industry. It will strive to deliver information, to stimulate ideas, to guide clothing designers in pioneering, reforming, and improving their work and to season people's lives. It will also provide guidance to consumers on increasing their taste level in order to urge them to lead a civilized, healthy, and intelligent life, and to become advocates and practitioners of new ideas, new culture, and new fashion.[11]

This statement of purpose for the fashion press was typical of the period: nearly every fashion magazine and newspaper of the 1980s spelled out similar goals and guidelines. Keeping practical goals in mind, many fashion magazines included patterns

**Figure 4.1**  The cover of the inaugural issue in 1985 of one of the most popular fashion magazines, *Shanghai Style.* Courtesy of *Shanghai Style.*

and instructions for making new clothing styles for those who did not have easy access to or were simply not satisfied with ready-to-wear fashions. In order to offer an encyclopedic overview of fashion, early issues of *Shanghai Style* featured sections such as "Forum of Techniques," "A Glance into Shanghai Window Displays," "Mix and Match," "Adornment," "Cosmetology," "Life Consultant," "Fashion in Shanghai," and "International Trends."

Fashion magazines varied in the depth and breadth of their coverage of international issues. But most of them positioned themselves as fashion mentors for the masses, whose fashion sense was believed to have been stunted over the previous decades. As fashion mentors, the fashion press attempted to be both politically and morally correct. Fashion took on a rather conservative look and was interpreted more as social appropriateness than as novelty. As argued in the article "Clothing—Mirror of the Era" published in *Modern Dress and Dress Making* in 1985:

> Every clothing designer hopes the clothing they design will be the most fashionable. Young women and men also compete to wear the most fashionable clothing. This is how it should be. But fashion is in no way odd, eccentric, or a display of novelty. Nor should it merely aim for artistic beauty. The basic function of clothing is to be worn, to protect the human body, to enable people to live a healthy, comfortable, and happy life in different weather conditions, seasons, and geographic environments, and to meet the broad and multifaceted needs of people's social lives and production.[12]

Since function was favored over fashion at the time, the fashion press rarely featured the controversial looks of the transitional period from the end of the 1970s to the early 1980s. Neither did it pay much attention to fashions that originated from TV shows and movies until these fashions were assimilated into the mainstream. According to mainstream views, the fashion pioneers who donned controversial looks were those who most needed fashion guidance. As a marginalized group, these fashion adventurers had no chance to express their aesthetic sense in the media. On the contrary, mainstream media stuck to conventional aesthetics and boycotted unfamiliar looks. Open-minded intellectuals were wary of defending new fashions and ideas because eccentricity and idiosyncrasy were socially risky. And criticism of novel fashions, especially those bearing a resemblance to fashions from the West or Hong Kong, was especially harsh in the mainstream media. Even *Fashion,* whose intent was to introduce international fashion trends to China, featured harsh criticism of trendy young women in the fourth issue in 1982:

> Still, there are some girls who are so concerned with being trendy. Looking for Hong Kong clothing everywhere, they imitate Hong Kong girls from head to toe: the finest bell-bottom pants, body-hugging T-shirts, high-heel leather shoes, sheepskin handbags, tinted sunglasses with foreign logos, disheveled hair, with painstakingly sewn fake items making up any gaps. This kind of adornment breaks away from reality. The new trends

sought after by these girls are not the kind of fashionable beauty that belong to our society, nor are they natural or harmonious.[13]

In keeping with their socialist goals and also confined by their limited means, early domestic fashion magazines adopted a simple and modest appearance. Published in black and white (often with color inserts) with a typical size of 17 by 24.8 cm (*Shanghai Style, Fashion,* and *Modern Dress & Dress Making* all used this format), these early fashion magazines focused on text instead of images. They aimed to provide practical information about new styles, clothing-care methods, pattern-making techniques, and makeup and offered mix-and-match tips. A small number of black-and-white photographs, graphics of stylized little flowers, and fashion illustrations occasionally accented the text. The majority of these early fashion magazines also put an emphasis on promoting local designs. The color-plate inserts usually featured new designs created by state-owned garment factories or models in rigid poses wearing outfits that had earned awards in fashion design contests.

Many fashion magazines also reserved space to discuss and showcase foreign fashions through both text and photographs. Some photographs were taken from local fashion shows held by prestigious designers from Paris or Japan. Since most believed modern fashion originated in the West, Western styles were considered more fashionable than domestic creations. Blond models with blue eyes made it onto Chinese magazine covers in the 1980s. *Fashion* often used Caucasian models as cover girls to justify, in a way, its fashionability, while most other fashion magazines, such as *Shanghai Style, China Garment,* and *Modern Dress and Dress Making,* consistently featured Chinese cover girls. Not surprisingly, fashion journalists and editors of the time rarely had the opportunity to report foreign news on-site (except for *Fashion,* which had its own journalists overseas) nor to attend the fashion shows that regularly took place in the world's fashion centers. Thus, information about new trends in the West, such as the "International Trends" section in *Shanghai Style,* was mainly compiled and translated from English-language media.

In the early years, these magazines were distributed mainly through subscriptions via local post offices and bookstores, which allowed them to reach every city in China. And their black-and-white, text-oriented format helped to keep production costs low: in the mid-1980s, *Shanghai Style* sold for ninety cents *renminbi, Fashion* for sixty cents *renminbi,* and *Modern Dress and Dress Making* for sixty-four cents *renminbi.* Prior to the widespread inclusion of high-fashion, name-brand advertisements, early fashion magazines financed themselves mainly through profits from sales and the support of their state-owned publishing houses. In its forty-eight-page first issue in 1985, *Shanghai Style* included a ten-page color insert showcasing new styles designed by local garment factories. The first issue of *Shanghai Style* also featured limited advertising on the inside and back covers, but by including a considerable amount of useful information catering to the practical needs of readers who craved new styles, *Shanghai Style* soon attracted legions of subscribers—it claimed to have a million readers per issue in its heyday. However, due to increased competition, the main audience of *Shanghai Style* in later years shifted to second- and third-tier cities.

Because of the text-oriented format, in the early years of the fashion press, magazine writers were more influential than photographers. Early fashion magazines enlisted their writers from the ranks of cultural critics, novelists, clothing designers, college professors, industry experts, and readers. This pool of talent was composed of multifaceted perspectives. Often, these outsiders held more important roles than in-house journalists and editors in terms of both the quality and quantity of articles they contributed. Since the fashion press aimed to offer advice and guidance on mass fashion and consumption, professional knowledge became a key ingredient. And, thus, plain, didactic language defined the style of magazine writing in this period.

With their great sensitivity to new fashions, fashion professionals were deemed ideal contributors to the fashion press. They were also among the first who had the opportunity to visit Western fashion centers after China first opened up to the world. Upon their return, they reported on Western fashions in the form of travelogues that often included eye-opening life experiences. Fashion critics with Western experience inevitably became authoritative judges of Western fashions and the favored spokesmen for Chinese fashion. They became the most sought-after writers by the fashion press.

On the other hand, chief editors of fashion magazines were usually former senior book editors from the magazine's publishing house. Selected for their political reliability as much as their rich editorial experience, they were often just as clueless as their readers as to what the current fashions were, especially in the early years of these newly created fashion magazines. Thus, unlike in the West, many Chinese chief editors of early fashion magazines generally did not consider themselves fashion insiders. At first, they had to rely heavily on other fashion professionals and younger editors who had a keen eye for fashion. In fact, the names of the editorial staff were not even listed in early fashion magazines. They appeared in the magazine only as a unit of the publishing house without being individually identified.

Young fashion magazine editors were drawn partly from the pool of editorial talent of the magazine's publishing house and partly from the pool of college graduates who had majored in journalism, literature, or fashion design. Their youth made their transition to the fashion world much smoother than that of their seniors. Young fashion editors proved to be susceptible to high fashion and were among the earliest to evolve into brand-name aficionados. The complete devotion of fashion editors to style was clearly reflected in their poetic and passionate depictions of new fashions, which consequently captured millions of young readers, most of whom became regular consumers of fashion magazines. The plain and instructional language that was initially used to describe fashion gradually shifted to the fanciful and entertaining. This drastic shift in the use of language in fashion journalism was directly linked to the changing role of fashion magazines, which had moved from socialist fashion mentor to lucrative business.

College professors in the fields of clothing or literature, such as Bao Mingxin and Yang Qingqing from Donghua University, Li Dangqi from Tsinghua University, Hu Yue and Yuan Ze from the Beijing Institute of Fashion Technology, and Gong Jing from Fudan University, also became prominent writers in the nascent fashion print media. A great deal of new fashion terms were coined or translated from English by college professors and scholars who regularly wrote about fashion. Keen fashion observers and shrewd critics in the fashion press quickly built up national reputations and a large readership, which gave these writers the ability to influence pop culture. Distinguished professors were singled out as authoritative spokesmen for the fashion industry. Through this position they helped to establish the aesthetic standards of modern Chinese fashion. Other than writing on fashion, they were also frequently invited to sit on panels for various design and modeling contests in China. Bao Mingxin is a good example of a college professor who made a substantial contribution to the Chinese fashion press. With the rising popularity of the fashion press, Bao rose to become a prominent fashion critic and was among the few Chinese scholars who had the opportunity to work in the West and become acquainted with Western fashion in the reform era. Bao's overseas experience enabled him to introduce the Western fashion system and lexicon to Chinese fashion readers.

Throughout the 1980s and 1990s, Western designers, fashion concepts, and theories were systematically introduced to Chinese by scholars like Bao via the mass media and scholarly books. The pioneering work of these scholars helped to bridge the gap in fashion aesthetics between China and the West. And the Chinese fashion media soon adopted the same fashion lexicon as the West to communicate fashion innovations and trends. Various assemblies of curvy lines, supple materials, ethnic patterns, tassel trims, and transparent outfits that were defined by the Western media as the "hippie look," the "romantic style," the "cosmonaut look," and so on became known to Chinese fashion readers. The seemingly meaningless lines, colors, patterns, and forms of dress now took on new meanings. Fashion critics brought fashion to life in ways that a Chinese audience could understand and relate at a basic level. Newly translated fashion terms from "A-line silhouette" to "chinoiserie," from "Op" to "Pop" art, from "paisley patterns" to "leg o' mutton sleeves" inspired readers of early fashion publications and motivated fresh talents to join this new world of fashion. Aside from introducing Western fashions, college professors also sought to spur the development of the Chinese fashion industry. For example, Bao panoramically surveyed the Chinese fashion industry with articles titled "Seeking Designers," "Consumer Decision," "Call for Fabrics," and "To Have Famous Brands or Famous Designers?"[14]

While introducing Western fashions, designers, and brands to Chinese readers, the fashion press also vigorously promoted domestic fashion designers and models. Early fashion magazines sponsored many national fashion design and modeling contests. *Fashion* magazine created the Chinese Fashion and Culture Award for fashion designers in 1983. To emphasize the compatibility of Chinese fashion with international fashion, international designers and critics from Japan and the United States were invited to judge the competition. *Fashion* also held one of the earliest Chinese fashion modeling contests in 1988, the goal of which was

> to improve the social status of models and publicize those who excel in modeling in order to boost the elegant and beautiful international image of Chinese models; to facilitate world trade in Chinese clothing; to enhance the overall quality of Chinese models; to discover new talents to fill various modeling teams; and also to uncover good-looking amateur photography models who are not tall, but good at posing, to help to improve the quality of fashion magazines and books.[15]

Upon its creation in 1985, *China Garment* cosponsored the first *Jinjian jiang* (Golden Scissors) National Clothing Design Contest to improve the quality of domestic design. Contemporaneous with the groundbreaking efforts of the fashion press to promote domestic design and national brands, numerous professional associations and fashion organizations were established at national and regional levels. With similar goals of promoting the clothing industry, the 1990s saw an explosion of fashion design and modeling contests. Also, since early magazines were intimately connected to traditional publishing houses that published books, they also published pattern books and collections of new styles.

However, the sense of responsibility toward both the people and the fashion industry that the early fashion press exhibited was later replaced by a more commercial drive to entertain. Instead of "guiding socialist production," fashion magazines tended to celebrate the luxury that Chinese life had long lacked and that was normally associated with a bourgeois lifestyle. As fashion writing became more popular, literary writers with sophisticated rhetorical skills began writing for fashion magazines and greatly accelerated the shift from professionalism to rhetoric in the 1990s. This shift pushed out many apparel experts as only those with a rhetorical flair could survive as regular writers for the fashion press.

Chinese literary writers have a long history of fashion writing. Zhang Ailing (Eileen Chang), one of China's most famous novelists, published "Geng yi ji" (A Chronicle of Changing Clothes) in *Gujin* (Ancient and Modern) in 1943. Writers from the Mandarin Duck and Butterfly literary school, such as Zhou Shoujuan and Jiang Hongjiao, were also major contributors to fashion criticism during the Republican period. Contemporary writers of the so-called "Little Women's Prose" movement that prevailed in the 1990s, such as Chen Danyan, Su Su, Nan Ni, Zhang Mei, Shi Wa, Huang Ai Dongxi, and Anni Baobei, also became a major force in fashion writing. Their writings were known for touching on the trivial aspects of everyday life. Their appreciation of nuances in fashion inspired not only ordinary readers, but also fashion designers, as increased attention to detail gradually raised the taste level of Chinese design. This group of writers also expanded the vocabulary and creative language used in fashion writing. The attention these writers gave to fashion, one of the hottest topics of the 1990s, also paid off with great fame: the marriage between fashion and literature in the fashion press turned out to be mutually beneficial.

When Hong Huang, publisher of *Shijie dushi* (iLook) and a celebrated writer herself, started to run *iLook* in 2000 she drew in many famous novelists and poets like Wang Shuo, Liu Suola, and Mang Ke. These writers attempted to bring depth to the seemingly superficial fashion press. Unfortunately, the serious and deep reflections of these writers proved too heavy for a fashion magazine. After a negative reaction from the market, Hong Huang made some major adjustments to her approach to covering fashion and ultimately accepted the beauty-seeking mission of the fashion press. As she put it: "I should really make *iLook* into a good consumer magazine, not a platform for my own views ... In reality, there are way more women who love beauty than who have a brain. Even some beauty-loving women do not like to use their brains, but all women who use their brains still seek beauty. My calculation was not clear before."[16]

Nevertheless, Hong Huang's vision did differentiate *iLook* from other glossy fashion magazines. For instance, the *iLook* "Monitor" section was set up to monitor and promote local designers and cultural innovations. Hong Huang believed that "we are not far away from an era where China has its own aesthetics and master fashion designers. We hope to get to know them while they are on their way to becoming such master fashion designers."[17] As part of *iLook*'s efforts to promote Chinese aesthetics, the magazine featured on its July 2008 cover a controversial look the Oscar award–winning makeup artist Ye Jintian had designed for a television drama based on the classic novel *Dream of the Red Chamber*. *iLook* defended this widely criticized look as "misunderstood aesthetics."

As the fashion press fully embraced outward beauty, its tolerance for body exposure and odd designs dramatically increased during the 1990s. Media attention meant sales. And sales were becoming increasingly important as large segments of the Chinese economy were privatizing. Hence, unlike the fashion press of the 80s that routinely criticized new and foreign fashions, the fashion press of the 90s welcomed fresh ideas and novel designs. In fact, nothing seemed off-limits to the fashion media in the 1990s. Criticisms of fashion were rare and, in most cases, sugarcoated. Fashion critics masterfully mixed witty sarcasm with disguised promotion.

Furthermore, many magazines tactfully advocated unconventional lifestyles and behaviors, which sometimes bordered on the immoral. For example, titles like "A Little Bit Boorish, A Little Bit Lovely,"[18] "Having How Many Men Will Make a Woman?"[19] and "Cohabitation Challenges Marriage?"[20] filled magazine covers. Fashion magazines also expanded their influence by tightening their relationship with the entertainment industry by employing movie and TV stars as models and participating in national film awards, popular TV shows, and other entertainment events. However, fashion magazines rarely attracted notable artists to contribute visual content, as *Harper's Bazaar* had with pop artists like Andy Warhol during the 1950s.

Despite this greater latitude, however, fashion magazines still generated controversy—sometimes unwittingly. Because the state censored all publications, directors and chief editors of fashion magazines were under enormous pressure to maintain a clean record. This naturally led to a form of self-censorship at every magazine. Despite taking precautions, however, they could not anticipate every controversy. In one such case at the end of 2001, a controversy erupted at China's earliest post-Mao fashion magazine, *Fashion*. The incident related to a notorious one-page fashion spread featuring a popular Chinese pop star, Zhao Wei, in a mini dress, in *Fashion*'s ninth issue of 2001. The whole spread was conceptualized and executed by *Fashion*'s New York studio, and the dress was designed by a young American designer. The pattern on half of the dress was identified as a reproduction of a Japanese military flag, and the look was accessorized with dark-colored high leather boots. Coupled with Zhao Wei's fashionably aloof facial expression, some Chinese readers interpreted the image as a representation of the Japanese militarism that severely wounded China during World War II, and attacked Zhao Wei as a traitor and "spokeswoman" for Japanese militarism. A nationwide repudiation of Zhao and the magazine followed that nearly destroyed Zhao's career. *Fashion* magazine temporarily ceased publication and its New York studio director apologized to the public and resigned.[21]

Less controversially, in the process of shifting from a text- to an image-oriented format in the 1990s, the total makeover was introduced in the fashion print media. This type of makeover came to be called *xingxiang sheji* (image design). At the end of the 1970s, the word "cosmetics" to ordinary Chinese meant only scented moisturizers and mosquito repellents, and makeup was something reserved for calendar girls and movie stars on magazine covers. Popular movie stars of the time such as Pan Hong, Liu Xiaoqing, and Xu Shanshan, who were featured on the covers of 1979's *Dazhong dianying* (Popular Cinema), wore light makeup with eyeliner, pinkish lipstick, and rouge. This was the farthest extent of "image design" in the early years of the reform era. But as the fashion press became more popular, image design evolved into a special service available to all image-conscious fashion readers.

The popularity of image design columns in the fashion print media gave birth to many masterful makeup artists and stylists who came to be called *xingxiang sheji-shi* (image designers). Many of them were also celebrated fashion writers. Image designers were first borrowed from the world of stage art by the fashion industry to coordinate hairdo, makeup, and clothing of models for fashion shows in China.[22] Fashion magazines turned image designers into stars who readers believed had the power to turn ugly ducklings into beautiful swans.

Yang Qingqing, one of the earliest Chinese image designers, who was also a young professor at Donghua University, rose to national prominence through her image-design columns in popular magazines and newspapers in the 1990s, including *Shanghai Style, Beautifying Life, Xiandai jiating* (Modern Family), *Shanghai Fashion Times,* and *Jiefang Daily*. The publicity Yang received can largely be attributed to a new method she used: contrasting "before and after" images. The effect of juxtaposing before and after images was visually shocking to Chinese, just as it had been to Western readers when this photographic technique first appeared in the West decades earlier. Yang used poetic and ornate language to describe the design and makeup process and the finished face. The detailed, step-by-step explanations of the design process that Yang provided proved invaluable to young women across the country. Cosmetics producers had found a popular promoter for their products, while the fashion media had discovered a best-selling columnist.

Similar image-design columns blossomed afterward with the same presentation of before and after images matched with poetic writing. The image design column in *Shanghai Style* has been popular since its inception (Fig. 4.2). And readers vied to be the first to have their faces made over and shown in magazines. In the early 1980s, applying makeup for most Chinese women consisted of rubbing skin lotion on the

**Figure 4.2** From the image design column "Fushi zhi xing" (Fashion Star) by image designer Qian Qian in *Shanghai Style. Courtesy of Shanghai Style.*

face and applying a few drops of scented mosquito repellent on the body. By the end of the 1990s—after the spread of image design columns in popular magazines—the bedroom dressers of fashionable Chinese women were filled with mascara, masks, foundation, blush, powder, false eyelashes, eyeliner, eye shadow, and lipstick.

Image designers also put together chic ensembles for their clients for photo shoots. An essential aspect of making the "before" image, as fashion critics frequently noted, was the photographer's strategic arrangement of lighting in order to magnify freckles, pimples, and wrinkles on the client's face. They also manipulated the lighting to smooth the skin for the "after" image. Therefore, there was always a great photographer behind a great image designer.[23] Technical advancements in graphic design software pushed the limits of what could be manipulated and changed in an image even further. However, this particular presentation of contrasting before and after images relied heavily on the impersonal medium of the fashion publication. But the reliance on fashion publication hindered the wider commercial success of image design for ordinary clients. Although many hair salons, beauty shops, and photo studios claimed to be "image design studios," successful cases were rare.

The popularity of image design reflected the growing influence magazines had on the appearance of Chinese women. The addition of features like image design columns also reflected the changing competitive landscape that fashion magazines faced compared to the 1980s. And as hybrid domestic-foreign titles overtook the market in the 90s, domestic fashion magazines were eventually forced to change their business models and formats even further.

Domestic fashion newspapers also changed their formats to compete in the new environment of the 1990s and 2000s. Unlike fashion magazines, which focused on the consumer market, many fashion newspapers, like *China Textile News* and *Zhongguo fushi bao* (China Fashion Weekly, launched in 1994), initially focused more on the industry. Thus, their readers consisted mainly of industry professionals, retailers, manufacturers, and college professors and students in the apparel or textile fields. However, in the mid-1990s more and more fashion newspapers began adopting a consumer-oriented approach to reporting fashion trends and events. Titles like *Fuzhuang shibao* (Fashion Times, launched in 1994), *Fushi daobao* (Fashion News, launched in 1995) and the *Shanghai Fashion Times* took this approach in order to gain a share of both the advertising and the rapidly growing consumer markets of the fashion magazine. Since most fashion newspapers are published weekly, restraints are put on reporting timely news compared to national daily newspapers. To differentiate themselves from daily newspapers, which used cheap black-and-white paper, many fashion newspapers resorted to full-color glossy paper. The new format made fashion newspapers look more like magazines than newspapers, and they attempted to present the fashion newspaper as a luxury product in itself in order to gain reader attention and a longer shelf life. These attempts to burnish brand image have become critical in the highly competitive fashion newspaper industry. Although quite costly, the use of high-quality, full-color art paper created a strong visual impression and had a great impact on consumers' perceptions of the role of these newspapers in the fashion world. This transformation, in a sense, reflected the rise of consumerism in general and the growing interest in luxury goods in China.

With the rise of consumer culture, fashion newspapers adopted modern marketing techniques and a wide variety of promotional tools. For example, the *Shanghai Fashion Times* chose the slogan "Let's Take the Hand of Fashion" and promoted itself as "the nation's first professional apparel newspaper published inside and outside the country." They also used lotteries and prize drawings in their efforts to increase subscription rates in 1997.[24] Other promotional tools fashion newspapers utilized included establishing readers' clubs, issuing club cards, periodically providing face-to-face fashion consultations for readers, and holding various meetings and symposia with readers.[25]

While fashion newspapers tweaked their content and marketing strategies, a number of mainstream newspapers began publishing fashion columns or weekend fashion specials. Their ability to attract a wide range of readers enabled them to compete with fashion newspapers. Influential titles include *Shanghai xingqi san* (Shanghai Wednesday), *Jingpin gouwu zhinan* (Life Style), *Xin nv bao* (New Women's Journal), and *Shenjiang fuwu daobao* (Shanghai Times). Some of these newspapers also began using full-color art paper in order to upgrade their visual quality. *Life Style* modeled its cover designs on glossy magazines and led the way in advancing newspaper layout.[26] In fact, *Life Style* soon moved beyond the conventions of magazine cover design and featured nearly no text on its covers. It opted for a minimalist design that simply paired a celebrity photograph and (occasionally) a brief title for the cover story.

Despite employing new marketing strategies and formats, however, many domestic fashion magazines and fashion newspapers struggled to contend with the rise of the hybrid domestic-foreign fashion title.

## Hybrid Domestic-Foreign Titles

Large-sized, glossy fashion magazines predominated city newsstands and kiosks in the 1990s. Fierce competition both from within and abroad forced many local magazines launched in the 1980s either to reform or to relaunch as domestic-foreign partnerships, or "hybrid" titles. Popular glossy fashion and women's titles from the 1990s onward included *Shishang* (Cosmopolitan), *Shijie shizhuang zhi yuan* (Elle), *How, Fengcai* (Frends), *Ruili* (Rayli) *Xiaosa Liren* (CHIC), *Dushi zhufu* (Hers), *Dushi liren* (City Beauty), *Hao zhufu* (Good), *Dadushi* (Metropolis), *Shijie dushi* (iLook) and *Shishang basha* (Harper's Bazaar). *Jiaren* (Marie Claire) and Chinese *Vogue* debuted in 2002 and 2005, respectively.

Most of these magazines were joint ventures with established foreign titles. In fact, fashion magazines found it difficult to survive without a licensing contract with a famous magazine title from abroad. The content and layout were modeled after the original foreign version and photographs were usually shared with the partnering title for a fee. Besides fashion, these glossy titles also touched on other aspects of life, such as love, emotions, health, people, culture, and entertainment, functioning as complete manuals for the fashionable urban lifestyle. In light of the rapidly growing consumer market for luxury products, fashion magazines considered themselves promoters of luxury consumption and guides of taste. In the 2000s, fashion magazines expanded into media groups that owned collections of titles ranging from fashion to interior design to housekeeping. The publication, distribution, marketing, and advertising management of dominant fashion media were entirely Westernized and operated as industry chains.

Unlike early indigenous fashion magazines that had a clear socialist goal in promoting mass fashion, hybrid titles were aimed at the leisure class and promoted luxurious lifestyles. Not only were the prices of these hybrid titles triple or quadruple those of indigenous titles, but the prices of the fashion brands featured in these magazines were also well beyond the reach of ordinary people. The image of the elite constructed by glossy titles suited the desires of the newly rich to distinguish themselves from the masses. The socialist fashion press had thus been transformed into an exclusive club for the Chinese elite and the growing urban middle class, while excluding the masses, especially people in rural areas.

Occupying the most prominent position in numerous kiosks and newsstands in every city in the 1990s, *Elle, Cosmopolitan,* and *Ruili* established their leading position in both circulation and advertising. These three magazines also established a series of spin-offs focusing on housekeeping, health, and interior design, which consolidated their dominance over the luxury magazine market. According to market research carried out in ten major cities in 2005 by Century Chinese International Media Consultation Inc. (CCMC), a media research firm, *Ruili, Cosmopolitan,* and *Elle*'s titles accounted for roughly eighty-five percent of the high-end glossy fashion-magazine market, leaving the dozens of other titles vying for the remaining fifteen percent.[27]

In 1988, *Elle* became the first glossy fashion title to land in China. *Elle* was launched as a joint venture between the Shanghai Translation Publishing House—a book publisher owned by the Shanghai Bureau of the Press and Printing Association (BPPA)—and Hachette Filipacchi. With a burgeoning consumer market for luxury brands, Robert Gutwillig, *Elle*'s international publishing director, admitted that *Elle* loved the idea of being the first Western consumer magazine to enter China: "We don't expect to make profits for five years, maybe ten years. We want to make investments there and become part of the scenery. It's market-making, not profit-making."[28] But *Elle*'s investment in China paid off sooner than expected, with *Elle* turning a profit since 1995.[29] With a price several times that of indigenous titles, *Elle* reached a circulation of 180,000 in 1996, according to Christine Debiais-Brendle, chief executive of Hachette Filipacchi Asia Pacific.[30]

The exploding consumer market also brought in more global fashion, cosmetics, and fragrance brands, which were in desperate need of high-profile media to convey their prestigious images in China. In the first half of the 1990s, *Elle* had almost no competition in the glossy fashion magazine market.[31] *Elle*'s exclusive position in the Chinese fashion world was in fact partially a result of China's tight control over the presence of Western magazines in China. As pointed out by the *New York Times* (January 1, 1996), Conde Nast failed to get approval from Chinese authorities to bring *Vogue* into China. Because of its high status and authoritative role in China's fashion arena, *Elle* attracted a slew of global brand-name advertisers. As Luo Zhaotian, director of *Elle*'s China edition, put it, "Anyone who can afford our magazine is someone our advertisers want to reach."[32] Thus, as with *Elle*'s other versions, the Chinese version also opened with page after page of big-brand advertisements. Its first issue featured fifty pages of ads and "advertisers include those already in the Chinese market, such as Christian Dior, and those wishing to have a stronger presence, such as L'Oreal."[33] Today, heavy advertising has become a common feature of every slick fashion title in China. Even the indigenous title, *iLook,* now features just as many luxury brands as *Elle.* While in the early years of the 1980s circulation was the sole criterion for success among state-run fashion periodicals, today the amount of advertising and the fame of the brands advertised in a magazine are the more critical gauges of success.

*Elle*'s historic arrival started a new "glossy" era in the history of the Chinese fashion press. Not only did *Elle* completely change the face of Chinese fashion magazines, it also demonstrated a successful business model. Thereafter, partnering with a well-known international title became virtually the norm when launching a new glossy title in China. Besides the imported paper stock and full-color printing, the content and layout of the 122-page *Elle* was also novel to the Chinese audience of the 1980s and inspirational to domestic start-ups. *Elle*'s Chinese staff worked with its international team to put together the editorial content to ensure a level of internationalism, something China longed for. The editorial team could also use any materials from *Elle*'s other editions around the world.[34] Fashion and beauty sections were the focus of Chinese edition of *Elle,* which provided Chinese women a "show window on the fashion of the world."[35]

Full-page fashion spreads also came to the Chinese fashion press via *Elle.* Producing a stunning visual effect, this form of fashion presentation soon became the heart of the slick fashion magazine in China. The eight-page fashion spread in the first issue of Chinese *Elle* was shot in Shanghai using local fashions with typesetting, color separation, finished artwork, and filming completed in Hong Kong.[36] Local fashion photographers and editors from other magazines took *Elle*'s fashion spread as a challenge to their own ability to produce full-page fashion shots of comparable quality. Seeking to meet the high aesthetic standards set by glossy titles like *ELLE, Metropolis,* originally an indigenous title launched in 1999, had difficulty finding a suitable local photographer to shoot a seven- to eight-page fashion story for each issue. On the bright side, foreign competition forced the domestic industry to adopt higher standards of quality for their productions. And in today's market, domestic photographers are comfortable working with international professionals and capable of shooting for any glossy titles. Thus, when *Metropolis* relaunched as *Biba* under copyright agreements with the French magazine *Biba* in 2004, it still produced many of its photographs and content locally, including full-page fashion spreads. Zhou Changqing, director of *Fashion* magazine, considered the production of fashion spreads the heart of a magazine's originality and its quality, determining how the entire magazine is perceived. *Fashion* also produced most of its fashion spreads locally, sometimes drawing on international photographic talent.[37]

As the focus of glossy titles shifted to large-sized photographs, images seemed to overpower text. And the power of photographers in defining the style of a fashion magazine was widely acknowledged. Consequently, a large number of fashion-related magazines competed for a relatively small number of local fashion photographers who were capable of producing large fashion shots. The shortage of fashion talent was also apparent in the editorial department. Vying for fashion editing and photographic manpower, magazines had high staff turnover rates, especially in the 2000s when Chinese *Harper's Bazaar, Marie Claire,* and *Vogue* entered the arena.

This lack of local fashion talent coupled with the immaturity of the Chinese fashion system contributed to the popularity of joint ventures between local magazines and foreign titles. On the other hand, the overabundance of partnerships between local and foreign magazines limited the opportunities for new editing and photographic talents to shine in indigenous magazines. Compared with hybrid titles, indigenous magazines were undercapitalized and had few resources. As Zhang Wenhe, editor of *Art and Design,* argued, "We must recognize that there is currently no fashion industry in our country, even the embryo hasn't been formed, and fashion magazines in China are no more than a clotheshorse for the international fashion industry."[38] A former senior fashion editor of *Elle,* Xie Li, had similar views and predicted a gloomy future for indigenous Chinese titles: "Local fashion magazines are so weak that they collapse at the first blow. Let's say there is no hope for a new local fashion magazine today."[39]

The success of another hybrid title, *Ruili,* can be largely attributed to its initial positioning as a pictorial fashion manual that sought to visually teach readers how to mix and match. *Ruili* had a fruitful partnership with the Japanese magazine *Housewives' Friend. Ruili* primarily relied on images purchased from its Japanese partner and quickly climbed to the top of the fashion magazine market. Knowing that busy young urban females were their target audience, shrewd editors of glossy titles adopted a philosophy of efficiency by distributing fashion information using a large number of images rather than text. They believed that readers of the fast-paced twenty-first century had no time to read long articles and thus preferred to browse through images. And so began the so-called image-reading era.

Furthermore, before the inception of *Ruili,* glossy titles like *Elle* were thoroughly Westernized, from models to content, and many Chinese readers felt that these titles promoted fashions that bore little relation to China. Readers of such glossy titles had no clue how to transfer the fashion displayed in their pages to their own bodies. Thus, their enthusiasm for these fashions was often a form of mere appreciation. But unlike other glossy titles, *Ruili* featured Asian models to whom readers related easily. The styles featured in *Ruili* were fashion forward, practical, and easy to implement, and the use of Asian models reduced the psychological distance between international fashion and Chinese readers. *Ruili*'s instant success inspired many local fashion titles to retool. *Shanghai Style,* for instance, followed *Ruili*'s lead to become more of a visual guide, providing its own mix-and-match examples.

A reader-centered marketing strategy also developed in the fashion press, especially as fashion magazines diversified their distribution channels in line with China's WTO obligations to admit foreign competitors and reform the media. Fashion magazines started to segment their readers based on demographics and lifestyle. And successful magazine publishers expanded their titles to cater to the varied interests of different market segments of a growing reader population. The *Ruili* Group today owns three top-selling fashion titles: *Ruili fushi meirong* (Rayli Fashion and Beauty), *Ruili yiren fengshang* (Rayli Her Style), and *Ruili shishang xianfeng* (Rayli Fashion Pioneer), plus *Ruili shishang jiaju* (Rayli Home). Magazines actively involved readers through various types of interactive activities, such as face-to-face meetings between fashion editors and readers on a monthly or yearly basis. *Ruili keai xianfeng* (Rayli Lovely Pioneer), the predecessor of *Ruili shishang xianfeng,* even allowed readers to visit its editorial department to foster a stronger bond with its readers and to promote avant-garde consumption behavior—*Ruili* wanted its readers not only to consume fashion information and advice, but also to "consume" fashion editors and their workplace. *Ruili*'s chief editor, Luo Jia, noted that urban youngsters with dyed blond, red, or neon-colored hair started hanging out in the hallways of the editorial department after this program was initiated.[40]

With intensified competition in a rather saturated market in the 2000s, existing magazines recognized the need for effective marketing, as well as for structural changes. Almost all early established state-run fashion magazines underwent reconstruction and some relaunched as hybrid titles. They changed names, layouts, and content and adopted full-color glossy art paper, growing bigger, heavier, and more expensive. The price of most high-end fashion magazines in the 2000s ranged from ten to twenty *yuan* ($1.43 to $2.86 USD).[41] Most of them aimed to attract twenty- to thirty-five-year-old white-collar urban female professionals. The growing number of middle-class female professionals sought out global fashions and tips on how to dress appropriately and fashionably at both work and play. As foreign businesses filled the most expensive office districts in major cities, Chinese employees were eager to blend into the global business culture in both spirit and appearance.

Collaborating with the French magazine *L'OFFICIEL, Fashion,* the oldest indigenous Chinese fashion title, became *L'OFFICIEL* in 2004. The magazine sold for twenty *yuan*—more than thirty-three times as expensive and twice as thick as its mid-1980s version. Its current price matches that of other leading fashion or women's titles such as Chinese *Vogue, Elle, Cosmopolitan,* and *Marie Claire.* To cope with the fast pace of fashion change and to compete with monthly hybrid titles, most indigenous magazines changed their publication schedules from seasonal or bimonthly to monthly or even semimonthly. Through restructuring and consolidation some have ceased publication altogether, *Modern Dress and Dress Making* among them.

From the 1990s on, the line between fashion magazine and women's magazine blurred. Most new magazines featured heavy fashion content and also touched on other material aspects of city life. Departing from *Ruili*'s predominant use of mix-and-match imagery, many other fashion titles such as *Harper's Bazaar, Cosmopolitan,* and *Elle* instead featured a variety of text-oriented sections such as "Features," "Lifestyle," "Emotions," "Culture," and "Entertainment." As respected fashion mentors, they seemed to have convinced their readers that fashion is not just about clothes and other aesthetic objects, but is rather a whole way of life. Accordingly, these magazines did not just provide fashion information and dressing tips; they offered a lifestyle complete with directions to the hippest bars, hottest movies, and trendiest streets to hang out on. Reading fashion magazines was also part of this new fashionable lifestyle that these magazines promoted. As *Elle*'s editorial director, Xiao Xue, stated in *Elle*'s twentieth-anniversary issue: "A magazine can establish a style and advocate a life attitude. I hope there is a day that *Elle* becomes an adjective. People may say, today what she wears is very Elle; her makeup is very Elle; this thing she makes is very Elle; she is very Elle!"[42]

Another local title, *Zhongguo shizhuang* (Best), owned by the Trends Group, joined with *Harper's Bazaar,* one of Hearst's prominent fashion titles, and relaunched as *Harper's Bazaar* in 2001. Headed by Su Mang, who previously worked for another Trends title, *Trends Health, Harper's Bazaar* managed to distinguish itself as a leading fashion magazine in China soon after its inception. As the fashion industry continued to solidify ties with the entertainment industry, *Harper's Bazaar* pioneered efforts to bring fashion and charity together after the SARS epidemic in 2003. Under slogans such as "Let Charity Be Fashion," *Harper's Bazaar* began sponsoring the annual "*Bazaar* Star Charity Night" in 2003. The event has attracted many influential Chinese celebrities and entrepreneurs from various fields and has grown more popular each year. Inspired by the words of *Harper's Bazaar*'s legendary editor in chief, Carmel Snow—*Harper's Bazaar* is for "the well-dressed woman with a well-dressed mind"—Su envisioned Chinese *Harper's Bazaar* as a place for Chinese devotees of fashion to retrieve the grace and delicacy they had lost in fashion.[43]

As the landscape of Chinese fashion changed drastically in the 2000s, *Harper's Bazaar* and other magazines found themselves in a new position. Su described the changes that took place at *Harper's Bazaar:*

Six years have passed [since *Harper's Bazaar* launched in China]. Our situation has changed from having no place to get clothing samples to now having a whole series of clothing samples shipped from overseas for fashion shoots, and from traveling thousands of miles to watch fashion shows overseas to now having all big brands vying for an international fashion show set in China. China has changed from a fashion desert to the largest market and a paradise for luxury brands.[44]

Capitalizing on this new fashion environment, the Trends Group became one of the most successful fashion print media groups in China. Trends also publishes Hearst's other popular titles in China, including *Cosmopolitan, Cosmogirl, Esquire, Good Housekeeping,* and *Popular Mechanics.*[45]

A relative latecomer to the intensely competitive fashion scene, the Chinese version of *Vogue* finally landed in China in September 2005 (Fig. 4.3), entering a market in which *Elle, Cosmopolitan, Ruili,* and *Harper's Bazaar* had established themselves years earlier. *Vogue* attempted to assert its authoritative role in fashion from its

**Figure 4.3** Cover of *Vogue* China's inaugural issue in September 2005 (photographed by Patrick Demarchelier). Courtesy of *Vogue* China.

inception in China with an ambitious slogan: "*Vogue,* Ultimate Fashion in China." *Vogue*'s editorial director, Zhang Yu (Angelica Cheung), the former editorial director of Chinese *Elle* and editor in chief of Hong Kong *Marie Claire,* made a clear distinction between *Vogue* and similar popular titles in an interview with the *Southern Metropolitan Daily:* "*Vogue* positioned itself very highly around the world. It is truly focused on dress. Most of our magazine's content is centered on dress, with a little on makeup. There is nothing about careers, love, or marriage relations."[46] Chinese *Vogue* also strove to maintain its luxurious visual appeal by assembling top stylists, photographers, and makeup artists from all over the world. Cheung believed that *Vogue* did not face the localization challenges that *Cosmopolitan* and *Elle* had faced because all of *Vogue*'s international versions were different. And *Vogue*'s fashion stories were not purchased from its foreign versions as was the case in many other Chinese hybrid titles. Instead, it combined fashion talent from both East and West, such as using photographers from abroad and models from China.[47]

Inheriting *Vogue*'s tradition of discovering and cultivating new talent, the debut issue of Chinese *Vogue* profiled four domestic clothing designers, representing the new faces of Chinese design. Nicknamed "the fashion bible," *Vogue*'s strong position in the fashion world helped to push Chinese designers and models onto the stage of international fashion. After landing the cover of *Vogue*'s debut issue, Du Juan, a Chinese model, gained contracts from top brands like Louis Vuitton and Roberto Cavalli and began flying to New York, Paris, Milan, and London as a highly sought after international supermodel.

With the brisk sales of the first 30,000 copies of the debut issue, which included a valuable handbag as a free gift, *Vogue*'s impact on the Chinese fashion print media market was almost immediate. Competing titles responded quickly to *Vogue*'s strong entrance. *Elle* launched TV advertisements and packaged a complimentary mascara valued at 168 *yuan* with its September issue in 2005, while the magazine itself sold for twenty *yuan*. *Ruili yiren fengshang* similarly offered a high-value gift with its September issue. Thereafter, free gifts became commonplace in the fashion magazine industry. Brooches, bracelets, cosmetics bags, hats, scarves, eye lotion, and even slippers were attached to magazines as free gifts in an effort to stimulate sales. *Harper's Bazaar* was one of the few magazines that did not give out free gifts, but it did offer extra value by increasing its number of pages to 618 for its October issue in 2005.[48] Finally, after an intense war of gifts, *Cosmopolitan, Ruili, Elle,* and *Vogue* united with over forty other fashion and women's magazines in September 2006 to call a truce.[49]

Although fashion pioneers on the streets of Shanghai today are virtually indistinguishable from their counterparts on the streets of New York, London, or Tokyo, outstanding fashion journalists and editors with a global vision who are fluent in the language of fashion are still in short supply in China. Thus, competition among fashion magazines for staff is perhaps even fiercer than competition for readers. Inspired by the powerful roles Anna Wintour, Carmel Snow, and Diana Vreeland have had in the fashion world as editors in chief for reputable fashion magazines, leading Chinese fashion titles were also eager to find their own glamorous leaders with an extraordinary fashion sense. Nearly every popular Chinese fashion magazine today has recruited a fashionable young woman as editor in chief or editorial director: Su Mang at *Harper's Bazaar,* Zhang Yu at *Vogue,* and Xiao Xue at *Elle.* Thus, the role of editor in chief as fashion outsider that prevailed in the early 1980s has been transformed to one of fashion opinion leader.

Furthermore, in line with the privatization of enterprises in every industry, fashion magazines no longer rely on their publishing houses for financial support, but are now able to generate enough advertising and sales revenue to fund themselves. However, similar content and layout in this category of magazines has intensified the already fierce competition. Recently, some magazines discovered underaddressed niche markets that they hoped to use to expand the horizons of the fashion press; for example, *Gediao* (MISS) targets urban single women, *Shaonv fushi* (Coco) targets teenage girls, and *Fuzhuang shejishi* (Fashion Designer) targets fashion designers.

Since the mid- to late 1990s, the internet has also played a critical role in communicating and spreading fashion trends in China. With over 253 million internet users, surpassing the online population of the United States for the first time in June 2008, the internet in China has become an important platform for delivering information, exchanging ideas, and conducting business.[50] Relatively loose controls over the internet by the government has made it the freest venue in which to publicize controversial ideas and to expose the darker sides of society. The internet has thus become a place where the young can be easily aroused and united on a number of topics, ranging from reviving Han Chinese traditional garb to more sensitive political issues.

Numerous fashion-related Web sites established by institutions, businesses, and individuals have targeted fashionable users mainly as a way to advertise traditional establishments. And popular shopping Web sites such as Eachnet, Taobao, Shishang, and Buyest have rapidly revolutionized the way people acquire and consume fashions, despite the lack of a mature credit card system in China. The Web sites of popular fashion magazines attract great numbers of readers to their various forums. With the increasing importance of the internet, magazines could no longer afford to ignore this fast-growing market. To some extent, the internet has endangered the development of traditional print media in China as the scarcity of fashion information available in the early 80s has given way to a deluge of fashion information available to increasing numbers of Chinese online. The internet has enabled Chinese to feel that they are now, finally, just as aware of international fashion—and just as fashionable—as their Western counterparts.

# –5–

# Importing Fashion Icons

Chinese fashion iconography throughout the twentieth century, from the *qipao* cal-endar girls of the 1920s and 1930s to the uniformed Red Guards of Cultural Revo-lution propaganda posters, offered models of what new, modern, liberated Chinese should look like. These idealized images of the "New China," whether in the turbu-lent years after the fall of the Qing Dynasty or in the convulsions of Mao's Cultural Revolution, influenced Chinese clothing choices and Chinese identity. But, for the most part, this fashion iconography lacked individual fashion icons: individuals, who, through the force of their own personality, sense of style, and personal popu-larity, influenced fashion on a mass scale.

To the extent that China did have individual fashion icons before the reform era, they were drawn from the world of politics rather than entertainment. The dress choices of Sun Zhongshan (Sun Yat-sen) and Mao Zedong had more influence on what Chinese wore than any pop star of today, and in this sense they could certainly be called "fashion icons" in their own right. Chinese emulated these fashion icons in part out of a desire to be politically correct, in part out of social pressure to conform, but also out of a genuine sense of enthusiasm and a desire to break with the past.

Even during the early years of the reform era, individual political leaders still retained enormous influence over what people chose to wear, as Hu Yaobang's popu-larization of the Western suit attests. But as the tight grip that had previously been maintained on outside cultural influence loosened, the personal became increasingly separated from the political, and the influence of politics and politicians on Chinese fashion began to wane. As these political models and traditional fashion systems were abandoned, people began to look abroad for a new, less politicized fashion iconography.

From the start of the reform era in 1978, China looked to the West for fashion in-spiration. But while a few foreign TV shows and movies aired on Chinese television in the early 80s, the government still maintained strict control over all forms of media in this period. Access to foreign entertainment and fashion media was still extremely limited, and the majority of the populace had no direct access to Western fashion. Without such access the Chinese lacked the criteria to judge what was fashionable according to "international standards," a byword for modernization in this period that signaled China's desire to join and compete with the international community.

At first, Western fashion trends and fads came to China through TV shows and movies imported from Hong Kong and Taiwan (see Chapter 2), but these fads were usually based on a particular character rather than on the actor as icon. In the restricted media environment of the day, it would have been difficult for any actor or entertainer from abroad to garner enough media exposure to transcend a particular role and become a fashion icon. So while a character in a Hong Kong television series might inspire many Chinese to adopt a similar hairstyle, the actor himself was not able to sustain any sort of influence over what people wore and could not serve as a real life model for fans desperate for a fashion mentor.

Into the 1990s, the development of a domestic entertainment industry that came to understand the importance of packaging and marketing—a mindset that had been virtually nonexistent in China's command economy—finally created the space necessary for the importation of more than just an occasional TV series or movie. And as Western-influenced entertainment products—above all pop music—became less controversial and were "officially" accepted by the mainstream media in the late 80s and early 90s, pop stars from Hong Kong and Taiwan came to fill the role of fashion icon and "super idol" (as they were called in Chinese). These pan-Chinese super idols were a natural choice for a country in search of fashion icons, since they were foreign, exotic, and Westernized, but at the same time still looked Chinese. Their shared cultural, ethnic, and linguistic heritage made it easier for mainland Chinese to identify with the stars of Greater China than with a Madonna or a Prince. Above all, imported pop icons from Hong Kong and Taiwan seemed to show the Chinese how they, too, could modernize and become fashionable according to "international standards" while still remaining Chinese.

## Light Music and Rock and Roll

Pop music has always been a close cousin of fashion: Elvis, the Beatles, Madonna, Cher, Jennifer Lopez, along with scores of other rock and pop stars have both influenced and been influenced by the world of fashion. This is no less true in Asia than it is in the West, but in China in particular the influence of pop stars on Chinese dress is a more recent phenomenon—and a phenomenon that only took hold once the music itself ceased to be politically controversial.

When China resumed foreign trade at the end of the 1970s, fashion and pop music came to China almost hand in hand, and both imports engendered debates that would last for years over their shared "decadent" nature. At first, this decadent music was brought into China via cassette tapes that were imported alongside cassette recorders. Still banned from radio airplay, early pop imports were popularized through private copying and sharing of these cassettes. The Taiwanese pop singer Deng Lijun (Teresa Teng) became wildly popular in this manner at the end of the 1970s and early 80s. Her songs featured soft rhythms and love themes, which made her soothing voice enticing to a generation of Chinese who had grown tired of the formulaic, "high-pitched, strong, fast, and hard" anthems of the Cultural Revolution. But while

Deng's songs were quite popular, mainland Chinese had to satisfy themselves with only hearing her, not seeing her: for political reasons, she never traveled to the mainland or appeared on Chinese television. Thus she had little discernible influence on fashion in China. Nevertheless, her voice launched the pop music industry on the mainland and set the stage for later pop music icons.

Song Xiangrui, a professor at the Wuhan Conservatory of Music, divides the early domestic development of Chinese pop music into two phases.[1] The first phase, which lasted from 1976 to 1979, featured "emotional songs." Songs of this era acknowledged the emotional needs of people, which had long been suppressed and ignored during the Cultural Revolution. But the purpose of these songs was not to entertain. Instead, they served only as a means of expressing politically healthy emotions. And the "artistic" merit of these songs was still judged, to a great extent, according to their political connotations and associations. The second phase, which began in 1980, featured "light music" that was more clearly influenced from abroad. At this point, people began to appreciate songs more for their entertainment value than for their perceived political correctness. The expression of emotion in this phase was more individual and was partially freed from political scrutiny despite continuing campaigns by the state to steer people away from the unhealthy and immoral influence of pop music.

Mainland singer Li Guyi became the target of one such campaign after the success of her song *Xianglian* (Hometown Love) in 1980. The state-run media attacked Li as a "criminal who corrupts the youth" and branded her "the mainland's Deng Lijun."[2] These criticisms reflected the serious doubts harbored by some elements in the government and society at large over new forms of music. But while they were officially condemned in the media, the popular appeal of singers like Li and Deng continued to grow.

The media, which the Communist Party called the "throat and tongue" of the Party, had long considered itself the guardian of public morals and political correctness. And throughout the early 80s the media widely criticized all forms of Western-influenced pop culture, including music, dress, art, and literature. In 1982, the editorial department of *People's Music* magazine published a guide called *How to Distinguish Yellow Songs,* which mainly consisted of articles originally featured in the *Wenhui Daily* and *People's Music.* According to the guide, "music or songs that propagate sexual, obscene, and decadent content are called 'yellow' music or songs, which corrupt people's hearts." This music, the guide cautioned, was merely a profit-making tool of capitalism.[3] The guide carefully scrutinized both lyrics and music, instructing unsuspecting listeners how to recognize the characteristics of these songs: "softened, restless, seductive, or quivering rhythms that create a sexy, frivolous, flirtatious, seductive effect." The use of "unclear, loose, artificial, and coquettish pronunciation" was another telltale sign of a yellow song.[4] The guide further explained the relationship of yellow songs to pop songs: "The phrase 'pop songs' (*liuxing gequ*) has a specific meaning in Chinese history. It is a generic term for all songs that are tender, cheesy, frivolous, and perplexing, with unhealthy content and tones. These songs are inferior and vulgar. Pop music usually includes yellow songs."[5] The "specific meaning in Chinese history" refers to the negative image pop songs had acquired through their association with the *guomindang* (Kuomintang) regime of the 1920s and 1930s. To avoid these historical connotations, pop music of the early 1980s went by the name "light music."

But young fans remained undeterred by the government's warnings against the evils of pop music. They hand copied music scores, recorded each other's cassette tapes, and taught themselves how to sing these "tasteless" songs. Teahouses featuring "light music" sprung up in an attempt to make money off of the pop music phenomenon, and the number of cassette tapes sold in 1983 reached 1.8 million, triple that of 1982.[6] The growing popularity of pop music was driven in part by the desire of many to live a new, fashionable lifestyle that intertwined fashionable activities such as singing, dancing, and the pursuit of trendy clothes. But by the end of 1983, the government perhaps thought that pop music had become a little too popular. Late that year, the Central Party Committee formally condemned pop music as a form of "spiritual pollution."[7]

In 1984, however, the fate of Chinese pop music took a dramatic turn. In an unexpected move, China Central Television (CCTV) invited two pop singers—Zhang Mingmin from Hong Kong and Xi Xiulan from Taiwan—to perform at its Spring Festival Gala, a nationally televised program that aired during the Chinese New Year. At a time when the media had routinely attacked pop music as both "spiritual pollution" and an obstacle to China's socialist goals, the sudden appearance of pop singers from abroad on CCTV, one of the most important propaganda outlets of the Communist Party, seemed contradictory. Some have speculated, however, that the invitation was a political gesture to the eventual reunification of China rather than any sort of official endorsement of pop music on the part of the government.[8] The intended political message was hinted at in the patriotic song sung by Zhang Mingmin, "My Chinese Heart." While Zhang gently pointed to his Western suit, he sang, "Although dressed in foreign clothes, my heart is still Chinese." But the politics of the invitations and any political message that the government hoped to send were too subtle for the public, which was far more interested in the music than the politics of musical diplomacy. On the whole, people interpreted the invitations as a shift in the government's official position on pop music and a signal of a relaxation in government controls on pop music. Shortly thereafter, provincial TV stations followed the example set by CCTV and started their own pop music programs, which the central government did not seem to want to restrict.

Another milestone in Chinese pop music was reached in 1986 when one hundred pop singers gathered in Beijing for a concert titled "Let the World Be Filled With Love," which many see as the birthplace of original Chinese pop music.[9] Inspired by the song "We Are the World," which was recorded by a group of popular Western musicians as a charity single in 1985 to raise funds for famine victims in Africa,

Chinese musicians organized this concert to pay tribute to the International Year of Peace. "We Are the World" made Chinese musicians realize that pop music could be more than just entertainment and could take on important social responsibilities. But the real significance of the concert in the history of Chinese pop music was the breakout performance of one singer: Cui Jian.

When Cui Jian appeared onstage and belted out "I have asked you endlessly, when will you go with me?"—the first line to his song "Nothing to My Name"—the audience was stunned.[10] Cui's performance that night challenged accepted notions of Chinese pop music and the appropriate way to present it. He appeared carefree and ragged with his long hair, his worn-out shirt with the sleeves rolled up, and his loose-fitting pants with unevenly rolled-up legs. Among all the other neatly dressed singers at the concert, he clearly stood out. And in a country that had always emphasized the collective, Cui was the first to declare—loudly—the significance of individual feelings. Cui later stated that it was this spirit of individuality in rock music that appealed to him.[11] All of these elements coalesced that night and by the end of his performance, in the midst of shock, cheers, and applause, China's first rock star had been born.

Western rock music had all of the characteristics that the Chinese authorities railed against: it was rebellious, libertine, individualistic, irrational, and morally suspect. According to *How to Distinguish Yellow Songs,* rock and roll represented the height of decadence: "When pop music turned into rock and roll, it became an incurable disease of capitalist societies."[12] Cui's music and image were both clearly influenced by this capitalist disease from the West, and he cited the Who, the Beatles, ABBA, and the Talking Heads as some of his favorite bands. But despite official condemnation, Cui Jian's popularity continued to grow.

Cui's growing popularity was due not only to his music, but also to his defiant attitude and his expression of bottled-up emotions with which many of the young could identify. Cui had a loud, brash musical style that was new to Chinese music if not to rock and roll. He shouted and yelled as much as sang, which both shocked and intrigued the younger generation. His lyrics were also shocking, especially to the government, which considered Cui a troublemaker and subsequently prevented him from holding an "official" concert for ages.[13]

In the realm of fashion, Cui's peculiar taste in dress also set the tone for Chinese rock and roll. In concert he often wore a military-style flat cap with a star on the front, a popular hat worn by the Red Guards during the Cultural Revolution. Wearing Cultural Revolution–era military garb as a performer was itself a provocative move: at a time when most of society was trying to forget the nightmares of that era, Cui Jian fearlessly called attention to it. His penchant for wearing this sort of military attire popularized military-style caps and unofficial army uniforms among urban rock fans in the late 80s, long after the general public had discarded them.

The rock musicians who followed in Cui's wake, including members of the popular rock bands Hei Bao and Tang Dynasty, also took their cues from Cui and donned similarly unconventional looks. They wore their hair long and sported outfits featuring loud patterns, such as dragons, Chinese characters, and polka dots. But although the first rock-and-roll fashion store in China opened in Beijing in 1993 (catering to aspiring rock stars and their fans), rock music in China never reached the heights it has in the West.[14] Rock's rebellious image and its tendency to veer toward the political limited its mass appeal and ultimately relegated it to a subculture of diehard fans. And while Cui Jian, China's own King of Rock and Roll, became a cultural icon of sorts, he and his rebellious music remained far outside the Chinese mainstream. Into the 90s, Cui and his fellow rockers were ultimately marginalized as a host of pop stars from Hong Kong and Taiwan took center stage on the mainland.

## Importing Superstars

By the mid- to late 1980s, the mainstream media fully recognized pop songs as a normal form of musical expression. No longer considered "spiritual pollution," pop singers and bands from abroad poured into the mainland market in the 1990s. And as imports from abroad became more popular, domestic stars started to lose their appeal. According to music critic Tie Cheng, pop music concerts at the end of the 1980s and early 1990s could not succeed without the participation of pop stars from Hong Kong or Taiwan. Album sales for mainland stars generally ranged from five hundred thousand to one million per album in the mid-80s. By the end of the 1980s and into early 1990s, that number had dropped to between ten and thirty thousand. In contrast, album sales for stars from Hong Kong or Taiwan averaged approximately three hundred thousand per album.[15] Mainland music critics at the time warned that the mainland pop music industry was in danger of colonization by pop music from Hong Kong, Southeast Asia, Europe, and America.[16]

These imports inaugurated a new era in the Chinese music industry in which singers were transformed into superstars, a process that shifted the audience's attention from the music to the image of the performer. As a critical element of this image, fashion became crucial to the development and success of superstars. And as less importance was placed on musicianship and greater emphasis was placed on "star quality," pop singers in the 90s began to branch out into TV and film. The entertainment industry made every effort to iconize these superstars using modern marketing tools and attracted millions of fans across the nation. Zealous fans collected their idols' photos, autographs, posters, CDs, and anything else they could get their hands on. And most important in terms of fashion diffusion, fans were easily influenced by the marketing efforts of their idols, from the products they advertised to the clothes they wore. Eventually, these superstars saturated all forms of entertainment media, from TV to radio, from magazines to newspapers, from billboards to posters, influencing an entire generation. In fact, having missed the chance to idolize pop stars during their own youth, many of the older generation also joined their sons and daughters in worshipping pop idols. In this sense, the influence of pop idols went beyond Chinese youth fashion and culture and extended to the whole society. The entertainment media squeezed every detail out of the personal lives of these pop idols, from their lovers to their childhoods, to their astrological signs to their living room decor. Thus ordinary fans were familiar with the image of their idols far beyond what was shown onstage. And the daily-wear fashions pop idols wore were also judged and imitated. Thus, through their music and images pop idols effectively communicated new lifestyles and fashion attitudes to their fans of all ages.

Debates arose over the demarcation between serious music and pop music, as well as the modernization of folk music.[17] But as pop music proved itself worthy of serious attention through its rapidly growing market, attention shifted from academic debates over the nature of pop music to the very practical question of how the mainland could produce its own superstars. Although mainland singers produced a number of hits, none of these singers became super idols who could set trends with their sustained national popularity and influence on popular culture.

However, a lesson that mainland music producers learned from their neighboring competitors was the importance of what they called *baozhuang* (packaging). The initially controversial concept of "packaging" consisted of a systematic process of making a musical product via modern marketing tools such as advertising, public relations, and promotions. From the producer's perspective, the emphasis on the musical product shifted from the songs to the singer in this process: the goal of packaging was to make pop stars, not just pop songs. The process included painstaking training of the singer, not only in singing but in stage performance, makeup, dress, and etiquette.[18] Serious musicians and singers on the mainland, however, considered this packaging process deceptive and misleading, and believed it served only to mask a lack of musicianship. Nevertheless, the mainland began to package its own singers as stars in the early 1990s. Under this embryonic star system, a few mainland singers such as Ai Jing, Mao Ning, and Yang Yuying became new stars of the mainland's pop music industry. But their influence on mass fashion was negligible because their images lacked novelty and, perhaps more important, exoticism.

With a more mature music industry equipped with more advanced packaging skills, packaged pop stars from Hong Kong and Taiwan were better prepared to function as fashion icons. When these pop stars metamorphosed into super idols on the mainland, they acquired the power to attract millions of loyal fans to fashion trends that they created or endorsed. The carefully designed images of super idols were ready-made and ready to be copied, from hairdos to clothing to footwear to makeup.

The worship of imported pop idols began with a short-lived infatuation with Fei Xiang (Kris Phillips), a pop star born in Taiwan to an American father and a Taiwanese mother. He became known overnight for his matchless voice, eye-catching dancing, and good looks when he first appeared on CCTV's 1987 Spring Festival Gala. His image included intriguing elements: he spoke perfect Chinese but looked like an incredibly handsome Westerner. Fei Xiang gave Chinese a chance to see firsthand what a glamorous pop star really looked like. With his charisma and good looks, he was more than just a singer. And unlike most singers from the mainland, he exuded energy and glamour onstage. Through both his dancing and the way he carried himself on and off the stage, Fei Xiang changed the focus of the pop performance from music to movement, from song to image. His sudden departure for Broadway in 1990 only stimulated the Chinese appetite for more idols. And despite his long absence from the Chinese music scene, Fei Xiang remains a popular figure in China even today, and he can still be spotted in ads and billboards in China, modeling clothing for Youngor and other Chinese brands.

The next big imported sensation was the Little Tigers, a boy band that first rose to stardom in the late 1980s in Taiwan. The band consisted of three handsome teenage boys: Wu Qilong (Nicky Wu), Su Youpeng (Alec Su), and Chen Zhipeng (Julian Chen). Miao Xiuli, the agent who discovered them, attributed the band's overwhelming success largely to their consciously designed image. "At that time boys generally did not manage their image. But the packaging of the Little Tigers team copied the operational model of Japanese band Boy's Brigade [a famous three-member boy band of the 1980s] which made people realize that Taiwanese boys were also cute and handsome."[19] The group was initially chosen and trained for a TV program for the Chinese Television System in Taiwan, and they quickly became regional pop idols because of their distinctive image, singing, and dancing.

As their albums were released on the mainland, especially after they held a series of concerts in Beijing, Shanghai, Wuhan, and Xi'an, the Little Tigers quickly expanded their fame among the mainland's youth in the early 1990s.[20] By that time, the mainland entertainment industry had matured enough to support a marketing plan designed to establish the Little Tigers as pop idols. Calendar posters of the three "little tigers" were everywhere, from bookstores to barbershops, and teenage boys began wearing their hair in "Little Tiger" styles. The band also had a major influence on the popularity of *taizi* (prince) trousers. Prince trousers featured many pleats around the waist (typically sixteen of them) that created a sense of fullness around the hips and thighs. At the hem, the trousers tapered into a natural fit. The fashion industry quickly capitalized on the popularity of the Little Tigers, contracting them as spokesmodels for various fashion brands.

The appearance of the Little Tigers greatly affected people's views of men's fashion. At the time, the general public still had rather conservative views regarding how men should adorn themselves, and compared to the growing variety of women's fashions, men's mass fashions in the 1980s were still generally marked by simplicity, neatness, and austerity. The arrival of these male pop icons, singing love songs to soft rhythms and dressed in the latest international fashions—and looking somewhat feminine according to mainstream views of the time—altered the ideal male image in China. The youth of the Little Tigers and the fact that they were performers lowered, in a sense, their masculinity requirements. Thus they could pull off somewhat feminine styles such as richly patterned vests and silky, looped neckties. Often dressed like school-boys, the band also donned Taiwanese school fashions.

Inspired by the great success of the Little Tigers, many other boy bands entered the mainland. Popular acts included another three-member boy band, Grasshopper, from Hong Kong. Although they were known more for their singing and dancing than anything else, their image was just as thoughtfully designed as that of the Little Tigers. In fact, at a reunion concert in 2005, they amplified the feminine trend that male entertainment artists had been slowly adopting over the years. All three members dressed in ultrafeminine styles with a touch of punk. One band member wore scarlet tights, hot pants, and a flamboyantly trimmed buttonless coat that revealed his bare, smooth chest. In the new millennium, decorations and trims and shiny, flowing, sheer fabrics became a mainstay of male fashion under the influence of pop icons.

In the 1990s, the "Four Heavenly Kings" of Canto pop from Hong Kong—Liu Dehua (Andy Lau), Zhang Xueyou (Jacky Cheung), Li Ming (Leon Lai), and Guo Fucheng (Aaron Kwok)—emerged and eclipsed the popularity of all other pop singers. All four of these pop stars shone in several spheres of entertainment. Andy Lau's career, for example, took off as a TV-drama actor in the early 1980s after his graduation from Television Broadcasts Limited's (TVB) star academy in Hong Kong. Aaron Kwok was originally a dancer. But they all shone for decades as pop singers, with legions of fans attracted to their individual qualities and specialties.

As super idols, they were highly sought after spokesmen for global brands. The brands they represented included a range of products, such as Pepsi, Cyma, Sony, and Benetton. Their ability to influence the fashion choices of millions of their fans turned them into fashion icons, with every change in their appearance noted by the media and copied by their legions of fans. Fans and the media incessantly compared the singing, acting, looks, and overall images of the four. The comparisons among them as well as with other pop stars helped the Chinese audience develop an eye for fashion. As the worship of these super idols helped to spread new fashions, some fans took it a step further, opting for plastic surgery to look like their idols. Compared to extreme instances of idol worship like this, the imitation of Aaron Kwok's hairstyle by teenage boys and young men in the early 1990s is easier to comprehend. Kwok left his hair full on the top but cut it short at the bottom, with eye-length bangs parted in the middle. Its shape resembled a mushroom and became known as "mush-room hair," but it was also called "Guo Fucheng *tou*" (Aaron Kwok hairstyle). Another pop idol of the time, Zhang Guorong (Leslie Cheung), told *Time* magazine, "I don't even put my litter outside the house anymore. People try to find things and sell them."[21] In the 90s, debates over whether fans should worship their idols, and what the acceptable limits of this worship should be, replaced debates over the decadence and political correctness of pop songs.

Amid the dominant influence of male superstars, Wang Fei (Faye Wong) stood out as the most popular female pop icon of the 1990s in greater China. Her mainland fans adored her as the "Heavenly Queen" of pop while her Japanese fans dubbed her the

"Diva of Asia." Because of her constantly changing image, she was also called the "chameleon Heavenly Queen." Also a model and an award-winning actress, Wang grew up in Beijing but first achieved fame in Hong Kong, where she began her music career in the late 80s. By March 2000, she had become the best-selling Canto-pop female star.[22]

Just like other super idols of the time, Wang Fei had a "packaged" image. However, the commercial aspects of her image did not undermine the artistic value of Wang's work in the eyes of her fans, nor did it hinder her popularity. According to a survey conducted on a popular Chinese Web site, Wang Fei's many fans were fully aware that Wang Fei, as a star, was really only a commercial product just like other commodities. But they could not resist Wang Fei's charm even knowing they were the target consumers of her product.[23] Ultimately, Wang's unique personality, fashion taste, and extraordinary singing and composing talents enchanted her fans, despite their cynicism regarding star packaging.

Wang's resistance to becoming overly packaged as a star, however, also contributed to her popularity. She struggled to maintain her independence and individuality and resisted being molded by a marketing machine, and earned a reputation for being low-key, carefree, and uncooperative with the media—all of which only attracted more media attention to her and added to her image as the "antistar." As her fame grew, Wang gained more control over the style of her music and her public image, including changing her original stage name, Wang Jingwen (Shirley Wong), back to her real name. Ironically, the great fame she attained through the star packaging system eventually awarded her the freedom to be herself and to keep distance from that system. Her personal taste in both music and fashion accordingly became even more critical to her subsequent success. At the height of her popularity, some believed that Wang had "surmounted the ordinary manufacturing process [of a star] of a record company" and become "an unconventional, anti-commercial cultural hero in an era of consumerism."[24] But Wang's rejection of commercialism itself became an integral part of her image that only generated even greater commercial success.

While Wang Fei resisted efforts on the part of the industry to overdesign and package her, her dress belied her carefree image. Working with the top stylists from Hong Kong, her concerts, music videos, and CD covers always featured cutting-edge, meticulously designed styling. Her highly refined and carefully designed outfits, makeup, and coiffures have often strongly contrasted with her laid-back, almost aloof, stage presence. But the common thread throughout Wang's career has been her daring sense of the avant-garde, whether in the creation of her image, her music, or her stage productions.

Since the early 1990s, after returning from New York, Wang made her presence felt in the fashion media. For the CD cover of her Western-influenced release of 1993, *100,000 Whys,* she donned a loose-fitting Bohemian sweater worn underneath an unbuttoned vest. Her ankle-length dress was matched with flat shoes and her hair was loosely coifed into two braids. Shortly after the release of the CD, the fashion media started to tout the Bohemian look. In greater China, she was also among the first to introduce the underwear-as-outerwear look, popularized in the West by Madonna in 1990. One memorable look showed her in a cropped black short-sleeved sweater matched with tight silver panties that could be seen under a see-through spaghetti-strap dress. Around the same time she sported a funky hairstyle with her hair tied into several knots along her hairline, which was widely copied in the music and fashion industries and which the media labeled the "pineapple hairstyle."[25] Her 1994 concerts saw her in dreadlocks, painted silver tears, and unusually long sleeves. And mass-produced sweaters, shirts, and coats featuring long sleeves soon appeared in stores. In the music video for the song *Renjian* (Mortal World) Wang Fei showcased punk-looking butterfly makeup with a colorful butterfly glued to her forehead above her left eyebrow. She also wore heavy red eye shadow and dark chocolate lipstick. This new image inspired a butterfly tattoo and embellishment fad in 1997. Chocolate lipstick also became the trendy color among chic young urban women. In her concerts of 1998 and 1999, Wang sported red cheeks that resembled a sunburn, as well as a big ponytail tied straight up. Her sunburned cheeks and big ponytail were widely copied not only in the music industry but also in the fashion world. Fashion models on magazine covers and in fashion spreads in 1999 often imitated this look.

By the early 2000s, Wang was firmly established as an influential super idol and fashion icon. She graced the covers of many fashion magazines throughout Asia, such as *Vogue* Taiwan, *Elle* Hong Kong and Japan, *Marie Claire* Hong Kong, and even *Time* magazine. However, her collaborations with the domestic fashion industry were rare. Unlike Madonna, who had relied on big-name designers such as Jean-Paul Gaultier, Chanel, and Christian Dior throughout her career, Wang relied on her own stylists from the music industry and her own sense of style. Also, aside from her performance image, Wang's everyday appearance has been featured in newspapers and magazines throughout her career, providing invaluable fashion inspirations that her fans could easily translate into everyday fashion.

Other pop singers from Hong Kong and Taiwan such as Qi Qin, Su Rui, Luo Dayou, Tan Yonglin, Wang Jie, Zhang Guorong, Mei Yanfang, Zhang Huimei, Ye Qianwen, Zheng Xiuwen, and Zhou Huajian debuted on the mainland from the mid-1980s into the 1990s. Their distinct musical and fashion styles suited the diversified tastes of the Chinese audience and drew many fans away from the dominant super idols.

In the new millennium, Zhou Jielun (Jay Chou or Chou Chieh-lun) and Li Yuchun emerged as new super idols and changed the notion of what a super idol should be. As a composer, songwriter, and singer from Taiwan, Chou was compared to Elvis by *Time* magazine because both "transcended conventional musical boundaries" and held "a strange power over fans' lives."[26] The media crowned him a "small Heavenly King" for his sweeping influence. But Chou charmed his fans with his music and his cool demeanor rather than his good looks:

He came to understand that it was the music that mattered, more than the looks and the moves and the image. He saw them come and go, pretty boys who could barely carry a tune, divas who had the attitude but not the talent, boy bands whose members were chosen for their dance steps instead of their voice chops. He saw that what made a performer memorable—what could make him, Jay Chou, special—were the songs themselves.[27]

This shift in focus from image back to song was in reality no more than a shift in marketing orientation—a shift that deemphasized the power of fashion. However, new super idols like Chou could no more escape the image-centered "packaging" of the entertainment industry than the idols who came before them.

In 2005, the mainland finally produced its own super idol—Li Yuchun, a Sichuanese music student. Li won a televised "Super Girl" singing contest, which was similar to the popular American TV show *American Idol,* and was the first show of its kind in mainland China. According to *Time* magazine, "The show drew the largest audiences in the history of Chinese television" by soliciting audience votes to decide the winner. The level of audience enthusiasm was both great and greatly unexpected, with some interpreting the overwhelming response to the democratic nature of the show as having deeper significance than mere entertainment. "After all, in China the opportunity to use votes to choose are relatively few," said Yu Guoming, a media expert at Renmin University.[28] Therefore, "Li represents unabashed individuality, and that's why she's a national icon."[29] In this sense, it did not matter who Li was. What mattered was how she was chosen: by the will of the people.

In the Chinese media, Li's victory was more often associated with the charm of her androgynous image than with her singing skills. She took a natural and somewhat careless approach to her image. However, as we have seen, antifashion looks are often transformed into popular fashions themselves. Li's democratic image coupled with her innocent, twenty-one-year-old look appealed to both men and women and was undeniably fashionable at the time. Numerous fans rejected other pop idols as prepackaged by the entertainment industry and instead turned to a super idol that they themselves had made—one who appeared more like the girl next door than a superstar.

After the Li Yuchun phenomenon, the internet allowed the democratization of the pop idol packaging process to continue, as several unknown singers released songs via the internet and became famous, first online and then in other media outlets. In these instances, the relationship between pop idols and their fans shifted from top-down imitation to crossover sharing.

## Japan Craze, Korea Craze

The Japan craze and Korea craze that began in the mid- to late 1990s were also instances in which the people, rather than star-making corporations, played a critical role in the initial selection of pop icons. In a sense, fashion diffusion also became more democratic as diversified, stratified tastes and preferences in fashion created demand for diversified sources of inspiration. Fashionable youth found their fashion inspirations in Japanese and Korean pop culture through multiple media channels, including TV dramas, films, animation, pop music, books, fashion magazines, the internet, and consumer products. And rapidly increasing levels of trade between China and Japan and China and Korea facilitated and stimulated cross-cultural communication, including the exchange of fashion ideas.

The Japan craze gave birth to the Chinese buzzword *ha ri,* which originated from a regional dialect of Taiwan. The word *ha* was widely used by Taiwanese youngsters to mean "crazy about something; madly infatuated; and to worship and imitate."[30] Thus *ha ri* (*ri* being the Chinese character for Japan) was the Chinese phrase used to describe the Chinese infatuation with and imitation of Japanese popular culture. In the 2000s, the Japan craze jumped from Taiwan to major cities on the mainland, such as Beijing and Shanghai. In the *Wenhui Weekly,* the "symptoms" of *ha ri* were described as follows:

> They rode skateboards outdoors, wore hip-hop clothes and gaudy headscarves, liked anime, such as *Chibi Maruko-chan, Doraemon, Sailor Moon, Slam Dunk,* and *Boys Over Flowers.* They watched Japanese movies and TV dramas like *Love Letter* and *True Love.* They wore platform shoes and skirts trimmed with short fringes. They had permed hair that looked like fibers. *How* magazine supplied them with spiritual nourishment. They were madly in love with Sakai Noriko, Namie Amuro, Utada Hikaru, and Kimura Takuya. But they were immune to Western fashion culture.[31]

The fever for Japanese pop culture was in fact a global trend that was especially prominent in the 1980s in the West. Japanese values and aesthetics were communicated to the world through Japan's world-famous animation, electronics, automobiles, and fashion designers. Fashionable youngsters in the West were also fond of anime, *Pokemon,* and *Hello Kitty* and influenced by the clothing styles of "Gothic Lolitas" or *yamanba.* As for Japan's Asian neighbors, shared cultural roots and greater media exposure led to an even deeper fascination with Japanese pop culture.

Looking back, Chinese had been copying Japanese fashions displayed in TV dramas and movies since the early 1980s. At the time, imported household electronics from Japan, such as Toshiba refrigerators, Hitachi color TV sets, and Sharp washing machines, had a reputation for quality and high cost: in the 80s, these products were status symbols for middle-class Chinese. These satisfying consumption experiences in the past further stimulated Chinese interest in Japanese material culture. In the mid-1990s, a strong interest in Japanese pop culture and fashion revived, coinciding with the airing by a number of Chinese TV stations of the greatly popular Japanese romantic TV drama *Tokyo Love Story.*

A key component of the Japan craze was an emphasis on a youthful look. The elements of this look in China included neon-colored hair; long eyelashes; pinkish, glossy, full lips; clear, smooth skin; polished nails adorned with patterned designs; short skirts worn over leg warmers; platform shoes; and *kawayi* (cute) accessories. Even the Japanese word *kawayi* was borrowed along with *kawayi* looks by Chinese youth who followed the *ha ri* fad.

But the Japan craze went beyond looks and fashion. It encompassed all of the fashionable items and activities that were associated with Japanese youth culture. Costume role-playing games or "cosplay" (a portmanteau of "costume play") became popular among college anime fans in Beijing, where college students formed cosplay groups and performed for the public. Well-known cosplay groups included "Twilight Anime," from Renmin University, "Truth Troupe" from Capital Normal University, and "Black and White" from the Beijing Institute of Technology. Thus some *ha ri* adherents not only watched anime but played at it as well (Fig. 5.1).[32]

In the 2000s, a few years after the Japan craze gained popularity, the Korea craze emerged. Termed *ha han* (*han* being the Chinese character for Korea), both the Korean and Japanese crazes had a strong impact on contemporary Chinese fashion at roughly the same time. In fact, Japanese design elements were often seamlessly mixed and matched with Korean design elements on the fashionably dressed Chinese body in this period. This amalgam was often apparent in styles like hair dyed red, yellow, and other neon colors; baggy pants with large legs and many decorative pockets, matched with T-shirts in cute prints (Fig. 5.2); and oversized overalls. Moreover, a variety of accessories made adherents of the Japan and Korea crazes stand out from others. Round necklaces or neckbands, multiple earrings or ear bands, bracelets, and sometimes nose rings were commonly used. The "Hello Kitty" character was frequently attached to their clothes, backpacks, or cell phones. Cell phones in

**Figure 5.1** Anime fans in cosplay costumes in Shanghai, December 2004. Courtesy of Yong He, photographer.

pastel colors that looked more like toys than phones were also commonplace. They painted their nails black or in pastel colors and wore platform shoes or sneakers, and often moved about the city on skateboards.

Followers of these trends were usually young Chinese born in the 80s or 90s who hailed from well-to-do urban families. And their conspicuous consumption of material goods also set them apart from their peers. Their Japanified and Koreanized tastes in fashion, music, and social activities also differentiated them from other subgroups. And gaining acceptance to a *ha ri* or a *ha han* social circle was often a competition based on both taste and levels of conspicuous consumption. Although a great number of fashionable youth blended Japanese and Korean influences together, many made a clear distinction between the two and identified themselves as followers of either Japanese or Korean fashions. Middle-school student Li Shan, a member of a prominent *ha* Korea group in Beijing, felt that "Japanese pop culture aims at people above eighteen years old, while Korean pop culture aims at people younger than nineteen years old."[33]

The Korea craze initially grew out of a Korean pop music fad. Korean pop songs were introduced to Chinese in major cities through a popular FM radio program called "Seoul Music Hall" in 1997, which built up a vast audience for Korean pop music in only a few years.[34] The colossal success of a concert held in Beijing in 2000 by H.O.T., a five-member South Korean boy band, in particular fueled Chinese interest in Korean pop culture and fashion. Chinese youth were soon imitating the dance

**Figure 5.2**   Chinese youngsters dressed in Japanese- and Korean-influenced styles on the streets of Shanghai in 2004. Courtesy of Yong He, photographer.

moves, hairstyles, and dress styles of H.O.T. members.[35] The feeling for H.O.T. here described by Li Shan was typical of H.O.T. fans:

> Nowadays in China, whether on the mainland, Hong Kong, or Taiwan, everywhere is filled with soft love songs. The boring, sickly sweet, hollow, and meaningless lyrics floating in the air make you sleepy ... Then, H.O.T. landed here like angels. They reject violence. They are against wars. They cherish the moment. They give us hope for the future ... Their shouting, "We are the future," reverberated to the heavens and shocked my heart. They woke us up from our numbness and sound slumber: we need to change the structure built by adults. The world is ours and we are the future! Who else in the Chinese pop music industry could have such an effect? So, I like H.O.T.[36]

The Korea craze was thus, for some, a form of youth rebellion against their parents' generation's fascination with Hong Kong and Taiwanese pop songs. The spiritual emptiness that the new generation saw reflected in Hong Kong and Taiwanese pop songs was exchanged for a new spirit that some found in Korean culture.

Post-Mao Chinese pop culture had always yearned for China's glorious past. TV channels were filled with dramas set in ancient times. And while the influx of TV dramas, music, and fashion from Hong Kong and Taiwan exposed China to Western influence, perhaps more importantly, it reconnected China with its traditional past and, to some extent, reestablished a sense of cultural continuity that had been severed during the Cultural Revolution. However, with the return of Hong Kong to China in 1997, increased communications and business connections developed between Hong Kong and the mainland. After two decades of increasing interaction, Hong Kong and Taiwan had lost the foreignness that had once appealed to Chinese who longed for the exotic. Chinese interest in the pop culture of Hong Kong and Taiwan thus also waned through fatigue. Thus the attraction of Hong Kong and Taiwan super idols started to wear off as well, as did their influence on fashion.

In the eyes of Chinese, the advanced economic development on display in Korean TV dramas embodied China's possible future, which resonated with their desire for modernization. At the same time, Korea provided a model for China in preserving its traditions and cultural values and roots in the process of modernization and globalization. Furthermore, Korean-made products, including fashion, were comparatively less expensive than those made in Japan, Europe, and America. Long-standing anti-Japanese sentiment in China also worked to the advantage of the Korea craze.

The sixth floor of Beijing's Xidan Shopping Center, which featured a great number of Korean products and fashions, was a hub of social activity for Korea-craze adherents.[37] However, the Korean fashions sported on the streets of Beijing or Shanghai had been specifically chosen or sometimes slightly modified to suit Chinese tastes. Just as Chinoise was never a truthful representation of Chinese style, fashions and styles popularized by the Korea wave were also inevitably filtered through the lens of Chinese aesthetics. And the majority of Korea-craze adherents perceived Korea only through its pop music, fashion, TV dramas, films, and consumer products. Misunderstandings and distortions were inevitable. However, it was this distance between the real Korea and the perceived Korea that really attracted Chinese, because in the end what mattered was Chinese interpretations and creations of fashion, regardless of what it was based on. "We like Beijing. Korea is so far away. We really do not have any sense of it. But their dress and their bands that are good at dancing are what we really want. But we do not have it. That's why we *ha* Korea," declared another Korea-fashion fan.[38]

The emergence of the Korea craze brought a set of new ideas, cultural associations and meanings, and exotic styles to a new generation of Chinese. However, in one sense, the Korea craze was just a repetition of what had happened twenty years earlier: it reconnected China with its past. As Pei Zhongxin, the Vice Minister of the Ministry of Culture and Tourism of Korea, pointed out when he attended the Asian Cultural Forum of Ministers, "The so-called 'Korea wave' is in fact China's rediscovery of its classical culture in Korean culture."[39] The Korea wave brought Chinese "packaged," modernized Oriental culture, containing the right mix of Euro-American and Asian cultures. Thus the fashion elements displayed in Korean culture seemed so familiar to Chinese through their linkage to China's past, yet novel due to their linkage to the West. This combination was extremely attractive, especially to a younger generation that was patriotic, anxious to find its cultural roots, and yet fashionably Westernized.

# –6–

# Reinvented Identity: The *Qipao* and *Tang*-Style Jacket

In an era of globalization in which popular fashion trends and ideas are increasingly borrowed from others, China felt an urgent need for a sartorial symbol of national identity of its own. India had the sari. Japan had the kimono. Korea had the *hanbok.* Vietnam, the *ao dai.* And Indonesia, the sarong. Compared to these proud symbols of national identity of China's neighbors, many of which had connections to China's own imperial past, China seemed to have nothing but fashions from the West. This discovery was rather embarrassing to a people who claimed to have inherited five thousand years of civilization and who had always taken the issue of national identity so seriously.

China's long, self-imposed isolation from the rest of the world after 1949 obscured in a way the need for such a symbol of national identity, even though nationalism remained a prominent feature of Chinese politics. It was only after China had opened up to the world in 1978 that the need for such an identity symbol became apparent. Rapid modernization coupled with the collapse of both the Marxist-Leninist-Maoist and Confucian value systems in the post-Mao era led to a pervasive sense of anomie and alienation in Chinese society as people lost their moral and spiritual moorings. Much like what Japan experienced in the 1970s during its own modern transformation, China found itself in the throes of a national identity crisis. On the one hand, many Chinese resented the idea of being culturally assimilated by the West. On the other hand, many Chinese were reluctant to appear merely traditional. Therefore, the Chinese attempted to find or create something new enough to differentiate themselves from the traditional Chinese image, yet familiar enough to make a meaningful connection to their cultural roots.

At the turn of the twentieth century, China faced a similar dilemma. Before the two Opium Wars (1839–1842; 1856–1860), China was largely an isolated, multicultural empire, and identity issues relating to dress mainly pertained to the differentiation of ethnic groups. During the Qing dynasty, issues of dress identity were particularly tense between Han Chinese (the majority) and the Manchu (the former ruling ethnic minority). But after the imperial door was forced open to foreign trade and influence after the Opium Wars, the need to unite all Chinese, including the powerful Nationalist Party and the budding Communist Party, in order to establish the identity of China as a nation-state, overpowered the tension between Chinese ethnic groups. Almost throughout the Republican era, "Nationalism became the ideological glue of campaigns against imperialism and the privileges of foreigners."[1]

> China's long struggle for autonomy and survival vis-à-vis Japan, culminating in the bru-
> tal struggle of 1937 to 1945, would do more than anything else to create a national sen-
> timent that was both deep and strong. The memory of that struggle, memorialized and
> cultivated in statues, plays, films and books for Chinese of all ages for over six decades,
> has made nationalism a prominent, apparently permanent, feature of China's political
> and cultural landscape. The Three People's Principles, Marxism, Maoism, even Deng
> Xiaoping "theory" have come and gone; Chinese nationalism remains the bedrock of
> any political legitimacy.[2]

## The Path to Modernization

Dressing had always played a critical role in marking ranks and classes in the strict hierarchical system of imperial China. What Chinese men, in particular, wore had always been of great political importance. Throughout Chinese history, transitions between Chinese dynasties were always accompanied by a transformation in dress. And when Manchu nomads, an ethnic minority living to the northeast of the Great Wall, conquered China and established the Qing dynasty in 1644, they forced all Han Chinese males to conform to the Manchu style of dress. This included requiring men to shave the front of their heads and wear a queue. However, the enforcement of the new dress code was met with vigorous resistance from Han Chinese. The Manchu ruler finally offered Han men a choice: they could keep either the heads or their hair.[3] More than 100,000 Ming loyalists were executed for not conforming to the Qing dress code.[4] In this brutal struggle between conqueror and the conquered, clothes were weapons. The Manchu wielded this weapon as a means of imposing their authority, while the Han clung to their own clothing styles as a means of resisting that imposition.[5]

To mitigate Han resentment, the Manchu ruler allowed for many exceptions to the new dress code. Under this compromise, Han Chinese females were exempted from the official dress code. Apparently, what women wore was considered less symbolic and meaningful and was thus less important to the new ruling class. Ordinary Han Chinese women therefore kept the dress style of the earlier Ming dynasty (1368 C.E.– 1644 C.E.) and maintained a distinct appearance from the Manchu women of the ruling class.

In the last decade of the Qing dynasty Manchu dress styles had become a particular focus of ethnic hatred. They were also viewed as a symbol of feudalism and imperialism, especially since Qing dynasty dress styles were linked in the Chinese mind to the humiliations Chinese had suffered at the hands of foreigners—China's defeat by Japan in 1895 in particular. Thus, Manchu dress was seen as an obstacle to the transformation of China into a strong and prosperous country.

Kang Youwei, a famous reformist in the late Qing dynasty, suggested that Emperor Guangxu set an example for the court and the people by cutting his queue and changing his clothes.[6] Although his suggestions were not adopted, some people had already adopted Westernized adornment. When China's ports were forced open after the two Opium Wars, Western fabrics and trims, accessories, and other material goods, along with Western missionaries, diplomats, businessmen, and travelers, began to enter China. These exotically adorned foreigners provided real-life fashion models for Chinese to observe and copy. Reformists and more radical revolutionaries began to adopt Western fashions as a means of modernizing the Chinese image.

Thus, in the early twentieth century, when the West was immersed in the orientalism of Paul Poiret's exotic couture designs, Chinese were busy stripping off the remnants of their imperial past in order to build a new, independent, modern country. As argued on August 11, 1934, in an article in *Shenbao,* an influential daily newspaper in Shanghai of the day, "Everything in China is too ancient. In today's world it won't work to remain ancient. But how shall China change? Undoubtedly, it needs a new life to replace the old one. This so-called new life, I dare to say, is to Westernize as much as possible." The essence of Westernization, as promoted during the May Fourth Movement, was Mr. Sai (science) and Mr. De (democracy), as intellectuals then called them. And according to the author's observation: "The essential spirit of Westernization is 'progress.' In other words, Westernization is modernization."[7]

At the beginning of the twentieth century, the most common formal wear for Han men was in the Qing dynasty style, consisting of a teal *changpao,* or long gown, and a black *magua,* or surcoat, matched with a dome-shaped cap. But during the Republican era (1912–1949) Westernization in many facets of Chinese life became apparent. Western styles quickly overtook large cities like Shanghai, where the colonized culture cultivated an inclination to anything Western. In Shanghai, men wore three types of Westernized attire: (1) military uniforms, including British, American, Russian, and Japanese styles; (2) Western suits and other traditional Western daily wear, worn by civil officials in Chinese embassies, employees of foreign firms, and students who had returned from overseas; and (3) Japanese-style government official attire and school uniforms.[8]

The traditional image of Chinese men adorned in long gowns made of gentle silks and satins in various colors was then replaced with one of Chinese men sporting Western attire in black or shades of gray made of firmer materials that fit the Western definition of masculinity. Western suits, shirts, ties, bowlers, and leather shoes, and Japanese-style school uniforms were often worn by revolutionary activists. Thus, the ruling class saw these styles as a sign of political dissidence.[9] But in the eyes of reformists and revolutionaries, Western attire signified a desire for change, progress, and modernization.

For the same reason, seeing dress as an explicit cultural symbol as well as a critical component of the nation's economy, many people also boycotted Western dress and products for patriotic reasons, especially Japanese products. Patriotic advertisements in *Shenbao* throughout 1919 featured calls for patriotic sentiment and antiforeign action to save the country through the boycott of Japanese products and the promotion of national goods.[10] However, these patriotic, antiforeign movements had little effect on fashion. And dress mixing Western and Chinese elements had come into vogue for both men and women by the 1920s.

Women modernized their image by bobbing or perming their hair, abandoning breast and foot binding, adopting Western undergarments and accessories, shortening the hemline, and eliminating fancy ornaments and trims from their dress. Four types of fashionable modern women were noted at the time: (1) the "study-abroad type," who totally adopted a Western style of dress; (2) the "school type," who combined Chinese and Western styles of dress; (3) the "boudoir type," who kept the Chinese style entirely; and (4) the "brothel type," who adorned themselves in obscene dresses that were neither fish, flesh, nor fowl [also a mixed style using all available means].[11] Fashionable Chinese women learned about Westernized styles both "directly through Western garments brought back to China by travelers returning from Europe or America and indirectly through fashion magazines and drawings and, later, photographs in periodicals."[12]

## The Evolving *Qipao*

At the beginning of the twentieth century, Han Chinese women wore an ensemble consisting of the *ao* (a padded or thickly lined jacket) and the *qun* (a pleated, floor-length skirt) during the winter, and the *shan* (a jacket without padding or with only a thin lining) and *qun* during the summer. Beneath the skirt, women wore a pair of loose-fitting trousers called *ku*. On less formal occasions, the *ao* was worn over the *ku* without a skirt. Especially in the early Republican era, the *ao ku* and *shan ku* ensembles were worn on various occasions.[13] But a variety of clothing styles, such as long or short vests, cloaks, and various skirts, were at the disposal of fashionable women at the time. By the 1920s, Western overcoats and full-skirted dresses, corsets, hats, gloves, watches, oval-shaped glasses, leather shoes, stockings, brassieres, handbags, silk scarves, and umbrellas became trendy items and were sometimes mixed with Chinese traditional dress forms, such as the *ao* and *ku*.

In contrast to the two- or three-piece ensembles that Han Chinese women wore, Manchu women in the Qing dynasty wore the *qipao,* which literary meant "banner gown," a voluminous floor-length, one-piece dress with side slits and a curved asymmetrical closure extending from the neckline to the underarm on the right side. *Qi,* or banner, originated from the "Eight Banners" of the Qing dynasty military and administrative divisions. The banner gown was worn over loose trousers and, on rare occasions, over court skirts. On formal occasions, the sleeves of the banner gown featured *mati xiu,* or horseshoe-shaped cuffs. In the late Qing, the mandarin collar replaced the round neckline of the early banner gowns, and more exaggerated collar shapes reaching the earlobes were sported on Han women's jackets. The banner gown was also decorated with elaborate bandings and piping and meticulously embroidered patterns.

Besides clothing, Han and Manchu women's appearances were further distinguished by their headwear and shoes. Manchu women's headwear in the late Qing was characterized by an insertion of a large stiff board to form a horizontal shape on top, which was called *dala chi.* And the hair of Han women was combed flat into a bun (or buns) held in the back with combs and hairpins. An embroidered headband hid hairlines and shaped a woman's face into an oval. Manchu women's shoes were constructed with a wooden platform attached to a silk upper.[14] Toward the mid- to late Qing, upper-class Han and Manchu women started to imitate each other's styles, and a look that mixed both Han and Manchu dress features became popular along with hybrid styles that mixed Chinese and Western features.

By the Republican era, the ethnic demarcation in dress was obscured. As Han Chinese regained power in Republican China, the need to mark ethnic identity was overshadowed by the need for new symbols that would represent the new China as a national state. To clarify the confusing messages displayed in various hybrid styles, the Republican government issued guidelines for men's and women's formal wear in 1912. The regular formal dress for women retained the traditional Han women's *ao qun* ensemble. But the thigh-length jacket closed in the center, which bore resemblance to men's jackets but differed from the normal asymmetrical closures of women's wear. It featured a fashionably high collar and embroideries all over. It also had two side slits and a back slit. Banding trims framed the tubular silhouette along the edges. The long jacket was matched with a heavily pleated floor-length skirt with an embroidered rectangular insertion draping down the front. The skirt ended with tassels all around the hem. However, this mode of dress did not become popular. Instead, the shortened and simplified *ao* and *qun,* referred to as "civilized new dress," came into vogue.

In 1927, the Republican government proposed a second dress form, the *qipao,* as a "national" garment for Chinese women.[15] This modern form of dress resembled the silhouette of the banner gown, also called the *qipao,* worn by Manchu women in the Qing dynasty. Thus, the Manchu women's banner gown is generally identified as one origin of the modern *qipao.* However, the modern *qipao* differed in many ways from the banner gown, with materials and matching accessories influenced by Western fashion. Thus, the new *qipao* came to embody one of the most notable modern, Westernized images of Chinese women in the twentieth century (Fig. 6.1). Aesthetically, the older Manchu banner gown emphasized the meticulously designed pattern with delicate banding edge trims. Auspicious animal and plant themes were common in the surface design, and complicated embellishments gave the materials a heavy look. The modern *qipao,* on the other hand, usually used lighter materials with printed abstract patterns. Compared to the commodious cut of the banner gown, the modern *qipao* was slimmer and shorter in the sleeves and the bodice. From the late

**Figure 6.1** A fashionably dressed lady with permed hair in a *qipao* matched with a Western-style overcoat, scarf, and leather shoes. Circa 1930s. Courtesy of the Fashion and Art Design Institute of Donghua University.

1930s on, the incorporation of Western construction techniques such as darts, set-in sleeves, and shoulder pads made the *qipao* even more formfitting, subtly revealing female body shapes. While the banner gown was worn with wooden platform shoes and loose trousers or leggings (tightly bound at the ankle, often embroidered at the hem) underneath, the modern *qipao* was worn with panties and nylon stockings and was accessorized with heeled leather shoes (Fig. 6.2). The Manchu banner gown reflected the Qing hierarchical sartorial code, and the use of pattern, color, and material strictly conformed to the sartorial code. But the modern *qipao* was democratic in nature and supposed to be classless: at least no restrictions were officially placed on its design and usage.[16]

The direct predecessor of the *qipao,* however, is believed to be an ankle-length vest, which originated from a Manchu women's calf-length long vest that was worn

**Figure 6.2** An ankle-length *qipao* with an abstract print and accessorized with high-heeled shoes. The backdrop also featured modern designs. Circa 1930s. Courtesy of the Fashion and Art Design Institute of Donghua University.

over a coat.[17] The *qipao* was first worn circa 1921 by female students in Shanghai and became a popular fashion among young ladies in urban centers by 1926.[18] With a flourishing pop culture, including pop music, fashion publications, large department stores, and a film industry, Shanghai had become China's fashion center and an active port. While flappers in the West waltzed in Chanel's little black dress, Shanghai's flappers, or so-called "social flowers," donned the *qipao* and enjoyed ballroom dancing and nightclub activities, such as drinking whiskey or brandy and watching dancing and singing spectacles put on by Russian girls.[19] Intimate interactions with the West in Shanghai, which had a large foreign population, made the city particularly susceptible to Western influence, which contributed to the birth of the modern *qipao*.

Chinese novelist Zhang Ailing believed that women started to wear the *qipao* because they wanted to look like men.[20] This explanation could be linked to the *qipao*'s more well-known name in the West, *cheongsam,* which in Cantonese literally means "long gown," the same name for a garment worn by Chinese men, especially scholars. This long gown featured the same mandarin collar, asymmetrical closure, and side slits as the *qipao.* Thus, the *qipao*'s Cantonese name seemed to indicate another origin of the *qipao:* the long gown worn by Chinese men. Hence, women's donning the one-piece *qipao* was viewed as symbolizing equality between the two genders. Song Qingling, Sun Zhongshan's (Sun Yat-sen) last wife, an American-educated, fashionable young woman, is pictured wearing the *qipao* in a photograph taken in 1925 in Beijing. Her *qipao* was plain, in a solid dark color with bell-shaped sleeves that were characteristic of the 1920s. Angular lines and a spacious cut gave no hint of her body shape. Overall, her *qipao* looked exactly like a man's plain long gown except for the flared sleeves.

Bearing a resemblance to both the Manchu women's banner gown and the Han men's long gown, along with evidence of Western influence on its fabrics, construction, and accessories, the *qipao* was embedded with modern meanings while still vested in a traditional frame. It became the most dominant urban female fashion of the 1930s and into the 1940s. The booming consumer culture encouraged urban women to act as modern consumers who would consume Paris or New York fashions like Parisians or New Yorkers. Changes in the *qipao*'s length, cut, sleeves, fabric, collar, and trim closely followed international fashion trends, especially in the 1930s. Along with the *qipao,* many other one-piece dresses were either imported from the West or locally made based on Western fashions and were worn by fashionable women. Hybrid styles, such as mixing the *qipao* silhouette with round, heart-shaped, or V-shaped necklines, were also in vogue. And the formfitting shape of the *qipao* of the 1930s, with its revealing high slits, matched with stockings and high heels reversed the *qipao*'s early androgynous image. Since then, the *qipao* has established itself as a classical form of dress epitomizing Chinese femininity. However, the body-confining silhouette of the *qipao* fashion was basically an urban phenomenon of the leisure class. Women in the countryside opted for the *ao ku* ensemble for its practicality. Although the *qipao* fashion had been adopted by women of all classes in the city by the 1940s, its middle- and upper-class urban image still remains even today.

The wars between China and Japan and between the Nationalist Party and the Communist Party during the 1940s massively affected China's fashion landscape, just as World War II had in the United States and Europe. The media called for patriotism and frugality in support of the war against the Japanese. At the same time, the use of Western construction techniques to modify the *qipao* became very common. While the length was shortened to mid-calf and sometimes to the knee, the collar was also narrowed with some added detachable lining for easy cleaning. Cap sleeves were popular, and sometimes sleeves were eliminated altogether for the summer. Prevailing "National Goods Movements" again urged people to use domestically produced fabrics, which led to the prevalence of the blue "patriotic fabric," as it was then called. Zippers and snap fasteners replaced the elaborate frog fasteners. The

early asymmetrical closure was expanded to various shapes, and curved symmetri-
cal closures were also common. The *qipao* form, with great variation, was widely
adopted for school uniforms, factory uniforms, daily wear, and formal wear. Meanwhile, as novel commodities, ready-made *qipao* provided additional options for the
rich and fashionable.[21]

After the establishment of the People's Republic of China in 1949, the bourgeois
image associated with the *qipao* was no longer in tune with the national spirit. Frugality, austerity, hardship, and egalitarianism instead marked this new spirit. Anything
bourgeois was looked down upon, and the *qipao* accordingly fell out of fashion.
Without the promulgation of any official dress codes, people opted for more egalitarian styles to reflect the new spirit, such as the Mao suit, youth jacket, *ganbu zhuang*
(cadre jacket), and *renmin zhuang* (people's jacket) for men, and Lenin suits and
*bulaji* for women. *Bulaji* was a Chinese translation of the Russian name for a loose-
fitting, short-sleeved, calf-length, waisted dress, which was usually made of flowered
or plaid fabrics in pastel colors.

The cadre jacket and people's jacket looked similarly plain and resembled the
Mao suit, and both were matched with loose pants. Lenin suits suited both men
and women and were especially popular among women. They were double-breasted
and often worn with a belt, which brought subtle decorative aspects to this plain and
proletarian jacket. Wool and wool synthetics were then considered luxury materials
that people saved for important occasions. Since Chinese communism modeled itself
on the Soviet Union, the Chinese copied many dress forms from the USSR. Popular
Soviet styles included *bulaji,* overalls, newsboy caps, and the Lenin suit. Meanwhile,
besides the effect of the Cold War, Chinese participation in the Korean War against
the United States further fueled anti-American and antiforeign sentiment in China
and caused the Chinese to shun anything Western during Mao's era.

Around 1956, when the government called for everyone to dress in flowery
clothes, the splendid past of the *qipao* seemed to have temporarily returned. But the
*qipao* was undoubtedly no longer considered proper daily wear shortly thereafter.
Only when high-level cadres, such as female diplomats or wives of political leaders,
visited foreign countries or attended state banquets did they don the *qipao,* perhaps
as a symbol of both national identity and fashion. For instance, Wang Guangmei,
wife of Chairman Liu Shaoqi, once wore the *qipao* and a pearl necklace on a visit
to Indonesia. This clothing choice was later held against her during the Cultural
Revolution when she was publicly paraded and humiliated by the Red Guard, who
forced her to wear a necklace of Ping-Pong balls. Her sense of fashion, coupled with
the political persecution of her husband, was labeled capitalist and bourgeois and she
was subsequently imprisoned for more than a decade. In contrast, Song Qingling,
because of her special status as "Mother of the Nation," was one of the fortunate few
in China who was able to wear the *qipao* throughout her entire life.[22]

While falling out of fashion on the mainland, the *qipao* fashion continued outside
of the People's Republic in Hong Kong, Taiwan, Singapore, and Malaysia, where

it was preserved as a symbol of Chinese cultural identity. In Hong Kong the *qipao* was consciously promoted as a form of "national dress."[23] Various venues in Hong Kong's entertainment and fashion industry, such as beauty pageants, films, fashion shows, and design exhibitions, continued to reinforce the *qipao* image as a cultural symbol signifying formality and nationality, even after the *qipao* fell out of fashion at the end of the 1960s in Hong Kong.

Attacked by the revolutionary Red Guard, the *qipao* fashion, along with any other perceived forms of "fashion," ceased to exist on the mainland by the end of the Cultural Revolution. And the strikingly "simple, practical, unworldly, androgynous, unfeminine, or downright ugly" styles of the Cultural Revolution finally came to symbolize China.[24] In the sea of monotonous blue and gray, outsiders divined a deeper meaning: uniformity in dress signified the desire for uniformity in thought and behavior.

In the 1980s, as the political focus suddenly shifted from class struggle to economic development, the focus of mass fashion also shifted from a frugal uniformity to more varied forms, including the revival of indigenous dress forms like the *qipao.* Many indigenous fashion magazines featured *qipao* on their covers (Fig. 6.3). But in spite of the state's conscious promotion of the *qipao,* many people had mixed feelings about it. It was modish, yet a fashion from a bygone era. It was feminine, yet backward looking. It was classic, yet looked out of place. Hesitations and doubts of this sort surrounded the revival of the *qipao* fashion. At the beginning of the reform era, the *qipao* made only a minor comeback despite the sense of many that the *qipao* fashion might make a full-scale return. In July 1983, the *Xinmin Evening News* attempted to quell fears related to donning the *qipao* in an article titled "Women Like to Wear the *Qipao:* There Is No Need to Fear."[25] The article related the story of a female comrade who had gone in and out of the Green Leaf Clothing Shop in Shanghai three times, wanting to buy a *qipao.* She was so hesitant because she was afraid others would consider it "too modish" and that leaders in her work unit would form negative opinions of her in the *qipao.*

During this period, the *qipao* was seen more often at fashion shows, trade exhibitions, in advertisements (Fig. 6.4), on mannequins in window displays, and on magazine covers than on the streets. After failing to come back as a mass fashion, however, the *qipao* became a standard uniform in the service industry among airline stewardesses, waitresses, and hostesses at various commercial events (Fig. 6.5). Through such uses of the *qipao,* its fashionability was unavoidably reduced. Its attraction to the fashion-seeking younger generation was lost, while the older generation was still leery of donning an outfit that only a few years earlier had been strictly taboo. The adoption of the *qipao* in the service industry also tarnished the *qipao*'s elegant and graceful image, which discouraged many from adopting it. Moreover, the formality and confinement that characterized the *qipao* form were increasingly incompatible with contemporary fashion, which centered on the casual and the comfortable. However, attempts to promote the *qipao* in the media did help to repopularize it as

**Figure 6.3** *Shanghai Style,* an indigenous fashion magazine, featured a *qipao* design on the cover of its second issue in 1986. Courtesy of *Shanghai Style.*

ceremonial attire for traditional holidays and special occasions, in addition to its use as a uniform in the service industry.

As a result of embracing Western fashions, urban street fashion in China in the 1980s lacked Chinese features. Only in remote rural areas, which were largely untouched by modern fashion trends, were indigenous dress forms preserved—and they were mainly worn by the elderly. Folk costumes were preserved in the dress of national minorities, which were also increasingly Westernized, following the path of the Han majority. However, increased foreign exposure made it an urgent task for Chinese to find a meaningful vestimentary symbol that would clearly mark them as Chinese. Serious debates arose not only over what the national costume should be, but also over whether there even is such a thing as a national costume. National flags, emblems, and anthems were officially designed and promulgated by the government. Should a national costume also be a new design issued by the government?

**Figure 6.4** A large billboard advertising local skin-care products on a street corner in Beijing in January 1979 features a young woman in the *qipao* with permed hair. Courtesy of Li Xiaobin, photographer.

Or should it be the *qipao*? Before the numerous debates on the mainland yielded any agreed-upon answers, Westerners had already come to associate the *qipao* with Chinese women. Besides the influence of Chinese outside the PRC, movie characters, pop stars, artists, and fashion designers all exerted a tremendous influence on Westerners' perceptions of the *qipao* as a national symbol of China. As early as the silent-movie era, Anna May Wong, an American-born actress of Chinese heritage, came to exemplify sensual Chinese beauty in luxuriously made *qipao*. Her signature Chinese hairstyle, tightly tied in a bun leaving straight-cut bangs, coupled with her slender figure, perfectly iconized the *qipao* image in the West.

A few decades later, in the hit romantic drama of 1961 *The World of Suzie Wong*, Hong Kong actress Nancy Kwan made her character—a Hong Kong prostitute named Suzie Wong—a remarkably sexy Asian icon in body-hugging *qipao* in violet, beige, orange, bright red, and yellow. *Life* magazine also featured Nancy Kwan in a golden *qipao* on its October 1960 cover. The various *qipao* Suzie Wong wore in the film were typical styles of the 1960s in Hong Kong: a high mandarin collar, a high slit, knee length, narrow piping, short sleeves or sleeveless, asymmetrical side closure, frog buttons, and a body-hugging silhouette. Although the film itself has often been criticized for its Eurocentric outlook and stereotypical views of Chinese women, it was an extremely effective advertisement for the *qipao* in the West. As a result, Suzie Wong became synonymous with the *qipao* at the time.

**Figure 6.5** Hostesses dressed in *qipao* at a ceremonial event at a bank in Shanghai, February 2004. Courtesy of Yong He, photographer.

About forty years later, the Hong Kong film *In the Mood for Love,* released in 2000 by Wong Kar-Wai, one of the most celebrated Chinese-language directors, again put the *qipao* in the international spotlight. The film harvested dozens of international awards, including best actor at Cannes in 2000, best foreign language film and best cinematography from the New York Film Critics Circle in 2001. *In the Mood for Love* featured limited dialogue with elaborate settings and a stunning wardrobe consisting of over twenty exquisite *qipao* for the lead role played by Maggie Cheung. Cheung played a married woman who falls in love with her neighbor, a married man, played by Tony Leung.

Set in 1960s Hong Kong, the film displayed the astonishing beauty of the *qipao* from the same period as *The World of Suzie Wong*. The *qipao* that Cheung donned, however, displayed a more prominent S-curve, with splendidly decorative fabrics with a postmodern flair. Wong Kar-Wai often dresses his romantic female leads in *qipao* of this type, re-creating a dreamlike, romanticized Hong Kong of the 1960s. In another award-winning film, *2046,* a loosely tied sequel to *In the Mood for Love,* Wong Kar-Wai again slipped stars Zhang Ziyi, Gong Li, and Carina Lau into exquisite *qipao* accessorized with fur, pearl necklaces, and brooches.

Chinoiserie has been part of the Western design vocabulary for hundreds of years. As fashion became increasingly multicultural, the *qipao* and other Chinese styles such as the dragon robe and the Mao suit offered inexhaustible sources of inspiration for Western designers. Yves Saint Laurent focused his 1977/1978 Fall/Winter collection on imperial Chinese themes, including richly embellished *qipao* forms, coinciding with the opening of China.[26] A year before Hong Kong rejoined China in 1997, he again reassembled elements of the *qipao* and other Chinese styles into his Fall/Winter ready-to-wear collection.

Indeed, the 1990s saw a proliferation of designs inspired by the *qipao* and other China motifs on Western fashion runways, especially around 1997.[27] A number of high fashion designers, such as Pierre Cardin, Karl Lagerfeld, Christian Lacroix, Valentino, John Galliano, Kenzo, Ungaro, Donna Karan, and Jean Paul Gaultier, played with Chinese design elements, with many of them making a direct reference to the *qipao* form in their couture or ready-to-wear collections. In addition, China-born designers or those with Chinese heritage, such as Vivienne Tam and Anna Sui, reinvented the *qipao* fashion and simultaneously reinforced the linkage between the *qipao* and a Chinese identity in the West. They experimented with the potential of the *qipao* form, claimed Vivienne Tam:

> When I design a cheongsam, I want it to be a clean translation of the dress's essence—almost an abstraction—beautiful, but without restriction. I've made it in stretch fabric, unconstructed, hugging the body with no darts. The collar is still there, but it doesn't have to stand stiff upright against the neck; it can be folded down into points or it can stretch. It's fun to experiment with the basic elements—to make a new slit where the side closure would be, use a zipper instead of frog fastenings, find ways of liberating the shape.[28]

The reinvention of the *qipao* form, in China or in the West, by Chinese or by outsiders, almost always stemmed from the same classic forms of the 1930s of Shanghai or 1960s Hong Kong. Throughout history, the *qipao* form constantly evolved, but with its essential features, such as the mandarin collar, body-hugging silhouette, side slits, asymmetrical closure, and frog fasteners, remaining relatively stable.

The attention the *qipao* was receiving in the West was reported on the mainland and affected Chinese views of the *qipao* serving as a symbol of Chinese identity. Gong Li, a renowned Chinese actress from the mainland, chose the *qipao* for her debut at the Venice International Film Festival in 1992. She wore a rather conservatively designed sleeveless *qipao* covered with white lace and trimmed with narrow banding. Her long white gloves added to the formality of her look, which matched the grandeur of the event. She was later spotted in various versions of the *qipao* with improved designs at Cannes. The *qipao,* in this case, in addition to being a symbol of national identity, came to mark Gong Li's own style. And in 2004 at Cannes, Gong Li again donned the *qipao*. Only this time the collar was open with a plunging neckline and an elegant train, designed by Yves Saint Laurent.

Compared to Gong Li's predilection for the *qipao,* Zhang Ziyi, another internationally famous Chinese actress from the mainland, swayed between the *qipao* and the *dudou* before finally settling on Western evening gowns for most of her red carpet appearances in the West. The *dudou* is a traditional form of undergarment that looks like an embroidered kerchief tied to the neck and back, and it became a fashionable item in the 1990s in China. Zhang sported a *dudou* dress at the fiftieth Berlin Film Festival, while at the seventy-third annual Academy Awards in 2001, she wore a richly patterned *qipao.*

With endorsements by internationally famous Chinese celebrities, high-profile directors, and fashion designers, the *qipao* once again became associated with avant-garde fashion and was often adopted by subcultural groups (Fig. 6.6). In China, it had again attracted notice after decades of anonymity. Mirroring the China fad in the West in the mid-1990s, China experienced its own China fad, marked by a revival of many traditional styles as street fashions, along with a renewed and

**Figure 6.6** Two lesbians dressed in stylish sleeveless *qipao* with high slits, depicted in a contemporary artwork by Shi Tou. 2006. Courtesy of Shi Tou, artist.

intensified interest in Chinese traditional culture. The *qipao, dudou, ao* or Chinese-style short jackets were all reinvented and combined with contemporary street styles (Fig. 6.7). In the summer of 1996, *Shanghai Style* pronounced the return of Chinese-style dress.[29]

Meanwhile, regarded as a deeply situated cultural symbol in the now highly Westernized Chinese society, the *qipao* became a popular form of wedding dress starting in the 1990s. Ceremonial *qipao* for weddings were usually in red, as this color is traditionally associated with good fortune and happiness. More traditional versions were embroidered with a phoenix pattern—the phoenix traditionally representing the empress, just as the dragon traditionally represented the emperor. A variety of *qipao* were available to suit both traditional and modern tastes, with lengths ranging from mini to maxi. Materials included silk, brocade, velvet, or rayon. Most were trimmed with piping, crystals, pearls, or rhinestones to add to their formality. Brides could purchase ready-made *qipao* in a broad price range. Or for a better fit, some brides had their *qipao* made to measure. In Shanghai, where the *qipao* fashion originated, many small shops specialized in producing and selling the *qipao,* such as the Longfeng Chinese Garment Corporation located on Nanjing Road. Meanwhile, the traditional *ao qun* ensemble, Western wedding gowns, and Western suits also secured their role as proper wedding attire. Brides wore different dresses for different occasions on the wedding day. While the *qipao* and *ao qun* could be absent from a city wedding, Western wedding gowns became nearly indispensable.

**Figure 6.7** The traditional undergarment *dudou* is here creatively matched with jeans and a tattoo, making a strong fashion statement. Courtesy of Yong He, photographer.

Despite the popularity of Western wedding gowns, however, at the turn of the millennium, when the Japan and Korea craze prevailed in fashion, the younger generation began returning to their own cultural roots. They resorted to traditional Han wedding practices in search of more culturally meaningful expressions for their wedding ceremonies. They substituted the *shenyi* for the *qipao*. The *shenyi* is a one-piece wrapped long gown that was worn by the Han Chinese (mainly the elite) from ancient times until the beginning of the Qing dynasty (1644–1911 C.E.), when the Manchus forced the Han to adopt Manchu styles of dress. Some modern Han Chinese thus sought to revive traditional Han wedding ceremonial practices, although a great deal of cultural meaning was lost in this modern translation.[30] The *shenyi*, along with many simplified versions of it, worn by both genders, was given the more generic name *hanfu*. *Hanfu* can be interpreted either as the dress of Han Chinese or the dress from the Han dynasty (206 B.C.E.–220 C.E.). In either case, *hanfu* suggests a close connection to the Han Chinese, who make up over ninety percent of China's population today. On the other hand, the association of the origin of the *qipao* with the Manchu minority automatically disqualified it as a national identity symbol in the eyes of some of the young Han generation.

Nevertheless, the heyday of the *qipao* as a modern street fashion had already passed, and the modernity that it signified was outmoded. Moreover, the *qipao* fashion was most closely associated with the Qing dynasty and Republican China, historical periods that Chinese were not particularly proud of, which also hindered its acceptance as a national costume by many Chinese: from its beginnings the *qipao* seemed to lack any real potential to become a symbol of nationality. However, it seems certain that the *qipao* will continue to evolve with global fashion as it did throughout the twentieth century. But whether it can retain its tacitly acknowledged symbolic status as the Chinese national costume remains to be seen.

## The Tang-Style Jacket, the *Zhongshan* Suit, and Chinese Nationality

In globalized cultures, traditional and cultural associations are largely preserved in women's dress, while men's dress is mostly Westernized and modernized. But in the imperial era, Chinese men's wear traditionally possessed more cultural and political significance than women's wear. However, unlike Chinese women, who had generally retained the *qipao* as a form of ceremonial dress, Chinese men entirely abandoned traditional styles such as the Qing-style long gown and horse jacket ensemble or the Han Chinese long gown. Thus, it is perhaps even harder for Chinese men of today to identify a form of dress that marks their national identity than it is for Chinese women. In fact, issues of national identity are present not only in the sartorial regime, but in economic, political, and cultural spheres as well. What does it really mean to be Chinese?

As American entrepreneur Kai Robert Worrell, currently an expat living in Shanghai, observed, "The problem in China is that consumers aren't sure what their identity is, which is a symptom of the society as a whole."[31] Globalization has fueled an upsurge in patriotism and nationalism in twenty-first-century China, and perceived slights to China from foreigners have generated stronger and stronger reactions from Chinese—and especially Chinese youth—in recent years. One prominent example is the reaction in China to protests that took place in many Western countries surrounding the Beijing 2008 Olympics torch relay. The protests by Westerners and Chinese political dissidents, mainly supporting freedom for Tibet, were widely viewed by Chinese youth as attempts to attack and humiliate China. Patriotic sentiments flooded every Chinese chat room, online forum, and Web site, and the protests generated a strong backlash in the business community in China. The internet community called for the boycott of French and American products and stores, as these two countries were the site of prominent pro-Tibetan protests. French big-box retailer Carrefour, luxury brand Louis Vuitton, and American fast-food chains, such as KFC and McDonald's, were boycotted or sabotaged by outraged Chinese youngsters. Even Hollywood star Sharon Stone, a friend of the Dalai Lama, got herself into trouble by remarks she made regarding the Sichuan earthquake of 2008. Christian Dior quickly dropped her from its ads in China.

A supporter of the Carrefour boycott, a popular young blogger named Acosta, explained his reasons for the passionate nationalistic reaction of many Chinese:

> "The sick man of East Asia"—this is a nickname every Chinese knows. In the early twentieth century, some magazine in Tianjin inquired: when could China participate in the Olympics? When could China host the Olympics? Such a dream has lasted for a hundred years. But people in the West do not know what the Olympics mean to the Chinese.
>
> Since 1840 China has continuously suffered from bullying and humiliation from Western big powers and a hundred years of consecutive wars and chaos—this is the history that every Chinese is familiar with. This humiliation and disgrace are buried in everyone's hearts and have dissolved in our blood and have been passed down from generation to generation. Every Chinese longs for respect and China's rapid rise. In the eyes of every Chinese, no disaster can match humiliation.[32]

The desire for respect and the sense of past national humiliation—and the desire to become modernized, international citizens of the world while still remaining Chinese—have complicated the choice of national dress for both Chinese men and women.

But the lack of an agreed-upon dress form to represent the Chinese to the world has stimulated new inventions. As a tradition of the Asian Pacific Economic Cooperation (APEC) summit, world leaders attending the summit dress in the national costume or a costume that reflects the culture of the host country. This unique combination of global economics and local dress posed a critical question to the Chinese: how could China preserve its unique culture in the face of the irreversible trend of globalization? When the APEC summit was held in Shanghai in 2001, mission teams were formed, drawing on the best talents from state-owned clothing corporations and research institutes, to compete for the right to design the APEC costume.[33] After two years of collaborative work, the individually tailored *xin tangzhuang* (new *tang*-style jacket), so named by its creators, came into being.[34] The jacket was designed in six colors: red, deep red, dark red, sapphire blue, green, and coffee brown. This new *tang*-style jacket featured a mandarin collar, circular motifs, knotted buttons, and contrasting piping along the edge of the collar and the middle closure. Right after the media published photos of Jiang Zemin, George W. Bush, Vladimir Putin, and other world leaders dressed in these eye-catching *tang*-style jackets at the summit, a *tang*-style jacket fad swept over the men's formal wear market in various cities of China (Fig. 6.8). Although the jacket was designed for both genders, its influential models were mostly men. Thus, the APEC jacket was mainly used for men's ceremonial wear. Right after the summit, tailors and specialized Chinese-clothing shops were inundated with customers seeking knockoffs of APEC clothing. This fad quickly spread to other types of Chinese-style clothing.

The Chinese media joyfully announced that this Chinese style clothing fad represented "the heightened international status of Chinese, as well as people's increased confidence in the nation."[35] After garnering an enormous amount of publicity because of APEC, many viewed the *tang*-style jacket as a possible form of national costume. But the fad did not last long as sales of APEC knockoffs plummeted in a few short years. The publicity the jacket received obscured the intention of its creation specifically for APEC: even the word *APEC* was incorporated into the circular motif of the jacket. To many, the function of the *tang*-style jacket was still ambiguous: should it serve as China's national costume, or was it merely an ad hoc creation that turned into a fad?

Commonly known as the *tang*-style jacket (without the "new"), the jacket form bears little relation to the clothing of the Tang dynasty (618 c.e.–907 c.e.). Instead, it actually resembles the Qing dynasty "horse jacket," a men's formal wear garment of the time. Rather than denoting any literal connection to the dress of the Tang period, the phrase "*tang*-style" here means only "Chinese-style." This is a common linguistic convention in Chinese, with Chinatowns and overseas Chinese called *tangren jie,* literary, "the streets of *tang* people" and *tangren* (*tang* people), respectively.[36] The word *tang* in these phrases makes a clear association with the Tang dynasty, which was one of the most prosperous and influential dynasties in Chinese history. Naming Chinatowns, Chinese-style clothing, and even the Chinese themselves after the Tang dynasty reflects the special feeling Chinese have for this glorious era, when China was one of the cultural and economic centers of the world. The infatuation with the Tang dynasty has also extended to many other fields, such as literature, films, and poetry. In addition, since the terms *tangren jie* and *tangren* both clearly marked Chinese identity outside of China, the name

**Figure 6.8** A wedding ceremony in Chenzhou, 2002. The groom is dressed in a *tang*-style jacket decorated with its characteristic round shapes, mandarin collar, and Chinese-knotted buttons. The bride is also adorned in a traditional-style jacket. Courtesy of Yanjiang Hou.

"*tang*-style jacket" accordingly labeled Chinese identity in an international setting like the APEC summit.

However, the *tang*-style jacket was also criticized for its overly decorative design and false representation of Chinese tradition. Hu Yue, a professor at the Beijing Institute of Fashion Technology, argued that the *tang*-style jacket "was not a design based on the real life of our people, but based on a misinterpretation of traditional dress, vague memories of the past, and shallow thinking."[37] Although the criteria for determining a national costume were never made explicit, it was clear that a national costume requires some level of authenticity in its cultural heritage.

As the new *tang*-style jacket failed to become a lasting and widespread form of national dress, Chinese men seemed to be left with no choice but Western attire. And many Chinese men opt to wear Western suits and ties when accompanying their *qipao*-clad wives on formal occasions. But some men still have special feelings for the *Zhongshan* (or Mao) suit. The *Zhongshan* suit was the most common type of Chinese men's formal wear for most of the twentieth century, and thus was considered a nationality symbol that differentiated modern China from its imperial past and marked the beginning of a democratized sartorial system in China.

The *Zhongshan* suit is believed to be originally a hybrid design based on existing Chinese student uniforms that combined elements of East and West.[38] When Sun Zhongshan (Sun Yat-sen) first promoted this new creation around the turn of the twentieth century, it gained political significance, with its various parts symbolizing important political ideas and social meanings. For instance, the five buttons on the front closure symbolized Dr. Sun's "Five-Power Constitution" under which the legislative, executive, judicial, examinative, and censorial branches of government were kept distinct. The four front patch pockets represented the four Chinese traditional moral principles of *li* (courtesy), *yi* (righteousness), *lian* (integrity), and *chi* (a sense of shame). The three buttons on each sleeve were tied to Sun's "Three Principles of the People": nationalism, democracy, and people's livelihood. These were the three founding principles of the Republican era, when Sun led a revolution against the Qing dynasty. The seamless back panel signified a peacefully united nation-state. This symbolism embedded in the *Zhongshan* suit prevented the arbitrary alteration of its form.

During Mao's era the original symbolic meaning of the *Zhongshan* suit was transformed to symbolize Maoist egalitarianism and frugality. The overwhelming popularity of the *Zhongshan* suit during Mao's era, especially as the favorite attire of Mao Zedong, Premiere Zhou Enlai, and other national leaders, made this dress form one of the most recognizable symbols of China of the Mao era. Thus it was widely known in the West as the "Mao suit," while in China it was still referred to as the *Zhongshan* suit. But the time of the Mao suit, in retrospect, was the time of Maoist class struggle, the time of the Anti-Rightist Movement, the time of the Great Leap Forward, the time of sending the young to the countryside, and the time of smashing the Four Olds. And Mao's era and its political and economic ideology were exactly what reformists like Deng Xiaoping wanted to break away from after Mao passed from the scene. Ironically, however, the reformist Deng kept his old habit of wearing the Mao suit. Compared to his image-conscious successors, he rarely seemed to concern himself with what Chinese should wear.

Nevertheless, the changed political climate, advanced economy, and Westernized lifestyle of the Reform era made the Mao suit look out of place in a modernized China. Political leaders of the mid-1980s such as Hu Yaobang and Zhao Ziyang vigorously promoted Western suits, along with reformist policies. Jiang Zemin and Li Peng, successors to Hu and Zhao, and Hu Jintao and Wen Jiabao, who are currently in power, also usually donned Western suits and ties. Thus, the Mao suit was abandoned not only by the public, but also by politically correct national leaders. The political meaning of this change in attire was reversed right after the June 4 "incident" in 1989. As noted by Mike Chinoy, a reporter for CNN, at the time of the crisis, Prime Minister Li Peng appeared in public in the Mao suit instead of a Western suit. Chinoy perceptively interpreted Li Peng's first public appearance after the June 4 incident: "The Mao suit is preferred attire for making statements that are harsher and more uncompromising in this political climate." For the same reason, the Mao suit seemed incompatible with the "open" spirit of twenty-first-century China.

Besides the cultural destruction of Mao's Cultural Revolution, the public's un-clear notion of Chinese identity and its indifference to it in the early post-Mao era also contributed to the fading of traditions and the disappearance of indigenous dress forms. Not only did Western attire completely change the look of the Chinese people, Western landscapes, skyscrapers, interior design, transportation and communication systems, products and brands, and even language completely changed the face of China itself in the post-Mao era. In addition, Western corporate culture, consumer culture, and pop culture also changed Chinese lifestyles, attitudes, and values. Grow-ing up in this thoroughly Westernized globalized society, Chinese youth became par-ticularly fascinated by the idea of recapturing lost traditions and reviving traditional dress forms. Like their Japanese and Korean neighbors who had Westernized earlier, Chinese came to recognize the danger of losing their traditions and culture entirely, and thus took measures to prevent this from happening, or more to the point, to res-cue what had already been lost.

Thus, some scholars viewed the revival of *hanfu,* or traditional Han Chinese clothing, undertaken by some young Chinese cyber communities in the new mil-lennium as an outbreak of Chinese identity anxiety, as well as a backlash against Western cultural colonization. Some began donning *hanfu* at weddings, social gath-erings, schools, worship ceremonies, and cultural festivals and on many other occa-sions (Fig. 6.9). Influenced by Japanese coming-of-age ceremonies, *hanfu* advocates adopted *hanfu* as part of the restoration of Chinese coming-of-age traditions, along with the practice of other traditional coming-of-age rituals. A chain school that spe-cializes in teaching children Confucian literature and the classics in Dalian, Shen-zhen, Zhenzhou, Wuchang, and other cities adopted *hanfu* as a school uniform for both its teachers and students. Influential Web sites and online forums, such as the Tianhan Ethnic Culture Web site, promoted *hanfu* and Chinese culture, with leaders of the *hanfu* forums diligently posting essays and images to educate the public on traditional sartorial codes, giving instructions for making proper *hanfu,* and organiz-ing *hanfu* gatherings and demonstrations. One such forum leader, "Zi Xi," designed a series of *hanfu* styles for the four seasons and for various formal and informal occasions. Summer versions featured short-sleeved hip-length tunics wrapped with a waist sash, matched with a pair of knee-length loose pants. Meanwhile, *hanfu* advocates pressed the media and official institutions to adopt their ideas and de-signs, including their designs for China's own academic regalia and designs for the Beijing Olympics. Various designs of *hanfu* for formal occasions shared common features, such as a loose-fitting long gown with large sleeves, banding trims, *bixi*

**Figure 6.9**   A wedding picture taken in a professional photo studio in Guangzhou in December 2008. The couple are wearing *hanfu,* featuring a V-neck, layers, and wide banding on the edges. Courtesy of Wenjuan Guo.

(a rectangular band hanging down from the waist), a layered look, and a wide waist sash instead of buttons.

Compared to the traditional *qipao* and the newly invented *tang*-style jacket, *hanfu* was especially favored by those who were concerned with the ethnic authenticity of national identity symbols. In their eyes, the *hanfu* form was "purely" Chinese in heritage because it had been established before "barbarian" invasions and before the Western influence of later eras. Thus, to them it had more legitimacy than the *qipao* and *tang*-style jacket as a symbol of China. However, the *hanfu* form that they promoted was also flawed: it was not any less of a new creation than the other two forms. First, the form of the *shenyi,* which is the basis of the *hanfu* form, constantly evolved throughout history. Contemporary *hanfu* thus displayed inconsistent forms and details depending on which dynasty their designs were based on. Second, many *hanfu* advocates were unfamiliar with Chinese history and historical costumes, and thus their *hanfu* designs were mainly copied from historical TV series, which were mostly contemporary creations that mixed traditional design elements with modern tastes for theatrical effect. Third, since most *hanfu* promoters had to make their own costumes on a limited budget, it was nearly impossible for them to duplicate the embroideries and other construction details of the *shenyi* from ancient times. Therefore, modern *hanfu* was inevitably a modernized and simplified version that lacked an identifiable uniform design, which again raised the question of authenticity as an identity symbol for all Chinese.

In addition, China is officially made up of fifty-six ethnic groups. Singling out Han Chinese traditional costume as a symbol of Chinese nationality neglected the folk dress of the other fifty-five ethnic minorities. The feverish promotion of *hanfu* by its promoters also frequently exposed nationalist and ethnocentric viewpoints. Some scholars, therefore, warned the *hanfu* movement that it would not only put Han Chinese in an ethnocentric position, but also endanger China through excessive nationalism. However, most people merely regarded promoting *hanfu* as a form of preserving Chinese traditions and culture, which has become a popular topic in the new millennium. For instance, to promote Chinese culture further, the government promulgated a change to the national holidays in 2008 so that people could celebrate traditional holidays such as *Qingming,* or Tomb-Sweeping Day; *Duanwu,* or Dragon Boat Festival; and *Zhongqiu,* or Mid-Autumn Festival. And the Beijing Olympics in 2008 used Chinese-style dresses for its ushers and other ceremonial staff that clearly assimilated the *qipao* form and other traditional design elements such as blue-and-white porcelain patterns, golden embroideries, and jade pendants. In this sense, the *hanfu* movement is just another manifestation of the search for cultural roots that began in the 1980s and continues today. However, despite growing publicity and interest, the government has not yet endorsed *hanfu*, and the *hanfu* movement remains a subcultural movement, with its members proudly wearing the *hanfu* in subways, malls, parks, and other public spaces.

Today, the Chinese seem to be caught in the same dilemma that their predecessors faced a hundred years ago: is the path to modernization yet again Westernization? Are Chinese once again forced to choose between keeping their heads (modernization) or keeping their hair (Chinese culture)—the choice their ancestors faced at the beginning of the Qing dynasty? As China's political and economic status has continued to rise, the Chinese media often proudly and confidently declare that the twenty-first century belongs to China. But what dress form will the Chinese wear in "their" new century?

# –7–

# The Evolution of the Fashion Industry: Designers and Models

In 2005, Wang Wei, a fashion designer from Shanghai in his early 30s, registered his fashion label, Wang Wei Gallery, in London and set up a studio in Shanghai. Dividing his time between London, Paris, Hong Kong, and Shanghai, Wang set out to enter the elite circle of international fashion designers. After his show at Shanghai Fashion Week in 2005 caught the eye of Vivienne Westwood, Wang was invited to the sidelines of London Fashion Week in 2006. He also won the 2006 Who's Next, an international fashion trade show in Paris. In 2007, he participated in the Vendome Luxury Salon show in Paris, and by 2008 his collections were selling at Riot, a high-end showroom in Los Angeles and New York. "We've seen Indian designers already establish themselves in the European market, and now the world is waiting for a global Chinese designer. In a few years, that could be me," remarked Wang.[1]

Wang's impressive entry into the world of international fashion is exactly what the Chinese fashion industry has long desired: innovative Chinese players on the international fashion stage. Firmly established as the world's production powerhouse and the number one exporter of apparel and footwear, the Chinese fashion industry has long dreamed of one day exporting China's own fashion labels rather than only the fruits of its cheap labor. But while the West has continued to lose manufacturing jobs to the outsourcing of production to that cheap labor, China has paid an increasingly high price for these new jobs in terms of industrial pollution. Nevertheless, like most other industries, the apparel industry has integrated at a global level. But in the globalized apparel supply chain, China's fashion designers have been largely ignored or have functioned only as "ghost" designers for fashion brands produced in China.

In the 2000s, policy makers called for fashion innovation in the hope that China would produce its own designers capable of competing on the international stage. As the *Washington Post* observed on June 17, 2006, "The question of whether China can pull off this transformation—from workshop of the world to cradle of invention—is key to the giant country's future." The national leadership fully recognized the necessity of this transformation. President Hu Jintao urged strategic structural adjustments in economic development in his report to the Seventeenth National People's Congress in 2007 that stressed "improving the capability of independent innovation and building an innovation-oriented country."[2] However, while individual fashion designers have learned to innovate, the Chinese fashion industry as a whole has never been innovation driven, and innovations on a large scale are yet to be realized.

## State Designers

Prior to the economic reforms launched in 1978, the garments of most urbanites (and of nearly all rural residents) were made either at home or in small tailor shops, either by hand or on home sewing machines. Home sewing machines were introduced to China in the 1920s and industrial models appeared in the 1960s, but it was not until after the economic reforms of the late 70s that the Chinese ready-to-wear industry started to cater to the needs of the masses.[3] Throughout the 1980s, government-funded garment research centers and magazines also published patterns and pattern books in an attempt to address the supply shortages of the ready-to-wear industry and to introduce current fashions to home sewers and tailors.

As China entered the 1980s, however, one of the obstacles to the widespread adoption of new fashions was the shortage of fabric. Rationing had first been introduced in the fall of 1954 in an effort to ensure the equal distribution of scarce consumer goods among China's vast population while still allowing exports to bring in valuable foreign currency. Into the early 1980s, ration coupons for popular goods were often secretly traded and used to barter for merchandise. In this environment of scarcity, especially in rural areas, people would often make or purchase new clothes only when their existing garments were beyond repair. Thus, fabric shortages and the rationing system still made fashion a luxury for many people.

China sought to overcome these problems through a combination of educational and industrial measures. The prescribed Chinese language textbook in elementary schools included stories aiming to teach frugality to the new generation of the 1980s. Premier Zhou Enlai, who often wore old clothes that had been patched rather than new clothes, was held up as an exemplar of such communist frugality. In May 1978, the party press organ, *People's Daily,* published an editorial titled "Overcoming the Challenge of Clothing Eight Hundred Million People" that reviewed the weak foundations of China's textile industry.[4] Ninety percent of the raw materials used in the textile industry came from agricultural products such as cotton, flax, silk, and wool. The article cited Mao's successor, Hua Guofeng, who urged the industry to "try hard to increase the production of agricultural materials and to vigorously develop chemical fibers." Subsequently, fabric shortages were partially alleviated through increased use of synthetic fibers as a means of increasing overall textile production. The industry also faced other technical problems: high shrinkage rates of cotton cloth, poor shape retention of knits, and fading of dyes and prints. The monotonous designs used for textile patterns and prints needed to be improved as well. Thus, prior to the elimination of the rationing system in 1983, clothing choices were still limited due to shortages, technical challenges faced by the industry, and the limited economic means of most Chinese.

In the 1980s, however, China's export-oriented apparel industry started to pay more attention to domestic markets, and the ready-to-wear industry began to replace home sewing and tailor shops, especially in urban areas. This shift in garment production called for greater variety and more creative designs from the industry. However, fashion trends in the 80s seemed to have less to do with the embryonic Chinese fashion industry and more to do with pop culture, especially TV shows and movies. Prevailing styles directly copied from TV shows generally bypassed clothing designers. And since new designs were so financially rewarding at the time, private clothing merchants contributed to the transformation of TV show costumes into everyday fashion. The number of private merchants and vendors mushroomed once private businesses were permitted by the state. In state-owned garment factories, new products were developed by clothing technicians and designers with limited training in modern design but great skill in pattern making and tailoring. Garnering numerous design awards, these clothing technicians and designers developed new mass-produced styles for the domestic market that generally featured conservative designs that bore little relation to contemporary international fashions.

Big names in Chinese clothing design in the 1980s were known only to the narrow circle of the apparel industry as their fame was tied to the state-owned garment factories or research institutions where they worked. Most consumers were concerned only with the physical garment itself and not with the designer behind the garment. More sophisticated consumers sought brand names that were either imported or produced and labeled by state-owned factories. These labels gave no indication of the designer, either. However, these factories relied heavily on their designers' creations to attract consumers and to compete with other state-owned factories from various cities. To reward "model" designers and to encourage budding young designers, large factories funded fashion exhibitions for their designers, sent their works overseas to international exhibitions and trade shows, and supported their participation in national or regional design competitions. State-owned fashion media helped to publicize their achievements and popularized the new concepts of fashion design and fashion designer. At the time, well-known designers in Shanghai included Qian Shilin of the Shanghai Qianjin Garment Factory, Jiang Hailiang and Jiang Yinmei of the Shanghai First Garment Factory, Jin Taijun and Ye Deqian of the Shanghai Clothing Research Institute, and Cheng Genfa of the Shanghai Clothing Factory.

These designers came from diverse backgrounds, but they were transformed by the state into China's first generation of fashion designers: they were responsible for large quantities of garment exports and new styles in the domestic marketplace in the 80s. They differed from their illiterate predecessors—tailors who worked at pre-Mao stores and shops—in that they had acquired some level of education, ranging from elementary school to high school. They learned tailoring and design in garment factories or stores as part of their apprenticeship during or before Mao's era. And while they might not know how to draw, they did understand the female body and had mastered traditional tailoring craftsmanship. They may not have known how to dress fashionably, but they definitely knew how to please the market. And though they might have earned only an average salary, they made a great fortune in foreign currency for the state. Their designs paid great attention to decorative details, structural lines, shapes of collars, the placement of buttons, and the quality of materials. This reflected the tailoring tradition in China that had long emphasized construction and sewing techniques, pattern design, and trims rather than innovative silhouettes. However, their creativity was limited not only by the scarcity of fashion resources, but also by the tastes of factory management and governmental authorities.

Qian Shilin, a prolific designer, was one of the fortunate few who had the power to make decisions regarding his designs. Among his numerous awards were first- and second-place prizes at the Fiftieth Paris International Garment Expo in 1985.[5] He grew up as a tailor's apprentice with little education but never ceased improving his tailoring skills and exploring new ideas. And Qian was one of the few experts in draping in China before most Chinese designers had even heard of it. The media described him as a taciturn man in his fifties who dressed like a typical middle-aged Chinese man of the 80s. Rising from modest roots, Qian's career path was fairly typical among first-generation designers.

Jin Taijun, on the contrary, came from a different world. His father and uncle founded one of the earliest clothing companies in Shanghai in 1917, the Shanghai Hongxiang Clothing Store. It quickly became a trendy, high-end store brand that attracted high-profile clientele such as Song Qingling, wife of Sun Zhongshan (Sun Yat-sen), and the famous actress Hu Die.[6] Jin Taijun was educated at the British Yucai School and inherited his father and uncle's design talent, and started his design career at the age of fourteen in the 1940s at the Hongxiang Clothing Store. The company purchased toile and patterns from Europe and America to keep their employees abreast of the latest international trends, and Jin often worked with the company's European designer and a European fitting model to come up with new ideas.[7] Hollywood movies of the 1930s and 1940s were one of his favorite sources of inspiration. Jin read international fashion magazines like *Vogue* and *Harper's Bazaar* along with foreign brand catalogues and designed for high-profile ladies of Shanghai: he seemed no less a fashion designer than his Western counterparts. He continued to lead the Hongxiang Company after the founding of the People's Republic in 1949 until the company was finally confiscated by the state in 1956.[8] Jin then worked for the Shanghai Municipal Clothing Company, the Shanghai Fifteenth Garment Factory, and the Shanghai Clothing Research Institute as both a designer and promoter of Chinese fashion both inside and outside of China.

The profits these early clothing designers generated for state-owned factories taught the apparel industry the value of design, which increased their focus on fashion designers in the 90s. But despite these advances in design made by the state's top designers, the Chinese fashion industry of the 80s still lacked "star" designers. Limited media exposure coupled with the society's unclear notion of fashion design made the public indifferent to early fashion designers. As private enterprises and joint ventures entered apparel production and distribution, the initial appeal of the new styles created by designers at state-owned factories faded. The rapidly growing domestic market called for charismatic, modern fashion designers who were responsible not only for producing garments but also for inventing new styles, looks, and meanings.

## The Cradle of China's Fashion Designers

The development of the Chinese fashion industry was closely linked with the development of the Chinese fashion education system. Nearly all of China's most influential fashion designers of the 1990s and 2000s were products of this state-run system. Determined to nurture China's own design talents, more than thirty national and regional universities set up clothing design programs in the late 70s and 80s.[9] Early esteemed clothing design programs were scattered mainly along the east coast: the Central Academy of Art and Design (now the Academy of Arts and Design at Tsinghua University) in Beijing, the Beijing Institute of Fashion Technology, China Textile University (now Donghua University) in Shanghai, the Suzhou Institute of Silk Textile Technology in Suzhou (now part of School of Art at Soochow University), Zhejiang Academy of Fine Arts (now China Academy of Art), and the Northwest Institute of Textile Science and Technology (now Xi'an Polytechnic University) in Xi'an.

The Central Academy of Art and Design created clothing design programs as early as 1958, two years after its founding. In 1980, it offered the first degree major in clothing design.[10] One founder of this program, Yuan Jieying, was a respected designer herself. She studied at the Central Academy of Fine Arts and the Central Academy of Art and Design and had been trained in both art and textiles. Her pioneering work was published in various media, and she wrote scores of books on fashion drawing, historical costume, fashion modeling, fashion design, and clothing designers. Since the 1960s, she has designed for diplomats, the staff of *Zhongnanhai* (the residential compound that houses the political leadership in Beijing), TV programs, the Paris International Garment Expo, the Asian Games, and performance groups traveling overseas.[11] Her early designs mainly focused on performance costumes and uniforms, but she also later designed for the marketplace. In 1988, breaking with the notion that fashion was only for the young, her "Fashion Design for Middle- and Old-Aged Women" made headlines in the *Renmin Daily, Beijing TV Station, Beijing Radio Station, Chinese Women's News, China Textile News,* and *Fashion.*[12]

Like Yuan, the majority of pioneering college educators and founders of clothing design programs had themselves received extensive training in the fine arts and had drawing skills comparable to those of professional artists. Li Keyu headed the Apparel Research Institute at the Beijing Institute of Fashion Technology, founded in 1988. She graduated from the Central Academy of Fine Arts in 1954 and soon became a prolific costume designer, but she later shifted her focus from performance costume to fashion design.[13] Li Xin was another pioneer in Chinese clothing design with a background in the fine arts. She also started by designing costumes for performers in opera and the theater. She worked for the Garment Design and Research Center of China, established in 1982, which was one of China's most prestigious apparel research and design institutions. She played a critical role in organizing and initiating China's fashion forecasting runway shows and national fashion design competitions such as the Golden Scissors Award and the Brother Cup.

Partially due to the fine arts background most of these pioneers shared, early clothing design programs placed a strong emphasis on drawing skills, and most fashion design programs required sketching and painting tests for admission. Standard courses in the clothing design major included sketching, watercolor or gouache painting, Chinese painting, fashion illustration, aesthetics, color theory, and anatomy. In addition to general education courses, classes were also offered in apparel construction, apparel machinery, flat pattern, draping, clothing design, graphic design, hand dyeing, fashion photography, textiles, art theory, and costume history. In the 1990s and 2000s, computer-aided design and three-dimensional design were added to the curriculum. Different institutions across the country had similar programs since all of them were state owned and regulated.

When a large number of college graduates entered the clothing design workforce in the 1990s, a debate erupted in the media over the precise nature of a fashion designer's job. In the early 90s, when high school graduates flocked to clothing design programs in large cities, they envisioned careers as artists and were thus highly motivated to master drawing skills. Design programs centered on this objective and attempted to mold all clothing design students into fine artists. But the most successful designers who came out of this system lamented the restrictive nature of fashion education in China. One of China's "Top Ten Fashion Designers of 1995," the budding young designer Ma Ke, commented, "Our experience, our education, and our past have all served to restrict our imaginations."[14] Another clothing design graduate, Yin Yan, recalled, "At the time, both students and teachers held art in high esteem and disdained cutting and sewing. They thought highly of design ideology and scholarly research, but disdained making anything by hand. These unrealistic and biased views were formed under the invisible biases of the society, but the ultimate cause was the rigid educational system and ideology."[15] Wang Wei also described his design education as "overly focused on drawing rather than creative concepts and commercial branding."[16]

The high-tailoring tradition that had been the hallmark of Chinese clothing stores in the early twentieth century was largely lost when the Chinese apparel industry modernized. The industry focused instead on streamlined mass production. This change in the industry was also reflected in the educational system. As Yin Yan noted, problems emerged under the art-oriented educational structure:

> Hundreds of designer-wannabes graduated in China every year. If you are fortunate enough to see their graduation designs, you would be shocked by their extraordinary imagination and expression. But you would also discover their common shortcomings: lack of their own understanding of garments, lack of refinement in pattern and apparel

construction, lack of knowledge and mastery of materials. Their works were more centered on whimsical exaggerations in order to express a theme or an inspiration, and reckless deconstruction of the natural structure and shape of the human body and garments, with the ultimate goal of creating a strong visual effect. You could not see garments designed for the human body in these works. The human being, in the eyes of these designers, tends to be a prop for the expression of the garments.[17]

Concerns and complaints of this kind were common in the media in the 1990s. Jin Taijun thus advised that the new generation of designers should "not just know how to draw, but should also know how to cut and sew."[18]

In many ways, college-educated designers seemed to be opposites of the first-generation designers, who had worked for state-owned factories for most of their lives. Many of these college-educated designers had good drawing skills but modest apparel construction skills. They were not afraid to come up with the most whimsical silhouettes and shapes, but they often ignored fine details. They also had easier access to international fashion information, garnered more media attention, and enjoyed greater career mobility compared to their predecessors.

But as these designers established their own labels, they discovered something they sorely lacked: business education. The pursuit of commercial success, an obvious aim for Western fashion designers for over a century, was controversial among China's early fashion designers. Ironically, at a time when the whole country began to chase after riches, many designers in the 80s and early 90s looked down their noses at anything commercial. They looked up to French haute couture, in which financial concerns never seemed to be an obstacle to artistic creation. In this idealistic era, the relationship between art and commerce seemed irreconcilable.

Were fashion designers just businessmen who knew how to draw? Or artists who knew how to do business? These questions still puzzle fashion designers of today who run their own labels. Many young designers acquired their initial business training in Hong Kong or in coastal cities where they worked for world-class labels, which familiarized them with fashion markets in all parts of the world.[19] Wang Wei attributed his business sense to his experience in Hong Kong working for S. B. Polo, where he became acquainted with the operations of international fashion brands. Furthermore, "Since the mid-1990s, foreign brands have poured in and have forced domestic designers to compete and learn from them," Wang Wei said. "Designers became the core of fashion commerce. They needed to balance the pursuit of artistic creativity and commercial success to give the product extra value."[20]

Although criticized for their drawing-oriented design offerings, university clothing design programs played a major role in developing the concepts of clothing design and fashion in China. By the mid-1990s, a bachelor's degree in clothing design or related fields was almost a necessity for anyone who aspired to join the "club" of clothing designers in China. From the point of view of institutions of higher education, clothing design was a Western concept, and thus they actively involved themselves in foreign exchange programs and activities. Clothing-design teachers visited or studied abroad in order to bring back more advanced pedagogical ideas and skills. For example, Wang Shanjue, who introduced clothing design at the Zhajiang Academy of Fine Arts, was invited by Pierre Cardin to visit Paris in 1985, where she familiarized herself with haute couture. Her designs displayed the fine hand tailoring of couture, and she later exhibited in France, Germany, Switzerland, the United States, Japan, Singapore, and Hong Kong.[21] As a manifestation of her educational philosophy, which was to teach the masses aesthetics and to develop China's own couturelike industry, she gave a series of lectures on clothing design on China Central Television. Another designer, Li Dangqi, joined the newly founded clothing design program at the Central Academy of Art and Design in 1984 after studying at the Tokyo University of the Arts for a year in the mid-80s. After returning from Japan, he designed uniforms for state organizations and corporations and published extensively on world clothing, clothing design, fashion colors, and aesthetics.[22] Shi Lin, a student of Yuan Jieying, taught clothing design at the Suzhou Institute of Silk Textile Technology in the mid-80s. She took the opportunity to study high tailoring with a famous Japanese designer, Kimoyilo, in Japan for over a year. She became known for her designs of elegantly draped evening dresses.[23] The couple Yuan Ze and Hu Yue both studied at the Hong Kong Polytechnic University and taught at the Suzhou Institute of Silk Textile Technology, and went on to teach at the Beijing Institute of Fashion Technology. They both designed and published a great deal on clothing design and introduced Paris fashion and couturiers to a Chinese audience.

These early global connections, along with China's increased interactions with the West across the board, helped clothing design education pioneers see the structure built around modern fashion designers. Many of these educators were simultaneously designers, critics, scholars, fashion writers, event organizers, and founders of a variety of fashion programs and organizations. And they owed much of their success to their overseas experiences. Applying new ideas and methods to various fields, their international experience eventually benefited the transformation of China's traditional apparel industry into a modern fashion system consisting of manufacturers, retailers, advertisers, designers, models, journalists, and editors. Since the 90s, foreign exchange activities in higher institutions, as well as in the industry as a whole, have continued to multiply. It probably would be difficult today to identify a professor of clothing design at a major university in China who has not visited or studied abroad.

Scholars and designers from abroad have also been invited to higher institutions in China to give seminars and fashion shows. Donghua University, for instance, has invited many guest and advisory professors from abroad. French high-fashion designers Emanuel Ungaro, Daniel Tribouillard, Sonia Rykiel, and Oliver Lapidus and Italian designers Gianfranco Ferre and Ottavio Missoni are currently advisory professors at Donghua.[24] These world-class fashion designers have broadened the horizons of both design students and teachers. Emanuel Ungaro has even invited graduate students from China to do fieldwork at his studio in Paris. In the new millennium, partnerships with other higher institutions outside of China have also become commonplace. Donghua has cooperative programs with more than ten institutions stretching from Asia to the United States, including Hong Kong Polytechnic University, Japan Bunka Fashion College, the European Institute of Design in Italy, the Fashion Institute of Technology in New York, the London College of Fashion, and Iowa State University, among others.[25]

Today, many international educational models coexist in China to provide a variety of offerings in clothing design education. For example, the Shanghai University–Paris International Institute of Fashion and Arts, headed by Jean-Herve Habay, a graduate of the University of Paris and formerly a senior fashion educator and administrator in Paris and Japan, created a fashion design and pattern-making major emphasizing cut-and-sew techniques. The institute assembled a truly international faculty team, with supermodel Naomi Campbell sitting on the advisory board.[26] The Raffles Design Institute at Donghua University in Shanghai, owned by the Raffles Group of Singapore, was one of the earliest establishments to offer international design education in the 90s in China. In addition to design courses, it also offered courses in apparel marketing, multimedia, and apparel administration, and it hired international lecturers and aimed to situate students in a global environment. The Raffles Group has also established many design institutions in other major cities in China, such as Beijing, Guangzhou, Huizhou, and Ningbo. Meanwhile, the IFA (International Fashion Academy) Paris Shanghai was founded in 2002 at the Shanghai University of Engineering Science, with many of its faculty members coming from prestigious labels such as Yves Saint Laurent, Chanel, Givenchy, LV, Nina Ricci, and Versace.[27]

In addition to their greater integration with the world of international fashion, institutions of higher education in China remain closely tied to the domestic fashion industry. Chinese fashion design professors take an active role in designing for the industry and for the state. For instance, professors at the Beijing Institute of Fashion Technology designed some of the ceremonial costumes for the 2008 Olympic Games.

## The Chinese Fashion System

While both China and the Chinese educational system have become increasingly globalized, the influence of Chinese fashion designers on the global market remains to be seen. What does it take to produce world-famous Chinese fashion designers or even couturiers? And what is required to turn Shanghai into a global fashion center? Fashion critic Bao Mingxin posited:

> As a cultural phenomenon, fashion needs to be cultivated in a specific environment. The reason Paris has become the world's fashion center is that it has sophisticated consumers and a fashion circle consisting of artists, designers, photographers, fashion models,

retailers of shoes, hats, leathers, furs, accessories, and fabrics. In this environment, fashion designers need teamwork rather than working in isolation—that is, to collaborate and cooperate with many other people. It is a misunderstanding or merely naïve to attribute the prosperity of the fashion industry to the individual success or failure of fashion designers.[28]

Kawamura employed the term "fashion system" "to describe organizations, institutions and individuals interacting with one another and to legitimate fashion designers and their creativity." In essence, the fashion system makes great designers instead of individual creativity.[29] This idea is in fact reflected in the Chinese government's systematic efforts to produce global fashion centers, along with world-famous designers and brands in China. Other than the burgeoning fashion education system and the fashion media, state-funded institutions, research and design centers, associations, organizations, fashion forecast runway shows, and national design competitions were established to further boost the development of the industry. A number of these subsystems were housed in large cities, such as Shanghai and Beijing, to facilitate communication.

Nicknamed the "Paris of the East," Shanghai has had a long history of fine fashion and garment production since before the establishment of the People's Republic in 1949, stretching back to the early years of the twentieth century. Due to its proximity to Hong Kong, in the 1980s Guangzhou challenged Shanghai's role as China's fashion center. But after Deng's decision to open up Pudong, a district of Shanghai, as a free-trade area, Shanghai solidified its position as the national center of fashion and commerce. The influence of the foreign concessions in Shanghai, which existed for nearly a century, had a long-lasting effect on the city's sense of modern fashion. Shanghainese were more familiar with and receptive to Western fashions and lifestyles than others and were proud of their splendid sartorial tradition. "Made in Shanghai" was once a symbol of both fashion and quality clothing. Always sensitive to new fashions, Shanghainese consciously maintained a fashionable image, and new styles initiated in Shanghai would soon spread throughout the country.

After thirty years of rapid growth and globalization, every high-end department store in Shanghai was filled with global brands, and every commercial district was filled with foreign boutiques, bars, and restaurants. In October 2000, the mayor of Shanghai, Xu Kuangdi, at the opening of the Shanghai International Fashion Center, stressed that Shanghai was more eager than ever to become one of the world's fashion centers, alongside Paris, London, New York, Milan, and Tokyo.[30]

State-funded research institutions and associations have been founded since the end of the 1970s in order to build a functioning fashion system, with all parts taking cooperative action to reach shared goals. The Shanghai Clothing Research Institute, established in 1979, initially enlisted over thirty of the best craftsmen and designers in Shanghai to design mainly for foreign trade shows and exhibitions.[31] Today it still serves as a design, research, informational, and technological entity. To facilitate apparel production and consumption, in 1980 the State Bureau of Standards issued a standardized sizing system based on a study of body measurements of 400,000 people across China. The size standards delineated height and chest measurements for tops and height and waist measurements for bottoms.

In December 1981, a fashion color conference was held in Shanghai with the participation of color experts from the Japan Fashion Color Association and Chinese Textile Bureau, institutions of higher education, research centers, and companies. Thereafter, the National Textiles Fashion Color Research Center was founded in Shanghai to research and forecast textile color trends. Its delegates attended international fashion color conferences and brought back global color trends information.[32]

In 1986, the Shanghai Garment Trade Association (SGTA) was founded to function as a liaison between Chinese and Western fashion industries and between the government and apparel companies. It regulated professional activities, planned future development, edited apparel books and magazines, provided professional consultancy, evaluated fashion designers, and organized research seminars, design contests, and exhibitions. With similar functions to the SGTA, but more focused on scholarly work and communication, the Shanghai Apparel and Accessories Society was formed in 1985, which cofounded the top-selling fashion magazine *Shanghai Style*.

Countless fashion events and activities took place in Shanghai after the reform era began, most of which were organized by these state-funded service entities, companies, and higher institutions. For example, in April 1978 the first Garment, Shoes, and Hats Design Exhibition presented 180 newly designed garment styles and over sixty types of shoes. Attending the exhibition, leaders from the Ministry of Commerce and the municipal government set guidelines for clothing design, stating that designs should be *meiguan* (beautiful), *dafang* (composed), *jiankang* (healthy) and *shiyong* (practical).[33] These were apparently guidelines not only for designers but for everyone along the fashion supply chain. Fashion editors were supposed to use these criteria when selecting images for publication, and fashion critics were supposed to apply these criteria when evaluating new designs. Designs or styles that did not meet these guidelines were deemed offensive "bizarre looks" and were generally condemned by the state media in the end of the 1970s and early 80s.

Another such notable event was the 1979 Shanghai Clothing Design Exhibition held at the Shanghai Art Pavilion, which was advertised in and covered by the *Jiefang Daily*. The event attracted over ten thousand people every day of the exhibition, and over a thousand items of dress and illustrations were displayed.[34] Since these events were endorsed and sponsored by the state, they relaxed the rigid dress code and served as an effective form of communication within the apparel field and educated the general public on fashion and what was deemed "appropriate" dress.

In the mid-1990s, these fashion events reached a new level with a wider range of international participation. After witnessing the success of the annual international fashion festival hosted in Dalian beginning in 1988, the Shanghai municipal government and the China Textile Association started an annual festival called the Shanghai

International Fashion Culture Festival (SIFCF) in 1995, which involved dozens of municipal bureaus, departments, corporations, associations, and the media. The festival was designed to expand Shanghai's international connections as well as to enhance its leading position in the Chinese fashion industry. The first festival included runway shows by world-famous fashion designers, an international fashion fair, the China Cup national design contest, an international fashion model contest, an international seminar, an exhibition of cultural relics, and sales activities. Celebrated designers Emanuel Ungaro, Daniel Tribouillard, Olivier Lapidus, and Gianfranco Ferre have put on runway shows at the SIFCFs over the years.

Over a decade later, the 2008 festival turned into a monthlong fashion extravaganza, attracting sponsorship from major Chinese fashion retailers, along with extensive media coverage. The SIFCF has now engaged all state-funded higher institutions with renowned clothing design programs in Shanghai, such as Donghua University, the Shanghai University of Engineering Science, the Shanghai Institute of Design at the China Academy of Art, and the Shanghai Institute of Visual Art at Fudan University. Students and teachers from these institutions showcased their designs at design contests at the festival. In addition to the China Cup, a major design contest in Shanghai with the goal of discovering new design talent among college design students, fashion brands sponsored many other design contests at the festival. To differentiate SIFCF from other fashion festivals in Beijing, Dalian, Ningbo, Chongqing, and other major cities, Shanghai Fashion Week was started in 2003 as part of SIFCF. It has featured runway shows by Salvatore Ferragamo, Vivienne Westwood, Lanvin, Armani, Jean Paul Gaultier, Vivienne Tam, Sonia Rykiel, and budding designers from Turkey, India, Korea, Australia, Indonesia, Germany, and Denmark.

Not to be outdone, Beijing has vied with Shanghai for the title of China's fashion capital. Beijing has just had as many associations, organizations, research centers, fashion newspapers and magazines, design and model contests, higher institutions, fashion events, and runways shows as Shanghai. Fashion magazines such as *Fashion* and *China Garment,* both based in Beijing, have promoted domestic fashions and designers. In the 1980s, *Fashion* initiated both design and modeling contests, which also helped to diffuse the concept of fashion among its young readers. The China Garment Design and Research Center, founded in 1982 in Beijing, began publishing *China Garment* in 1985. Collaborating with *China Garment,* the center started to release a semiannual fashion trend forecast in 1986. The first trend forecast identified four main trends: "sporty casual," "natural and unrestrained," "pioneering," and "elegant and refined." Each trend was further described by cut, color, and fabric.[35] The fashion trend forecast has now evolved into a semiannual large-scale televised runway show produced by local designers.

Since 1993, the China Fashion Designers Association (CFDA), headquartered in Beijing, has enrolled hundreds of domestic fashion designers and national experts and scholars in the apparel field, hoping "to unite, innovate, and establish a team of world-class fashion designers."[36] It attempted to function simultaneously as an authoritative gatekeeper for the fashion industry by formulating "rules for the evaluation of Chinese fashion designers" and "rules for national and international fashion design competitions."[37] The CFDA began an honorary list of the Top Ten Fashion Designers in China in 1995 and created the most prestigious title for domestic fashion designers beginning in 1997: the Golden Peak Award. This award was intended to be the Chinese version of the French Golden Needle Award. The association has also established cooperative relations with similar organizations in various countries, such as the French Federation of Fashion and of Ready-to-Wear of Couturiers and Fashion Designers, the Japan Fashion Designers Association, and the Korea Fashion Designers Association. Utilizing state resources, CFDA has played an active and authoritative role in recognizing and promoting local designers.

Meanwhile, the China National Garments Association, founded in 1991, aimed to nurture Chinese local brands and enlisted most domestic brand names as members.[38] Since 1998, the association has held the annual China International Clothing and Accessories Fair (CHIC), previously sponsored by the China Textile Industry Bureau and the State Economic and Trade Commission since 1993. At the first fair, Valentino, Gianfranco Ferre, and Pierre Cardin wowed the Chinese with their runway spectacles. President Jiang Zemin met with Ferre and Valentino, a gesture the *New York Times* read as fashion "turning into a serious business in China."[39] Pierre Cardin's fashion business had already turned into a Cardin empire with forty-three stores and twenty-seven licenses in China by that time. Ferre also firmly believed that China had a promising future in fashion. "I would put my hand in the fire if these people in ten years have not gone very far in fashion," said Ferre to the *International Herald Tribune*.[40] CHIC has now become one of the largest Asian and world fashion fairs, attracting the participation of over a thousand domestic and international clothing brands from over twenty countries or areas.[41] Many famous domestic brands debut their fall/winter collections or their fashion forecast runway shows at the fair, followed by press conferences and business conferences.

The Brother Cup China International Young Fashion Designers Contest, which was sponsored by Brother Industry Ltd. of Japan and lasted for ten years (1993–2002), used to be a major event at the end of CHIC and was perhaps the most covered fashion design competition in China. The Brother Cup positioned itself as a competition of wearable art. Unconcerned with wearability, the competition encouraged innovation in clothing forms. In other words, it actually encouraged "bizarreness," which had been the target of media attacks only a few years earlier. This also seemed contrary to the design guidelines set forth by state officials at the first Garment, Shoes, and Hats Design Exhibition. Therefore, the ideology reflected in the competition itself was a critical innovation in the fashion industry. In a sense, it altered the notion of fashion design in China, which traditionally emphasized cut-and-sew techniques. Full of unconstrained ideas, odd shapes, and showy materials, the runway at the Brother Cup became the favorite of both the media and fashion designers.

Junior designers and clothing design students viewed it as a doorway to fame. Nearly all of the previous winners of the Brother Cup, especially those from the mainland, became influential designers. Their victories gained them enormous publicity and also won them opportunities to hold personal runway shows at state-funded fairs such as CHIC.

However, the Brother Cup was also criticized for sending the wrong message to young designers and design students, many of whom focused on drawing skills, showmanship, and theatrical effect while ignoring the body form and the market. Many designs at the Brother Cup were criticized for being overly designed and sensational. After seeing designs made of paper, plastics, hemp ropes, garbage bags, wood, tin cans, and galvanized iron, Liu Ruipu, a professor at the Beijing Institute of Fashion Technology, asked, "Was the Brother Cup useful for the industry? Did it elevate or inhibit ready-to-wear brands? Is it wearable art or wearable pollution? Did it cultivate fashion designers or did it foster a spirit of impetuousness?"[42]

Compared to the controversial Brother Cup, the Golden Scissors Award, created in 1985, represented mainstream aesthetics and reflected the fine techniques of cut-and-sew. If the Brother Cup represented the highest honor for innovative designs, the Golden Scissors Award was the highest honor for practical designs that encouraged "practical, sellable, and fashionable clothing."[43] These criteria practically excluded the participation of college clothing design students and ensured that the winners would have an industrial background or support.

However, since major contests and events were largely funded, organized, and operated by the state, many problems inevitably emerged, including issues over fairness, transparency, plagiarism, and commercial corruption, among others.[44] The state's monopoly on these events and media coverage helped to produce big-name designers, but at the same time it inhibited the growth of talented unknown designers because of the lack of a free and competitive environment. The pressure to conform to mainstream aesthetics also stifled creativity.

Nevertheless, the 90s saw the proliferation of fashion design contests, modeling contests, festivals, fairs, fashion shows, and exhibitions in nearly all major cities. Other than in Shanghai and Beijing, a number of garment associations were founded in Guangzhou, Hunan, Hainan, Hangzhou, Wuxi, Shenzhen, Shanxi, Sichuan, and other major cities. These regional associations actively organized various fashion events and activities to promote their local fashion industries.

As part of China's fashion triad and the fashion center of the south, Guangzhou mirrored the fashion boom in Shanghai and established its role as the southern fashion hub in the 1980s. Guangzhou clothing was once characterized by brisk and invigorating designs and competitive prices. Clothing vendors from nearby cities went directly to Guangzhou to replenish their stocks. As Valery Garrett noted: "The influence coming from Hong Kong via Guangdong province: a neat reversal of the 1920s and 1930s era, when fashion originated in Shanghai and filtered down via Guangzhou to Hong Kong."[45] The emergence of a massive number of garment factories in southeastern cities such as Shenzhen, Zhuhai, Shantou, and Xiamen—the first four "Special Economic Zones"—strengthened the influence of southern fashion, especially in the 1980s. Still the economic center of the south, Guangzhou's national influence on fashion receded in the 1990s and 2000s. Guangzhou also has an International Garments Festival, but its influence was regionalized, along with its declining number of fashion media outlets.

## Rising Stars: The More National, the More International

Big-name domestic designers nearly exclusively came out of a system of regional and national fashion design contests in the 90s, which initially screened their participants based on fashion illustrations. This screening process excluded most designers from state factories, whose specialty was tailoring instead of drawing. This gave an advantage to college clothing design majors. Compared to the previous generation, whose designs were tied to the state, these designers had acquired more freedom to develop individually. They frequently changed jobs, moving from one famous brand to another, or from brands to higher institutions and vice versa. Many also created their own brands. This generation defined the image of the modern Chinese fashion designer: creative, charismatic, independent, and expensive to hire. The proliferation of Chinese fashion media coupled with expanded financial means greatly elevated the status of fashion designers. It was only then that Chinese clothing designers finally shed their image as "modern tailors."

In his signature head scarf or a flamboyant hat and sunglasses, Liu Yang met Chinese expectations of what a fashion designer should look like. After graduating in clothing design from the Guangzhou Academy of Art in 1987, Liu entered the state-owned Guangdong Silk Import and Export Corporation. He became famous overnight by winning many awards at the China Youth Fashion Design Competition in 1989. Since then, Liu Yang has won a handful of influential national awards, including the prestigious Golden Peak Award in 1998. He made the Chinese fashion designers' Top Ten list in both 1995 and 1998.

His sensitivity to fashion stemmed from his own image consciousness. When he was awarded a "Model Student of Lei Feng" award (established by Mao Zedong in 1963; Lei Feng was a soldier of the Liberation Army and a role model for youngsters), he wore long hair and bell-bottom jeans, a typically rebellious "bizarre look" of the 80s. The contradictions surrounding his image have extended throughout his career until today. He dyed his hair yellow and donned red pants when he graduated as one of fifty-two students nationally honored for excelling "in both morality and academics" in the late 80s, at a time when hair dyeing was viewed as a sign of questionable morality.[46] He experimented with different images hoping to change how society viewed fashion designers (Fig. 7.1). He also hoped to change the views of his father, who had condemned his career choice.

**Figure 7.1** Charismatic fashion designer Liu Yang surrounded by models. Courtesy of Liu Yang, fashion designer.

With a monthly salary of 125 *renminbi,* or roughly thirty-one dollars at the time, he pushed for an individual fashion show the hard way: "With no money to buy accessories, I hand-molded the earrings from iron sheets. I could not afford fitting models, so I tried these clothes on myself in front of a broken mirror that I found on the street."[47] But his designs impressed the audience as well as the critics. In a feature story for *Shanghai Style* in 1993, fashion critic Bao Mingxin described Liu Yang as a rare Chinese fashion designer who had charisma.[48]

Liu's combination of unusual star quality and design skills commanded the respect of the domestic fashion media in the 90s. His straw-woven design series, *ye zhi qu* (joys of the wild), which he debuted in 1990, displayed an organic mixture of Chinese and Western elements (Fig. 7.2). His intricate patterns featured abstract geometric shapes with quasi-religious associations. But his later designs were more market oriented and displayed a unique romantic flair (Fig. 7.3). Unlike most designs of the time, Liu's designs rarely featured traditional Chinese elements like the mandarin collar, dragon motifs, or banding and piping and instead used large flowery patterns,

**Figure 7.2** Liu Yang's straw-woven design series, *ye zhi qu* (joys of the wild). 1990. Courtesy of Liu Yang, fashion designer.

silky materials for menswear, shiny leather decorated with rivets, and zebra patterns. However, his designs were often criticized at the time for lacking national character.[49] He defended himself against these criticisms with his unique understanding of national character: "It was hard for our fashion to enter the international marketplace in the past. One of the important reasons is that we misunderstood the meaning of national character, through, for example, drawing Chinese paintings on the surface of a *qipao*." He continued, "However, if national character can be incorporated in one's design without a decent understanding of international fashion trends and aesthetics, why doesn't one just regard jade clothes sewn with golden thread unearthed from Mawangdui [an ancient Chinese tomb dating from 168 B.C.E.] as fashion?"[50] His regard for international standards of fashion also influenced the way he sees foreign competition, which Liu considered a positive means for Chinese designers to learn and to improve: "Only competition leads to advancement."[51]

With star designers like Liu Yang on the rise, big-production runway shows became more common in the 90s. At the end of each show, a neatly groomed fashion designer, looking like a Chinese version of Karl Lagerfeld or John Galliano, would come onstage surrounded by elegant models to receive the applause of the audience. Such sensational domestic success ignited the desire of star designers to quickly gain international recognition.

Inspired by the domestic media's enthusiastic portrayal of the proliferation of Chinese elements on the Western runway and the example set by Hong Kong fashion designers emerging on the world fashion scene, most mainland designers at the

**Figure 7.3** Liu Yang's design, with his typical romantic flair, for domestic brand Xuanni showcased at a grand fashion show at the 2001 CHIC. Courtesy of Liu Yang, fashion designer.

time were firmly convinced that the path to international fame and recognition lay in China's rich sartorial history. Early attempts by Chinese fashion designers to become players on the stage of international fashion were predicated on the idea that the more their designs appeared Chinese, the more international appeal their designs would have. The Chinese media encapsulated this sentiment in the slogan "the more national, the more international." A sense of patriotism also contributed to the desire of designers to showcase Chinese culture and aesthetics, which also contributed to the spread of Chinese styles on domestic runways. Some designers were also driven by the desire to find an authenticity in their aesthetics that would set their designs apart from those of Western designers. In any case, Chinese-style designs predominated on the Chinese runway in the 90s.

For instance, most winning designs in the influential Brother Cup contained powerful cultural associations, such as Wu Haiyan's *Dingsheng shidai* (An Era of Great

Prosperity) series in 1993. Wu was then a teacher at the Zhejiang Academy of Fine Arts. The series featured flowing robes and long blouses matched with long skirts that were inspired by the fashions of the Tang dynasty. The blouses and robes were decorated with hand-painted, square-framed patterns with the colors of the mural paintings of Dunhuang. Accessorized with handheld prop lanterns, these looks could not be any more Chinese. Wu's success at the Brother Cup opened the door to more and bigger prizes. She was a rising star on the Chinese runway beginning in the 90s, making the Top Ten list in 1995 and 1997 and winning the Golden Peak in 2001, and she held numerous runway shows in China and abroad.

The winning series from the second year of the Brother Cup was named *Qinyong,* or Qin Dynasty Terracotta Warriors, a name directly suggesting cultural connections. The series was designed by Ma Ke, a budding designer from Guangzhou who graduated from the Suzhou Institute of Silk Textile Technology in 1992. Her creations imitated the shapes, textures, and colors of ancient tomb figurines but were made of leather and other contemporary materials. Later winning designs at the Brother Cup were influenced by Chinese folk art paper cutting, Tibetan Buddhist costumes, and fan shapes in abstract forms.

Another renowned designer, Liu Xiaogang, shone on Shanghai's runways in the early 90s with his many Chinese culture–inspired creations. He also pioneered China's Pop art–inspired designs, featuring newspaper materials and Coca-Cola bottle decorations. Awarded the first master's degree in fashion design in Shanghai, Liu also won many design competitions. His many culturally themed designs included evening dresses inspired by Dunhuang wall paintings; Qing-style coats with circular and ornamental scepter patterns; and blouses, vests, and loose pants featuring mandarin collars, frog fasteners, and white-and-blue porcelain patterns.[52]

This multiplication of Chinese themes on the domestic runway created a separate fashion world in which Chinese designers indulged themselves in the glories of China's past. Their intent was to convey deep cultural meanings through their creations. This trend peaked when Hu Xiaodan, a Beijing designer, debuted his "Moving Forbidden City" in 1995. In this grand series, Hu dressed models to look like different architectural elements of the Forbidden City: hats, shoulders, chests, and entire dresses were shaped like the pavilion, tiled roof, clock, and door knockers of the Forbidden City. These shapes were also meticulously decorated with zoomorphic ornaments, door studs, tassels, dragons, lotuses, and other plant and animal patterns. The collection was meant to display undiluted Chinese aesthetics. To minimize Western influence, Hu even trained his models to walk with "Chinese flair." Although domestic fashion critics and fellow designers faulted Hu's collection for its irrelevance to contemporary fashion, his designs were welcomed at many international exhibitions such as the Dusseldorf International Fashion Exhibition, where a Chinese national flag was raised for the first time.[53] In the following years, Hu toured the world, visiting Paris, New York, London, Tokyo, Brazil, Argentina, and Egypt. His shows often went beyond the runway and functioned as a form of cultural exchange, serving as part of China's diplomatic program. Amid his sensational success on the stage, Chinese fashion designers started to question whether fashion, in essence, was for the show or for the market, and whether the Chinese runway had already alienated itself from the cosmopolitanism of contemporary fashion.

These many star designers originally had few connections with the apparel industry: their design talents were discovered and validated by design contests, not by the market. But to sustain their status as fashion designers, many of them resorted to the industry. On the other hand, influential big-name domestic clothing brands normally relied on quality control and large economies of scale to gain market share rather than on innovative designs. In-house designers in these big brands were no different than pattern makers or cutters. However, after robust growth in the 80s, big domestic brands in the 90s faced intensified competition, especially from global brands that had recently entered China. As consumers became more and more conscious of international trends and brand names, the pressure to improve designs and to gain more publicity finally led to a marriage between domestic star designers and big brands.

In 1996, Zhang Zhaoda, also known as Mark Cheung, contracted as the chief designer for the Shanshan Group, based in Ningbo city. The Shanshan Group was famous for its suits and shirts and was arguably the largest garment group in China at the time. Zhang built his early career in the United States designing for high-fashion brands such as Oleg Cassini and A. J. Barj. His first runway show was held in the United States after he established the Mark Cheung label in 1991.[54] In the mid-90s, he shifted his focus to the mainland and found fast success, becoming the first recipient of the Golden Peak Award. The Shanshan Group also contracted another star designer, Wang Xinyuan, as its design director. A graduate of the Suzhou Institute of Silk Textile Technology in 1985, Wang's early Hong Kong experience designing for JMT and winning a competition among young Hong Kong fashion designers helped him secure this much-coveted position. Wang founded the Xinyuan Clothing Company in 1992 and became a well-known figure through his various roles as a business owner, designer, and judge of modeling contests and through his involvement in professional associations (Fig. 7.4). This unprecedented partnership between Shanshan and two star designers made headlines for its astronomical cost more than anything else. Both designers garnered yearly salaries of one million *yuan*.[55]

The Shanshan Group spent even more on its first runway show to promote its newly launched brand, FIRS for Ladies, designed by Zhang Zhaoda and Wang Xinyuan. The first show included over two hundred ensembles and generated enough publicity to make the huge expense worthwhile. From the very beginning, FIRS for Ladies was highly positioned as a top brand in women's career wear, with an ambitious goal of building the first China-made global brand comparable in design, quality, and prestige to its Western counterparts.[56] Following the show, FIRS boutiques spread from Shanghai to Shenyang. FIRS put on big production runway shows twice per year, mirroring the custom of the Western high-fashion system. Its catalogue was

**Figure 7.4**   A design from Wang Xinyuan's runway show at the Ningbo International Fashion Festival in 2002 (left). Wang's design at the fashion forecast runway show held by China Central Television in 2006 (right). Courtesy of Wang Xinyuan, fashion designer.

produced in Paris using Chinese supermodels, including Chen Juanhong and Ma Yanli.[57] But this fairytale-like marriage lasted only two years.

Wu Xuekai, a young graduate from the Tianjin Institute of Textile Science and Technology (now part of Tianjin Polytechnic University) and winner of the Brother Cup in 1996, replaced Zhang and Wang to serve as chief director of designers for the FIRS Collection for menswear in 1999, while FIRS for Ladies lost the media spotlight. Wu produced the "Gene 2000" runway show to promote FIRS Collection, which was broadcast by a variety of domestic media outlets and France Television (FTV). FIRS for Ladies was finally sold in 2003. Wang Xinyuan attributed the failure of FIRS for Ladies to the immaturity of the high-end market for Chinese local brands at the time.[58]

This (seemingly) mutually beneficial arrangement between famous designers and famous enterprises attracted not only the Shanshan Group, but a lot of others as well. Wu Xuewei, brother of Wu Xuekai, became chief director of designers for YINGDAK in 1997, a brand known for its leather and fur. Liu Yang contracted with ROMON in 1998, a large Ningbo manufacturer of menswear, and with SEPTWOLVES, a men's casual-wear brand, and also with Youngor, a brand known for its suits and shirts. China Garment Group Limited contracted Wu Haiyan in 1998. Chen Wen, a Donghua graduate and professor, joined Kangsai, a manufacturer for men's casual wear, as chief designer in 1995, and then Weipeng jeans, and Edenbo, a men's casual-wear brand. Thus, by the beginning of the new millennium nearly all the big-name designers had secured big contracts with domestic big brands or manufacturers. But often the tension between the designers' artistic visions and the brands' market goals turned designers into mere public relations tools that were used to secure publicity and enhance the brand's image. Brilliant and innovative ideas born on the runway frequently died there. Also, working with large enterprises, many designers also simultaneously operated their own brands or companies. This confusing relationship between star designers and their contracted enterprises often led to even more confused brand positioning.

Meanwhile, some large companies hired foreign designers to implement their international design vision. In May 1997, an influential garment and accessory manufacturer and retailer, the Taihe Group in Wuhan, announced a contract with French designer Aubry Marty, which cost the company 1.5 million Chinese *yuan*—perhaps the most expensive contract in the history of the Chinese garment industry. [59]

On the other hand, shrewd brand owners with comparatively limited financial means recruited less famous but talented designers to their design teams. For example, Chen Yifei, one of the most commercially successful painters in China, started to build his visual arts and fashion empire in Shanghai upon returning from New York, where he had made a fortune selling oil paintings to Western industrialists like Armand Hammer.[60] He stressed his notion of "big art," in which art, beauty, and style could and should be manifested in every aspect of everyday life. [61] With this in mind, he invested in a variety of areas relating to visual arts and fashion, such as film production, high-end clothing brands, modeling agencies, home furnishings, publishing, and city planning.

In 1997, Chen created Layefe, a women's wear brand headed by Wang Yiyang, and Sanyi, a younger brand, headed by Chen Xiang and Hu Rong. A year later, the LEYEFE brand was launched for menswear, headed by Wang Wei, and then Layefe Street for casual wear, headed by Zhang Da. All of the head designers were graduates of or young teachers from Donghua University, except Zhang Da, who was a teacher at the Northwest Institute of Textile Science and Technology in Xi'an. These young designers' sense of fashion and solid skills helped Chen to popularize most of these brands among Shanghai's white-collar consumers. Apparently, Chen also influenced these young designers with his international outlook and fine taste, considering the fact that nearly all of his head designers later became big names in the industry. The launch issue of Chinese *Vogue* declared Wang Yiyang, Hu Rong, Zhang Da, and Wang Wei, all of whom previously worked for Chen Yifei, as "China's new force in design." After a few years of collaboration with Chen, these designers created their own labels sold in China and abroad.

In fact, a wave of new designer labels and studios emerged in urban centers in the new millennium. Wang Yiyang launched ZUCZUG in 2002 and CHAGANG in 2004; Zhang Da founded Boundless in 2005; Wang Wei created Wang Wei Gallery in 2005 (Fig. 7.5); and Hu Rong launched Decoster in 2000. Ma Ke established Wuyong (Useless) in 2006, ten years after the launch of her first label, Exception. Wu Xuewei and Wu Xuekai created the made-to-measure label WXW & WXK and the ready-to-wear label WU.D in 2006. And Chen Wen launched the casual wear label CHENWENSTUDIO in 2005. Less restricted by owners or investors, these designers had more freedom to convey and promote their ideas and to decide how much "art" they should include to make their work marketable. Some labels clearly demonstrated their designer's notions of what contemporary Chinese fashion should look like. Their designs displayed a clear market orientation that catered to internationalized urban tastes: they did not fear appearing "non-Chinese." Looking to the future, Wang Wei believes that "brands will be developed globally and regional differences will be smaller."[62] However, the pursuit of an Oriental aesthetic and philosophy continues to underpin their modern looks.

Wang Yiyang's ZUCZUG is a brand designed for white-collar women who lead a fashionable, urban lifestyle but desire to differentiate themselves by a taste for the fashions of local, rather than foreign, designers. ZUCZUG's designs feature neutral colors, a soft cut, and unexpected details. Consumers of this brand might have jobs that require frequent business trips to Europe or the United States, where they have easy access to international fashion; however, only domestic designer labels like

**Figure 7.5** Wang Wei's architectural design from his 2006 fall/winter collection (left). A white overcoat with a multilayered collar decorated with delicate gathers from Wang's 2007 spring/summer collection (right). Courtesy of Wang Wei, fashion designer.

ZUCZUG, which are not widespread or widely known, seem to assure them of their sophisticated taste. By early 2007, ZUCZUG had expanded to thirty stores.[63] As his business has grown, designer Wang Yiyang has remained low-key and laid-back, seemingly indifferent to big production runway shows, mainly due to differences in the fashion retailing system in China. "In Paris, buyers are the ultimate audience of the runway, but here the runway is merely for show," he said. And he is anything but a showman. His travels to Europe with Chen Yifei in the early years of his career expanded his horizons but nearly crushed his confidence in his own culture and fashion environment. His experiences abroad forced him to contemplate fundamental questions, such as "what is fashion?" and "whom do I design for?"[64] As he told the *Jingji guancha bao* (Economic Observer), "For a long time, I was in a denial regarding my current condition. What you saw overseas became your ideal. Based on this illusion you deny the current environment. Nothing is what it is, nothing is right." But by the time he created his second brand, CHAGANG (Teapot), he seemed to have found the answer to those puzzling questions. He decorated his CHAGANG stores with shelves full of white teapots and clearly communicated his search for an Oriental aesthetic, but one that was not founded on Western notions of "Chineseness." Wang translated his childhood memories of frugality into fashion looks, utilizing minimalist cuts and decorations, blue or other gray tones, and odd shapes (Fig. 7.6).

As a close friend and former colleague of Wang, Zhang Da displayed similar characteristics in his designs: neutral tones and minimalist cuts. But his designs

**Figure 7.6** Wang Yiyang's artsy looks and models at a fashion show in the 798 Art Zone in Beijing in September 2006. Courtesy of Wang Yiyang, fashion designer.

targeted a smaller, higher-end market. Zhang's professional design career took off after he won an Italian design contest, Mittel Moda, and he subsequently studied at the prestigious fashion house Fausto Sarli in Rome in 1998. After working for Yifei for three years, he created his PARALLEL studio in Shanghai in 2004 and launched Boundless the following year. The name Boundless accurately depicts his ideal—to push the boundaries of design. He sells his designs at the prestigious showroom Younik located at Bund 18 in Shanghai and in Beijing's famous 798 Art Zone. As a historically iconic building, Bund 18 is now Shanghai's landmark of luxury fashion: it has housed Cartier, Ports, and Zegna and also a Vivienne Westwood exhibition.

Amid these world-class brands, the originality of Zhang Da's designs sprang from Oriental philosophy, literature, garden design, and sartorial culture. Not only did Zhang abandon the aesthetics expressed in Western chinoise designs, which are based mainly on Qing dynasty styles, he has also been reluctant to adopt the current standards of beauty and fashion established in the West.[65] He advocates a more fundamental change in Chinese views of what is beautiful and fashionable—views that are currently influenced by Western views. "You are done if you follow what they [the West] understand as Chinese," he warns. Maintaining a distance from the world of international high fashion thus helps Zhang to define a modernism that is unique to China.

These daring views are manifested in his designs, which are a cross between fashion and art. Zhang's avant-garde flat collection, exhibited as part of "China Design Now" at the Victoria and Albert Museum in London in March 2008, is a bold example of his design philosophy. The flat-cut O-shirts (as he calls them), pants, tops, and dresses of this collection look like oversized discs, pieces of paper, or strange two-dimensional geometric shapes when not worn on the body. But when worn, they drape on the body in elegant and clever ways. A minimalist Oriental aesthetic

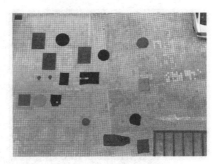

**Figure 7.7**  One look in Zhang Da's flat-cut O-shirt series, which appears to be a two-dimensional round shape when not on the body (left). Zhang's flat-cut series lying flat on the ground (right). Courtesy of Zhang Da, fashion designer.

is reflected in both the final form of these garments and in his process of cutting and sewing. For example, O-shirts all feature a perfectly circular silhouette with vertical and horizontal cutouts (Fig. 7.7).

Zhang Da and his generation are in search of not only new forms of dress, but also a new fashion lexicon that will differentiate not only China from the West, but also their generation from their predecessors (Fig. 7.8). They have been presented with great opportunities brought about by China's rapid economic advancement and increased global interconnectedness. While the high-end market has been exclusively dominated by global luxury brands, the growing urban middle class offers an enticing niche market for local designers. Designers of this new generation have responded to the hopes and dreams of their consumers with passion, imagination, and daring. They are not restrained by either old ways of thinking or Western views.

**Figure 7.8** Minimalist cuts and neutral colors are characteristic of Zhang Da's looks. Courtesy of Zhang Da, fashion designer.

However, they are limited by systemic deficiencies in the industry such as the lack of globally literate management talent. The division of labor is thus lacking in labels run by Chinese designers, and the designer himself has to play many roles. Zhang Da described the relationship between a designer and his company as that of a musician and his band: "There will be good musicians in a few years in China, but it will take a long time for a good band to emerge."[66]

## Going Global: The More International, the More National

While following his own original vision, Zhang Da still frankly acknowledged that "the power [of fashion] is in the West. All of us need to exhibit in Paris in order for the world to see ... Westerners come to China for the market, but Chinese go to the West for the recognition."[67] Chinese fashion designers need recognition from the West much as Japanese designers did in the 1980s. In the eyes of young Chinese designers, any new Chinese aesthetic discovered by the new generation of Chinese designers will only add another form of originality and exoticism to Western fashion but will not be a dominant force in global fashion.

But how could Chinese earn the respect of the international fashion world? The previous generation, as we have seen, believed that highlighting Chinese characteristics in their designs was the path to international acceptance. However, this quickly degenerated into tacking on traditional Chinese design elements that had little connection to international fashion. The next generation of designers, Zhang Da among them, took the opposite path: they deemphasized stereotypical Chinese elements and instead tried to express their individual creativity. Only in this way, they believed, could their "Chineseness" be truly expressed. Therefore, the mantra "the more international, the more national" replaced the earlier dictum "the more national, the more international." This reversal was clearly manifested in the designs of Chinese designers in this period.

Post-Mao designers from the mainland began their journey to the West as early as the 1980s. In March 1989, Ma Ling, a twenty-one-year-old actress and fashion designer, held her first runway show in Paris after participating in a Hong Kong fashion fair.[68] Her designs, inspired by the *qipao* form, were praised for their "combination of oriental charm with Western culture."[69] Twenty years later, Chinese designers have made it to nearly all renowned fashion weeks in Paris, London, Milan, New York, and Tokyo. But the road to the world's top fashion arena was not as smooth as it looked on the runway.

Designer Wang Xinyuan, also the vice president and secretary-general of the Shanghai International Fashion Federation, finally secured the first Chinese entry ticket to Milan Fashion Week in 2006. He directed the China day show with eight renowned Chinese brands including FIRS at the 2006 Milan Fashion Week. Various Italian, French, and Chinese TV stations covered the shows. To the Chinese fashion industry, what was shown seemed less important than the fact that Chinese brands and designers had made it to the prestigious stage of Milan Fashion Week. This type of governmental effort and its success in promoting Chinese brands inspired other designers.

A year later, Ji Wenbo, a winner of the 2004 Golden Peak Award from the coastal city of Xiamen, got the only entry ticket to the 2007 Milan Fashion Week as a mainland fashion designer.[70] After Western couturiers and Hong Kong designers had already stormed the runways of Western high fashion with Chinese styles year after year over the previous two decades, his collection of stylish terracotta warriors brought Chinese elements back to the runway, wowing the audience in Milan.[71] He dressed his modern warriors in fashionable leather coats, jackets, and leather shoes. But the carved, elongated headband, the Qin-dynasty hairstyle, and the color palette had hints of ancient armor. Ji successfully reinvigorated the exoticism and excitement that were associated with Chinese themes on the stage of world fashion.

Another high-profile fashion designer, and also a professor at the prestigious China Academy of Art, Wu Haiyan, participated in the "Power of Asia" runway show at Japan Fashion Week in Tokyo in 1996 (Fig. 7.9). Wu is especially known for her classic silk fashions with suggestive Chinese-style patterns and embroideries, often accessorized with extravagant hairstyles and headwear (Fig. 7.10). She plays with ribbons, feathers, hand painting, ruffles, and Chinese props such as oversized birdcages to add a dash of Chinese flair to her glamorous collections (Fig. 7.11). On top of her professorship, Wu Haiyan runs her own textile and clothing design company, WHY DESIGN, based in Beijing with a branch in Hangzhou. As a prolific designer, she has exhibited her works in a number of world cities, including Paris, Tokyo, and Hamburg.

Another designer, Liu Heng (Chris Liu), showcased his collections at the 2005 London Fashion Week. Born in Xinjiang, he studied fashion design in Xi'an and then obtained his master's degree from the London College of Fashion. His designs lacked any perceptible Chinese influence and featured marketable, trendy fashions: clear or pastel colors, clean cuts, and thoughtful details. While Chris Liu shone in London, Han Feng, another mainland-born international designer, became known to the worlds of New York fashion and opera. She studied painting and sculpture at the Zhejiang Academy of Fine Arts in Hangzhou and moved to New York in 1985. Her design career started with pleated scarves, which led to a presentation of her first line of women's clothing in New York in 1994.[72] Her work was exhibited together with works of Wang Yiyang, Ma Ke, and Zhang Da at "China Design Now" at the Victoria and Albert Museum in early 2008.

Ma Ke also secured an elusive prime spot at the 2007 Paris Fashion Week, where she presented her Wuyong, or Useless, collection. Her creations attracted much attention in both art and fashion circles.[73] Instead of showcasing her clothes on a regular runway, her models stood on lit boxes, which made it look like a sculpture exhibition. The clothes were made of layers and layers of discarded items such as

**Figure 7.9** Wu Haiyan's looks shown in the Power of Asia runway show at Japan Fashion Week in Tokyo in 1996. Courtesy of Wu Haiyan, fashion designer.

**Figure 7.10** Wu Haiyan's futuristic silk collection from 2006, bridging fashion and decorative art. Courtesy of Wu Haiyan, fashion designer.

**Figure 7.11** Lv Yan, a Chinese supermodel showcasing Wu Haiyan's design with an intricately painted pattern on a silky skirt in 2001 (left). Surrealistic birdcages decorate the runway at Wu's fashion show in 2001, echoing the Chinese elements that imbue Wu's designs (right). Courtesy of Wu Haiyan, fashion designer.

sheets covered with old paint, meshed knits, and intensive gathers. All the coats and dresses featured magnificent volume, earthy colors, and rich textures that were linked to the theme of the show: soil. Young and middle-aged models wore soil-like makeup and simple, tight caps of the same color. Ma Ke made a strong statement about her philosophy of fashion, or what fashion could convey. She drew attention to nature, which has largely been forgotten in flamboyant Paris high fashion and demonstrated how useless items in nature have their own unique beauty and value, even for fashion.

Her 2008 Wuyong collection was shown at Paris Haute Couture Week in July 2008. Being the first Chinese designer ever to make it to Haute Couture Week, Ma Ke continued to make her antifashion statement. Her creations and her unusual presentation of the clothes pointed to a new direction that challenged the ideals of current haute couture. Amid demonstrations of hand spinning, weaving, and dyeing in the gardens of the Palais Royal, her male and female models moved slowly in unison, incorporating elements of tai chi and yoga. Her simply cut, handmade loose shirts, trousers, and pleated skirts were made of natural fibers such as cotton, linen, and wool and accessorized with recyclable shoes. The collection featured brown, blue, grey, black, and white colors, all hand dyed with natural dyes.[74] As the name of the theme, "Luxurious Frugality," indicated, Ma Ke advocated frugality and simplicity, a revolutionary concept in haute couture, which has long been marked by extravagance and excess. Her pseudo-peasant clothes perhaps reminded her of her childhood in the 1970s, when all Chinese lived an environmentally friendly, frugal life. This shared memory of frugality also influenced other Chinese designers born in the same period, such as Wang Yiyang, whose work is frequently compared with that of Ma Ke. Perhaps Ma Ke's "peasant look" will become an updated version of Chanel's "poor look" for a new millennium.

Ma Ke's unique ways of connecting fashion with deeply rooted emotions, nature, and even the natural process of deterioration attracted renowned Chinese director Jia Zhangke, winner of the Golden Lion in Venice in 2007. Jia directed a documentary named after Ma's "Wuyong" collection, which contrasted Ma Ke's ideas of frugality and earthy designs with the hard lives of Chinese miners, peasants, and tailors in remote villages. In the documentary, Ma discussed her pursuit of the pure feelings expressed in the needle and thread, in the natural process of producing and consuming clothing, and in the deep meanings fashion can convey. "The essential needs of human beings across time and space are the same. I hope to express something that is more enduring than my life in my creations. It has nothing to do with science, technology, or economics."[75]

## From Factory Girls to Supermodels

In the world of modern fashion, fashion designers and models rely on each other to legitimize and glamorize their professions. The image of the modern fashion designer is therefore inextricably linked to fashion models. However, when Pierre Cardin held his historic fashion shows in Beijing and Shanghai in 1979, China had not encountered a real fashion model since the founding of the People's Republic. The twelve French and Japanese models Cardin brought with him to his Beijing debut opened Chinese eyes to the profession of fashion modeling. The remarkable visual and psychological shock Cardin's magnificent shows produced inspired the manager of Shanghai Garment Company, Zhang Chenglin, to assemble China's own modeling team.[76]

The state-owned Shanghai Garment Company was one of the largest and most competitive entities in the Chinese garment industry at the time. It formed the first modeling team of the post-Mao era in 1980. More than ten models were chosen for the team from factory workers at forty-four garment factories.[77] The minimum height requirement was 1.68 meters (5 feet 6 inches).[78] But the selection criteria went beyond body shape requirements to include screening of the applicant's family and friends in order to gauge how they would cope with the tremendous social pressure that becoming a model would entail.[79] Some models struggled to adapt to their new profession as many viewed modeling as an immoral profession. In a report in August 1982, *Xinmin Evening News* confirmed that Chinese models were working to promote the Four Modernizations rather than merely satisfying vulgar and inferior tastes. A clear distinction had to be made between Chinese models and their counterparts in the West.

At the debut runway show of the new modeling team held in 1981 in the Shanghai Friendship Movie Theater, the models showed 186 sets of new designs and historical costumes.[80] The goal of the show was merely to demonstrate modeling to the public, but the team later walked for domestic producers seeking to export apparel overseas. However, the social pressure models were under was heightened as the influence of their shows expanded. Some wondered, "What exactly do fashion shows promote? A capitalist life?" and "What is a fashion show? Isn't it just bizarre dress plus beautiful women?"[81]

At first, these models modeled only part-time and returned to their factory posts after the shows. Their training encompassed not only fitness, body movement, and makeup techniques, but also sewing.[82] To avoid sensitive associations with the capitalist lifestyle, these models were called *shizhuang yanyuan* (fashion actors).[83] In fact, this term accurately indicates how fashion shows were perceived at the time: pure entertainment. Based on this notion of fashion shows, design works were often split into two categories: "performance design" and "utilitarian design." Performance designs emphasized theatrical visuals for the stage instead of functionality and utility. And much as with designers, the government promoted the modeling system through a series of competitions. Models became famous through modeling contests rather than through the marketplace or association with brands.

Thereafter, modeling teams sprouted up all over China, with a large number of them formed merely to provide a novel form of entertainment. While many modeling teams put on shows in nightclubs, in hotels, and in the streets, institutions of higher education launched modeling programs to legitimize modeling as serious profession. The Suzhou Institute of Silk Textile Technology established China's first modeling degree program in 1989. This two-year program admitted young women with drawing skills who had passed the national college entrance exam. In the first year, fourteen young women were selected. They studied Chinese literature, English, aesthetics, advertising photography, music, and morality, in addition to fitness and body movement, dance, makeup, and garment construction and design.[84] A year later, China Textile University (later renamed Donghua University) created a similar modeling program, offering a baccalaureate that offered would-be models a similar education to that of other college majors. The program required courses in music, dancing, fashion photography, fashion show choreography, fashion color, illustration, garment construction, materials, flat pattern, fashion design, accessory design, apparel production and management, trend forecasting, 3D-Studio, and styling, in addition to professional modeling training.[85] Although the program was set up to attract fresh talent, it also attracted famous models, such as Ma Yanli and Xie Dongna, who wanted to acquire a college education. College education elevated the social status of models but simultaneously excluded talented models who failed to pass the college entrance exam.

Meanwhile, enterprising businessmen launched a number of nondegree modeling schools. "Some training schools can be crude and officials complained that some are just scams. But the demand remains strong."[86] Tang Ling, a tall, slender fifteen-year-old, when asked by the *New York Times* why she applied to a modeling school in 1990, replied: "I have seen models on television and I always envied them. They look so pretty and wear nice clothes ... I came because I have a dream," she said. "I love this. I would love to travel around the world and be the best model of the century." The glamour associated with the runway alone was already extremely appealing to aspiring models in a country where individual glamour had been strictly taboo not long ago. The prospect of international fame also appealed to many. However, social pressure on models remained even in the early 90s. A political commissar at the Beijing Port Authority bristled when his daughter answered an ad for a modeling school in the *Beijing Evening News.* He thought such "frivolous capitalist practices" as modeling and fashion were not suitable for his sixteen-year-old daughter. Some modeling schools, therefore, took precautions to reduce parents' worries and came up with slogans like, "Be not just fashion models, but model people."[87]

For over a decade, Chinese models were organized under the leadership of a team director, who was often appointed by a large, state-owned company. The director decided whether or not to undertake a show, as well as who got to walk at the show. They made decisions regarding the recruitment of models, salaries, and the choreography of the shows.[88] China's structural transformation from a planned economy to a market economy, however, altered the way modeling teams operated. Many teams became independent business entities that supported their models through performance revenue, which finally led to the establishment of private modeling agencies. Zhang Jian, a textiles graduate, grasped the opportunity in this newly emerging yet promising profession and founded the Beijing Fashion Performance Team in the mid-80s. A number of models from his team became famous, such as Zhang Jinqiu, who later starred in the film "Evening Liaison," directed by Chen Yifei. He later established the Beijing Fashion Performance Team, the China Fashion Art Performance Group, New Silk Road Models, Inc., and, finally, the Concept 98 Models Agency.[89]

The first modeling agency in Shanghai, the Zhaoping Modeling Agency, was founded in the mid-90s, followed by the Yifei New Silk Road Models Agency. This lucrative market also attracted investment from abroad, which brought to life the Starz People Model Agency and Oriental Modeling and Media. Both agencies were based in Shanghai and housed dozens of top models in China. Intensified competition through foreign investment brought with it new operational systems. Under the new operational system, the agency took 20 percent to 70 percent of a contracted model's yearly earnings in agent's fees, while in the past models were paid a monthly salary regardless of individual market value.[90] This new system also gave models greater career mobility.

Similar to the glamorization of the fashion design profession in China, the modeling profession also made itself the focus of the media spotlight through various modeling contests. In the early years of its development, TV stations and fashion magazines put on influential modeling contests. For example, the Xunda Cup, held by Shanghai TV Station in 1989, attracted participants from famous modeling teams such as the Shanghai Garment Company, the Shanghai Seventh Silk Printing and Dyeing Factory, and China Textile University.[91] Modeling contests have become an indispensable component of various fashion events and festivals all over China. Large annual fashion festivals, such as the China International Clothing and Accessories Fair, the Shanghai International Fashion Culture Festival (SIFCF), and the Dalian International Fashion Festival, regularly hold modeling contests to discover new faces for the burgeoning industry. The first winner of the SIFCF modeling contest in 1995, Ma Yanli, from the Shanghai Garment Company's model team, was a former rowing athlete. Her victory made her a highly sought after model by renowned domestic brands. She became the face of FIRS in the late 90s and later launched the made-to-measure label MARYMA in 2004.

Meanwhile, selective trials for international modeling contests such as the Elite Model Look and Supermodel of the World also attracted new modeling talent. Peng Li, a model from a team in Beijing, was one of the first Chinese models to win an international modeling contest. Her victory in an Italian modeling contest in 1988 made headlines in the domestic media. Four years later, Chen Juanhong was awarded Supermodel of the World in Los Angeles after winning the national selective trail in 1991, which made her the first Chinese supermodel. Her transition from a textile factory worker to a model on the Hangzhou Xidebao Models Team permanently altered the Chinese modeling profession. After her victory, model agent Wang Yiming brought her to the vibrant city of Shenzhen. Soon afterward, this shy young girl from a small town in Zhejiang province, with her distinctive height (179 cm or 5 feet 10 inches) and poise, would grace the covers of dozens of Chinese fashion magazines and would model for a variety of top international labels.[92]

Most top Chinese models followed the career path of Ma Yanli and Chen Juanhong—winning modeling contests brought them overnight success. Since modeling contests had the power to turn low-paid athletes or factory girls into top-earning supermodels, winning a contest became the ultimate goal of new models and their agencies. Many models train solely for modeling contests. But modeling contests have been widely criticized for their lack of professionalism and under-the-table manipulation of results. Nevertheless, the number of modeling contests in China has grown year after year. In 2000 alone there were as many as fourteen national modeling contests.[93] However, many of these contests were controlled by large modeling agencies. And it was an open secret that models who weren't contracted to the modeling agency holding the contest had no chance of winning, regardless of their quality, fashion editors Sun Xinghua and Shen Mu revealed.[94] In protest of this sort of manipulation, the famous models agent Zhang Jian along with supermodel Chen Juanhong both withdrew from the Best Professional Models contest at China International Fashion Week in 2000. At the press conference announcing the withdrawal,

Chen Juanhong spoke for seventeen modeling agencies and announced a proposal to oppose monopoly.

However, since domestic modeling contests could hardly provide any international exposure, top models relied on international fashion shows to move their careers forward. The fashion shows of couturiers and international top designers, which were being held more and more frequently in China, offered Chinese models opportunities to work with the world's top talents in fashion design, makeup, fashion photography, styling, and media. Walking at a top designer's fashion show often meant instant international publicity and the opportunity to work in the West. The *New York Times* covered Valentino's first fashion show in China in 1993, which starred model Bao Haiqing: "As Valentino took his bows on the runway for the first time in China, Bao Haiqing towered beside him, her tall, willowy figure suggesting a fresh, supple vine wrapped in a swirl of glistening black Italian cloth." Bao was from the same modeling team as Chen Juanhong and was also discovered and trained by Wang Yiming.[95] But the eighteen-year-old Bao commented, "We don't understand Western clothes … We don't know how we're supposed to feel when we wear them."[96]

But this initial unease with Western clothes dissipated as top Chinese models began working frequently for top labels both inside and outside of China. And Chinese models soon began competing with their Western counterparts for spots in fashion shows in the world's fashion centers. Li Xin, a six-foot-tall basketball player, started her modeling adventure in Paris in 1996 after her participation in China's Elite Model Look contest.[97] Her distinctive "Asian look" charmed such fashion designers and labels as Yves Saint Laurent, Givenchy, Giorgio Armani, Christian Dior, and Jean Paul Gaultier.[98] In addition to shooting advertisements for BMW and Cartier Jewelry, she made frequent trips to New York, Paris, Milan, and London, walking at various fashion shows. As one of the most notable Asian supermodels, she was featured in various versions of *Vogue, Elle, Harper's Bazaar, W,* and *Marie Claire,* among others.[99] Another notable Asian face on the Western runway was Li Fang. *Fashion* magazine described her as John Galliano's favorite Chinese model. Like Li Xin, Li Fang also played basketball. She secured a contract with the New Silk Road Models Agency after entering China's Elite Model Look contest in 1998.[100] In 2000, she went to Paris and soon got the opportunity to walk for Dior, Balmain, and Hermes.[101]

Compared to the former basketball players Li Xin and Li Fang, Lv Yan, another Chinese supermodel who worked in Paris, had an even more dramatic change in her career and life on her way to becoming one of the world's supermodels. Coming from a poor family in the countryside, Lv Yan was a peasant worker in Beijing. In 1998, two important men in Lv Yan's life—top fashion makeup artist Li Dongtian and photographer Feng Hai—discovered this unusual new face for the popular Chinese fashion magazine *Fashion Miss,* successor of *Modern Dress and Dress Making.* Afterward, Lv Yan landed on the cover of nearly every Chinese fashion magazine.[102]

She ranked second in the 2000 Elite Model Look contest, the best finish for a Chinese model yet. Her first month in Paris brought her 20,000 francs, a surreal sum for a girl whose parents earned only 400 RMB (271 francs) per month in the countryside in Jiangxi province.[103] In Paris, she got a contract with French Metropolitan Models, walked for Dior and Lacroix, and shot advertisements for Hermes and L'Oreal.[104]

Lv Yan's meteoric rise revolutionized the beauty standards of the Chinese modeling profession. Her tiny eyes, high cheekbones, flat nose, thick lips, and freckles were the exact opposite of what Chinese normally considered beautiful. But fashion professionals like Li Dongtian and Feng Hai were deeply touched by her unusual beauty and unique temperament and considered her the "most Asian" of Asian faces. While the Chinese media were in the habit of portraying her as the "lucky, ugly beauty," *Elle* France, *Paris Match,* British *Pure,* and Italian *Amica* were simply in love with her.

As more and more international fashion magazines have entered China, Chinese models have had greater opportunities for international exposure. Entering China in 2005, the debut issue of the Chinese version of *Vogue* featured five top Chinese models standing next to blond Australian Gemma Ward. Ward was the youngest model ever to land the cover of American *Vogue* and the face for Calvin Klein's perfume "Obsession Night for Men" after Kate Moss. *Vogue* China not only put these Chinese models at the forefront of the fashion stage, it also introduced them to top professionals like renowned photographer Patrick Demarchelier, who shot for *Vogue* China's debut cover. Du Juan, one of the first cover girls in *Vogue* China, quickly emerged as a popular face on the international runway in spring 2006, walking for couturiers like Chanel, Valentino, Givenchy, and Jean Paul Gaultier.[105] She was the first Chinese model to grace the cover of *Vogue* France and also appeared in global ad campaigns for Yves Saint Laurent, Roberto Cavalli, Gap, Louis Vuitton, and Swarovski.[106] She currently holds a contract with IMG Models, an international modeling agency that also represents Kate Moss, Naomi Campbell, Cindy Crawford, and Heidi Klum.

While Chinese models are making names for themselves on the international runway, most Chinese designers and brands have opted for exotic, fresh Western looks for their runway shows, advertisements, and catalogues. The increase in international opportunities for a few top models paled in comparison to the reduction of jobs for the majority of Chinese models. On the one hand, the luxury-brand market, which is largely dominated by global brands, has a limited need for local models. On the other hand, most local designer brands are struggling to expand, and their ability to generate top-paying modeling jobs is also limited. Thus, the limited scale of China's modeling profession calls into question whether China really has its own modeling industry yet. But as the first decade of the new millennium comes to a close, Chinese models are indisputably ahead of designers in their quest to reach the forefront of international fashion.

# –8–

# Importing Dreams of Luxury:
# Western Brand Names

We are finished here in the West—our moment has come and gone. This is all about China and India and Russia. It is the beginning of the reawakening of cultures that have historically worshipped luxury and haven't had it for so long.[1]

Tom Ford

Over two thousand years ago, the West sought out the luxuries of China in the form of silk, spices, and precious stone. These exotic goods, traded along the Silk Road, brought new symbols of status and power to the Roman world, where the fineries of the Far East were as highly prized by the ancient Italians as the luxury brands of their progeny are prized in China today. The silk that once flowed out of China to Europe now flows back into China with the labels of European designers securely and prominently displayed, serving as new signs of status and power in a globalized world. This reversal, however, also indicates that China has come full circle. An ancient empire that celebrated luxury and the exquisite, China turned in on itself in the twentieth century and attempted to smash, both physically and spiritually, that feudal culture of privilege and status. But by the end of the century, it became clear that not even a Cultural Revolution could extinguish the dreams of luxury of the Chinese people.

China has become one of the fastest-growing markets in the world for luxury labels, and by 2008 nearly every global label had a presence in China. With sales exceeding $6 billion, China was the third largest luxury goods consumer in the world in 2004, accounting for 12 percent of the world's total. China is projected to consume roughly 29 percent of the world's luxury goods in 2015, supplanting Japan as the largest luxury brands consumer.[2] Global labels are attracted to the Chinese market not only because of the stunning growth that has already taken place, but also because the potential for further expansion is so great: a luxury market built on a population base of 1.3 billion consumers is too tempting for any luxury brand to pass up. Editor in chief of *Harper's Bazaar* China, Su Mang, and her colleagues firmly believe that luxury products will dominate Chinese fashion in the near term.[3]

## First Encounters with Foreigners

Since luxury brands first appeared in China in the early years of the post-Mao era, they have been irrevocably linked with foreigners and Chinese notions of foreignness. As we have seen, these issues are fraught with controversy and touch on highly sensitive questions of national identity and China's own deep sense of past humiliation at the hands of foreign powers. At the end of the 1970s, this was further complicated by antagonisms generated by the global contest between communism and capitalism.

But after the end of the Cultural Revolution many Chinese were eager to understand the "wicked" yet "wealthy" West. Newspapers advocated friendship gestures to people from all over the world, including the American people, whom the Chinese officially disparaged for decades. However, only privileged comrades had the opportunity to travel to Hong Kong or Western countries. Upon their return, they became conduits of Western fashion and the luxurious Western lifestyle. Since the majority of the populace still had no access to information from outside of China, those with relatives overseas were envied. As these privileged few relayed tales of their personal encounters with the comparative splendor of capitalist material culture, faith in local fashions and lifestyles on the mainland began to erode. Consequently, this led to the rejection of elements of Chinese culture, practices, and beliefs throughout Chinese society: most people seemed reluctant to be associated with old Chinese traditions, in either appearance or thought. In this environment virtually anything Western came into vogue—a development that the Chinese government and the more conservative elements of society viewed with chagrin. Even Western philosophy attracted many adherents, and intellectuals could suddenly be heard quoting Sartre, Nietzsche, and Camus in everyday conversations as a way of displaying their familiarity with the West. College students were also entranced by the works of novelists like Hugo, Tolstoy, Turgenev, and Rolland. The adoption of such nonmaterial Western culture preceded the adoption of material items like fashion brands and other products. In a country still mired in poverty, luxury culture was practically nonexistent in China at the time. The concept of fashion still seemed strange and foreign to many, and the Chinese were only just beginning to decipher its meaning and how it could relate to their own daily lives.

But everyone understood that fashion was tied up with the wealthy foreigners who began to appear on the streets of China's big cities at the end of the 1970s. The thaw in relations with the West brought about by the Open Door policy allowed foreign visitors to China for the first time in decades. This provided a convenient means for ordinary Chinese who could not travel abroad to examine foreigners and their styles of dress. As Cohen and Cohen noted, these examinations seemed to become a national pastime:

> The Chinese do not hide their immense curiosity about non-Chinese. They stare with forthright intensity and at as close as a range as possible, up to three inches—even in

the urban centers that are standard sight-seeing stops. One often sees groups of Chinese assembled outside the leading hotels waiting to catch a glimpse of the exotic foreigners, and at the excellent zoos of Peking, Shanghai, and Canton the people stare at foreigners while the foreigners stare at the animals.[4]

In another instance of this new national pastime, one hundred thousand people surrounded and stared at a foreign tourist group visiting Lanzhou in 1978.[5] These episodes took place largely because, at the time, foreigners seemed extraterrestrial to most Chinese, not only because of their exotic appearance but also because they were representatives of the "Far West," an "immoral" land of wealth and plenty. Moreover, the very concept of "foreignness" was itself sensational to a people who had been isolated for decades. Inevitably, many if not all of these foreign visitors donned "bizarre" dress and other novel styles, as can be seen in pictures of tourists from the time (Fig. 8.1).

## Luxury Brands Come to China

The early excitement engendered by sightings of foreigners in China at the end of the 70s gradually waned as businessmen, investors, and designers from the West

**Figure 8.1** A group of curious Chinese observe a foreign blond in jeans and permed hair in 1980 in the Forbidden City. Courtesy of Li Xiaobin, photographer.

flocked to the newly opened Chinese market. The first haute couture designer to enter China's newly opened door was Pierre Cardin. Around the same time Yves Saint Laurent's Chinese Collection of 1977–78 was making headlines in Paris, Cardin held fashion shows in Beijing and Shanghai in 1979, in an era when fear of Western "spiritual pollution" still concerned the Chinese authorities. Due to their "sensitive" nature, only professionals were permitted to attend Cardin's shows. Nevertheless, the shows were a sensation. Paris fashion, a perfect manifestation of the capitalist lifestyle, had been a taboo subject for decades in China, and its vivid display in front of the Chinese audience left them speechless. In the words of the company, "China was grey—Pierre Cardin gave it color."[6]

Cardin's debut fashion show would become one of the most memorable East-meets-West fashion milestones in post-Mao China. Cardin brought with him a Western fashion lexicon new to the Chinese: fashion shows, fashion models, fashion designers, and luxury brands. In some sense, it was risky for Cardin to blaze a new trail in the still staunchly communist Chinese state of the late 70s, but Cardin did not return to Paris empty-handed. His suits soon became a symbol of prestige among China's nouveau riche, and many other Cardin luxury products came to be produced and sold in China.

As the popularity of Western suits dramatically increased in the 80s after China's political leaders gave them the official seal of approval, Cardin, as one of the few brand-name producers of suits in China at the time, benefited enormously. In fact, in the 80s and into the 90s Pierre Cardin became virtually synonymous with fashion. "We cannot find another brand that so overwhelmingly controlled [the Chinese] people, controlled those in the mainstream society, like Pierre Cardin," declared Wang Weiming in 1994, a popular fashion critic. He continued, "Pierre Cardin has become a model, a symbol, a signal that could not be any stronger. It signifies all required qualities in a commercial society: dignity, precision, manners, commitment, trust, ambition, and even arrogance."[7] When Valentino first came to China in 1993, he was asked at his press conference whether he was wearing Pierre Cardin.[8] With a fashion empire that dominated China's luxury market for over a decade, Pierre Cardin had become the most famous Frenchman in China by the end of the twentieth century.

After Cardin's foray into China at the end of the 70s, other brands soon followed. As one of the first post-Mao luxury brands sold in China, Nike opened its first factory in China as a joint venture in 1981. Nike's high-quality, stylish, exotic designs coupled with the prestige associated with English-language labels (which were explicitly linked to the economically advanced and fashion-forward West) gave the Chinese an early taste of the appeal of brand-name fashion. Focusing on sports and athletes, Nike adopted a similar marketing strategy in China to the one that had been so successful for them in the United States. They sponsored the Chinese national basketball team in 1981 and in 1994 helped to establish China's first professional sports league, in soccer. Nike later sponsored top athletes like Yao Ming and Olympic gold medalist Liu Xiang. After his groundbreaking victory in the 2004 Olympic Games,

Liu became a national hero amid a Nike ad campaign that stressed Chinese national pride.⁹ Nike's collaboration with the Chinese sports world turned out to be a long-term, fruitful, and market-savvy move for the company. First sold in the state-owned Beijing Friendship Store in 1982, Nike China grew into a billion-dollar enterprise by 2008, with a network comprised of 180 private contract manufacturers.¹⁰

After Pierre Cardin and Nike, exclusive fashion brands like Yves Saint Laurent soon followed. Saint Laurent opened his fashion exhibition at Beijing's Palace of Fine Arts to the public in May 1985 (Fig. 8.2). However, the head of the Chinese Writers' Association described his clothes as "too sexy" for Chinese women. And another Chinese official wondered how the clothes were supposed to be worn.¹¹ Photographer Li Xiaobin made similar comments about the disconnect between Saint Laurent's avant-garde designs and the Chinese audience. Although high fashion was no longer the taboo subject it had once been, its appeal early on was still limited because the Chinese audience was just beginning to discover international trends. If jeans were still considered "bizarre," one can imagine the typical Chinese perception of the avant-garde designs of high-fashion designers in this era. But high-fashion brands and designers like Louis Vuitton, Hugo Boss, Valentino, Ferre, Emanuel Ungaro, Gucci, Prada, Dior, Chanel, Burberry, Versace, and Fendi also soon made their way to China, along with many other world-class designers and luxury brands.

**Figure 8.2** Yves Saint Laurent held his public exhibition at Beijing's Palace of Fine Arts in May 1985, an early encounter with Paris high fashion in the post-Mao era. Courtesy of Li Xiaobin, photographer.

Despite some initial confusion and hesitation in the face of daring international fashion, the Chinese developed an appetite for foreign brand names (and foreign-sounding brand names) relatively early in the post-Mao era. As both legally and illegally imported trendy merchandise, such as sunglasses, watches, sneakers, and suits, made its way to the mainland, the Chinese consumer began paying attention to foreign labels, often quite literally. Brand labels themselves became "fashion accessories" that were often intentionally left on the lenses of sunglasses and on the sleeves of suits as a sign of prestige (Fig. 8.3). However, brand names were too vague of a concept for most Chinese to connect with company image or meaning. It really did not matter what the label read as long as it had foreign words on it and was designed with an exotic look. At the time, the brand-unconscious majority probably thought that the label was not supposed to be removed, having never encountered dress items with labels on them before. Leaving labels on sunglasses was a short-lived fad in the late 70s and early 80s, but labels could still be spotted on suits even in 2008.

As the Chinese became more brand aware in the 80s, the richest Chinese bought Cardin, while the luxury brands of the less well heeled included Nike, Goldlion (a Hong Kong brand known for men's leather accessories), Montagut (a French apparel brand popular in Hong Kong since the 1970s), Lacoste (a French casual wear apparel brand), and Playboy (an American casual wear apparel brand). Various popular brands that originated or were sold in Hong Kong were either smuggled in or imported to the mainland market. With housing generally provided for by the state

**Figure 8.3** Labels were intentionally left on the lenses of sunglasses as a fashionable and prestigious accessory in themselves. In Beijing's Beihai Park in 1980. Courtesy of Li Xiaobin, photographer.

and cars too far out of reach for ordinary people, a large portion of family income in cities was put into fashion consumption. However, the pursuit of fashion and luxury products, along with pop culture and material wealth, was still considered a suspect activity for good citizens, who in the eyes of the conservative majority ought to devote themselves to the pursuit of knowledge and national goals. But a daring, materialistic minority led the way down a new path.

At first, legally imported luxury brands were sold in friendship stores and so-called internal shops in large cities. Friendship stores mainly catered to the needs of expatriates and foreign visitors to China, and they were not accessible to the general public. But Chinese employees of such stores often sneaked in relatives and friends so they could purchase foreign products like 555 State Express cigarettes, Swiss watches, jewelry, and Nike apparel. Meanwhile, high-level cadres or the privileged would sometimes have the opportunity to make a purchase in friendship stores or internal shops. In her autobiography, *Life and Death in Shanghai,* Nien Cheng, a high-level manager for Shell Oil during the Mao era who was subsequently imprisoned during the Cultural Revolution, recalled celebrating the Chinese New Year in 1980 after she was released from prison with a friend at the Shanghai Exhibition Hall, where an internal shop was located:

> My young friend was impatient to get to the 'internal' shop at the exhibition hall, which was well known to the Shanghai public but inaccessible. She told me that she had boasted to her friends and neighbors that she was coming with me to the party; consequently they had all asked her to utilize the opportunity to buy them commodities they had long coveted but had been unable to obtain in the ordinary shops ... Much to my young friend's disappointment, when we got there we found that a large crowd had preceded us and that the staff was regulating admission into the shop. We had to join the line and wait. When we finally got in, half of the things she wanted were sold out. However, we still managed to spend several thousand *yuan* on items ranging from cashmere coat material to steel saucepans.[12]

At a time when workers in Shanghai earned an average monthly salary of approximately seventy-three *yuan,* the one-time expenditure of several thousand *yuan* on imported goods described here is one indication of the pent-up demand for imported items (which were often equated with luxury) in China as early as 1980. Although friendship stores and internal shops gradually began to open to the public in the mid-80s, products sold through friendship stores were still conspicuous status symbols until the early years of the 1990s when other stores began selling foreign brands.

As foreign brands moved from restricted friendship stores to privately owned venues, foreign brands seeking to crack the Chinese market encountered challenges that were often the result of cultural misunderstandings regarding Chinese views of foreign brands. When Giorgio Armani opened his store in Beijing, he chose to use a red lacquer Chinese-style door for the front of the store. Armani later cited this design choice as one of the company's first mistakes in China. "The first lesson with the Beijing store was that the Chinese want the Armani that you get in Europe. They want the Armani they see in magazines, on TV. The mistake I made at first in China was that I made the store too Chinese in decoration, and they didn't like it."[13] The Chinese-style door was later replaced. However, Armani's initial mistake revealed the Chinese desire for luxury brands that were authentically foreign and not connected to China's traditional past in any way.

## Embracing Brand Names and Luxury

In the 1990s, the influx of casual wear brand names, along with the leisure culture they promoted, transformed Chinese cities. Formality had been the hallmark of Chinese aesthetics for centuries, but as foreign fashions took hold a new informality became the norm. Respectable Chinese clothing had always featured a smooth and neat surface, a structured silhouette, and defined edge lines, which were associated with the disciplined, restrained, and conforming behaviors that Chinese culture emphasized. Typical examples of such clothing included the Mao suit, the *qipao,* and the *changshan,* or men's long robe. On the other hand, casual sweatshirts, T-shirts, sweatpants, and knitted sweaters lacked a defined structural look and often used textured and soft materials. More important, the spirit behind casual brands and most street fashions was carefree, laid-back, and individualistic. Thus, adopting these brand-name fashions not only changed Chinese appearance, it also signified a change in life attitudes and behaviors.

After the controversies over fashion and culture of the 1980s, people finally came to accept new ideas as well as more casual and individualistic expressions in dress. Sensing the need to further change Chinese urban culture in order to spur its sales, Puma, a German casual wear brand, promoted street culture in the mid-1990s in Shanghai. At the time, fashion critic Wang Weiming questioned whether street culture could thrive in a city with a highly controlled social and political structure that was deeply immersed in Confucian culture.[14] After all, only a few years earlier state-owned stores had refused to sell jeans because of their foreign appearance and the rebellious spirit they expressed. But by the mid 1990s, all stores were selling jeans brands like Puma, Fun, Apple, 5th Street Jeans, and Lee.

The majority of the younger generation in the 1990s embraced global brand names without any of the governmental restrictions that marked their parents' first encounters with Western fashions in the late 70s and early 80s. They took pride in owning popular labels like the Hong Kong brands Giordano, Bossini, and Baleno; the Australian brand Jeanswest; German brands Puma and Adidas; and American brands Nike, Lee, and Esprit. Many of these brands were brought to the mainland market by Hong Kong franchisers or licensers. Discarding the Mao suit and the military style, many urban youngsters donned casual outfits completed with white running shoes.

However, at first the market remained immature, and many were unable to differentiate various foreign brand names. "Anyone can be a luxury brand in China if they market the right image," said Chris Torrens, editorial director of consulting firm Access Asia.[15] This was especially true in the 1980s and early 1990s. As a result, virtually all homegrown fashion brands adopted an English or French name as a marketing strategy to capitalize on the prestige associated with foreign brand names. But the effective ad campaigns and promotional events of global brands started to make brand wearers aware of the hierarchy of brand names, which were differentiated not only by price but also by brand image. It was only then that Chinese consumers separated casual wear brands from luxury brands like Louis Vuitton, Armani, YSL, Prada, Chanel, Burberry, Gucci, Versace, and Hugo Boss. And since casual wear brands were more affordable, they dominated urban youth fashion in China in this period. As the market matured, Chinese fashion editors stressed the notion that "choosing your shoe is choosing your lifestyle."[16] And, eventually, brand-conscious youth could tell the difference between Giordano and Esprit.

With a more sophisticated retail environment and more affluent customers, large urban centers like Beijing or Shanghai were usually the safest venues for luxury brands to launch in China. For example, Louis Vuitton opened its first store in the Palace Hotel in Beijing in 1992 and another store in Shanghai Center three years later (Fig. 8.4). In 2005, LV relaunched its three-story flagship store in the China World Shopping Mall in Beijing, where it sells both women's and men's clothing and shoes as well as other accessories such as handbags, watches, jewelry, and glasses. Louis Vuitton claims it has never lost any money in any store in China since

**Figure 8.4** Louis Vuitton's large handbag advertisement in one of Shanghai's most prosperous commercial districts, Nanjing Road West, June 2004. Courtesy of Yong He, photographer.

its launch in 1992.[17] However, according to Jiang Yifeng, a senior editor of *Shanghai Style* who investigated luxury stores like PCD Stores, Jin Jiang Dickson Center, and Maison Mode in Shanghai in 1996, very few luxury brands seemed to have actually made money by then, considering their high investments in stores and marketing, high tariffs and luxury taxes, and the limited size of the market. A department manager in Shanghai's PCD Stores told Jiang, "It looks like none of the brands [sold in PCD] is making a profit."[18] However, getting into the fast-growing market first and getting acquainted with Chinese consumers proved a worthy investment over the long run. As Pollo Zegna told Jiang: "Although the Chinese market accounted for the smallest share in the Zegna global family, it is the most loved as the Zegna family sees it as a child."[19] The child grew up quickly. Zegna first entered China in 1991 in Beijing's Palace Hotel and had expanded to nineteen shops by 1999 and to fifty-two by early 2005.[20] Its three-story flagship store in Shanghai's luxury property, Bund 18, opened in January 2005, becoming Zegna's largest store in Asia.[21] Only a month before, Bund 18 had celebrated the opening ceremony of Cartier's flagship store with local celebrities and other luxury patrons who arrived wrapped in LV furs and carrying LV handbags (Fig. 8.5).

**Figure 8.5**   The opening of Cartier's flagship store in December 2004 at Shanghai's luxury property, Bund 18, attended by Chinese celebrities and prestigious luxury patrons. Courtesy of Yong He, photographer.

Armani also first tackled the Chinese market in large urban centers like Beijing and Shanghai, opening the Giorgio Armani boutique in Beijing's Palace Hotel in 1998, his first shop in China. In 2002, he launched the Armani/Chater House in Hong Kong, his largest multibrand store outside of Milan.[22] In 2004, Boutique Giorgio Armani, Emporio Armani, Armani Fiori, and Armani Dolci all opened in Shanghai's prominent high-end shopping space, Three on the Bund.[23] Armani sells not only suits but also accessories, cosmetics, calla lilies, and chocolates to Chinese luxury hunters. To celebrate the opening of his first store in Shanghai, Armani paid his first visit to China in April 2004 (Fig. 8.6). His impression of Shanghai explained his ambitious and aggressive expansion in China: "I don't know that the Chinese realize how futuristic Shanghai is, how much more avant-garde it is than, say, New York was, or Chicago, or Paris, or any of these other big cities."[24] However, despite the double-digit growth rate in retail sales in greater China, Paul Wight, Armani's China retail director, admitted that Armani's stores are not yet profitable in China.[25]

Nevertheless, luxury stores continued to open all over China. As the number of rich inlanders rose and brands began reaping profits, luxury stores expanded to second- or third-tier inland cities, often through franchising or licensing arrangements. By 2008, Louis Vuitton had stores in eighteen cities scattered across China from the northern cities of Changchun and Shenyang to southern cities like Sanya and Kunming. And Armani stores have also opened in both coastal and inland cities like

**Figure 8.6** Giorgio Armani's fashion show in Shanghai celebrating the opening of his first store in Shanghai in April 2004, when the designer first visited China. Courtesy of Yong He, photographer.

Dalian, Wenzhou, Chengdu, Chongqing, Guangzhou, Hangzhou, Harbin, Kunming, Nanjing, Qingdao, Suzhou, Tianjin, and Wuhan.

## Luxury Brands and Class

By the early years of the new millennium, the hype surrounding Western brands was apparent not only in the clothing and accessory industries—an obsession with brand names permeated all aspects of material culture, from food, cell phones, cars, home furnishings, and houses to lifestyles. Thanks to their initial positioning, many popular Western fast-food and coffee chains were considered affordable "luxury" brands by the masses. McDonald's, Kentucky Fried Chicken, Pizza Hut, and Starbucks became more than popular places to eat or have a coffee, turning into fashionable places to hang out with friends, colleagues, or business associates. The buzz surrounding Western brand names and Western culture has penetrated all aspects of urban life. White-collar urban workers grew accustomed to calling each other by English names. And consumers of all classes could readily identify the brand names that matched their own socioeconomic stations, as Mao's egalitarian China rapidly stratified upon the arrival of Western brand names.

As Chinese society became increasingly unequal and the gap between rich and poor expanded, the elite coalesced in order to advance or reconfirm their social standing. For example, in May 1993, the "Richman Club" was founded in Shanghai for the nouveau riche. As its not so subtle name implied, members of the Richman Club were eager to display their newfound status—members had a conspicuous letter R and their names embroidered on their clothing to signify their membership in this exclusive club.[26] The famous Chang'an Club, founded the same year in Beijing, attracted owners and CEOs of global businesses. Club members paid a $9,000 initiation fee (a staggering sum in China at the time). By 2008 the initiation fee had climbed to $20,000, with a $1,500 annual membership fee. The Owen Salon, founded in 1996 in Beijing, excluded entrepreneurs whose net worth was less than 300 million *yuan*.[27] While the richest Chinese formed their clubs and salons, less affluent but equally class-conscious white-collar women in Shanghai found ways to display their class solidarity through brands: the Italian shoe brand Le Saunda and the American shoe brand Nine West.[28]

While during the nonmaterialistic 80s socially appropriate topics of conversation were college life, books, poets, philosophers, novelists, and movies, in the 90s interest shifted to more materialistic concerns. Conversation turned to business, the stock market, brand names, and condos. This new obsession with material wealth encouraged luxury consumption not only among the elite, but also among the aspiring middle class. *Fortune* magazine described how Zhao Xinyu got her first Prada:

> It was 1990. After years as a soprano with the Harbin Opera, she had moved to Beijing ... she and a couple of friends launched a nightclub—and hit the jackpot. Zhao

remembers marching to a luxury boutique at Beijing's Palace Hotel, her pockets bulging with cash, and pacing back and forth in front of the shop window for a "very long time" before plunging inside. For a single Prada handbag, she counted out a stack of notes worth $1,000—more money than the average Beijinger would see in a year. She thought the purchase so extravagant that for months after, she says, "I hardly dared use the bag for fear I'd wear it out."[29]

By 2004 Zhao had become a regular patron of the latest Prada, Dior, and YSL, often spending thousands of dollars per month, supported by her husband's flourishing real estate business. "I'll scrimp on food, but not on clothes," she said.[30] Her attitude toward clothes and brand names is typical of middle- and upper-class Chinese of the new millennium.

As getting rich has become the main goal of China, luxury consumption became both a means and an end. Besides the enjoyment of spending, the prestige embedded in brand names served as a tool for social and economic advancement. This mentality was perfectly encapsulated by fashion critic Ka Fei: "Famous brands aren't food, but at least they enable you to obtain food more easily."[31] Clothes are highly visible symbols of status, and luxury brands in particular usually feature a conspicuous logo or identifiable patterns. When most people in the country had limited means to display wealth and to communicate identity, dress seemed an easily accessible choice for everyone. A nicely dressed body communicates wealth and career success. Thus, an individual clad in high-quality branded clothes tends to receive nicer social treatment and also has better opportunities for social advancement. While this is certainly the case in every society, in a traditionally hierarchical society like China, theses forces are exaggerated. As a result, branded fashion is not trivial in post-Mao Chinese life, especially since the 1990s, when Chinese suddenly encountered so many Western brands.

In the meantime, the rapidly emerging middle class started to make more expensive purchases like cars and houses in the suburbs. Audi, Mercedes, Porsche, and BMW became favored auto brands. Bentley, Ferrari, Hummer, and Rolls-Royce have also become popular with China's superrich. Bentley sold 338 cars in greater China in 2007, a 93 percent increase over the previous year. And the mainland market has become its fifth largest and fastest-growing market worldwide (Fig. 8.7).[32] China has also taken over Japan and become the largest Asian market for Rolls-Royce.[33] With all the buzz surrounding luxury cars and lifestyles, Formula One auto racing made a timely debut in Shanghai in 2004. And the city has been hosting Formula One races annually since then. To make the racing events even more luxurious, organizers scheduled Italian high-fashion shows during intermissions between races (Fig. 8.8). Responding to China's growing appetite for luxury, the annual global luxury exhibition Top Marques Shanghai launched in 2005 with a staggering 250 million *yuan* in sales.[34]

Luxury brands have become one of the biggest beneficiaries of China's booming economy. By September 2008 Armani had expanded to fifty-seven stores in

**Figure 8.7** A day laborer pulls his cart past a conspicuous Bentley billboard on Nanjing Road West in Shanghai, October 2004. Courtesy of Yong He, photographer.

greater China, with ten more slated to open. Hugo Boss has stores in forty-one cities in China. Salvatore Ferragamo is present in nineteen cities. And Louis Vuitton has over thirty stores in greater China. In fact, the world's largest luxury company, LVMH Group, which houses fashion and leather goods brands like Louis Vuitton, Givenchy, Celine, Kenzo, Donna Karan, and Fendi as well as Dior, Kenzo, and Givenchy perfumes, had thirty-one brands in China in October 2007 and over 900 retail stores in more than thirty-five cities across the country.[35] The sales figures from these many stores have also been impressive in the new millennium. For example, sales for Gucci China rose 168 percent in 2007, after a 65 percent increase in the previous year. And Ferragamo also reported a 34.2 percent rise in its record net profit in 2007.[36]

As luxury consumption in the Chinese market began to thrive in the 2000s, Chinese also began to frequent luxury stores overseas as international travel for work and leisure became more widespread. After the government relaxed visa restrictions to Hong Kong in July 2003, increasing numbers of tourists from the mainland visited Hong Kong. The sales of luxury stores in Hong Kong also expanded. Statistics from the Hong Kong Tourism Board revealed that Chinese tourists spend the most per capita among all tourists to Hong Kong.[37] According to Chinese custom, travelers are obligated to bring back gifts for relatives, colleagues, and friends after long journeys, which probably contributes to Chinese spending habits abroad.

**Figure 8.8**    An Italian fashion show during a Formula One car race in Shanghai, June 6, 2004. Courtesy of Yong He, photographer.

European luxury retailers, especially in France and Italy, also began to see a stream of Chinese tourists making large cash purchases as European countries conditionally opened to Chinese tourism after September 2004. Paris's upscale Galeries Lafayette department store began posting signs in Mandarin and is equipped with Mandarin-speaking staff to accommodate Chinese tourists.[38] "Chinese travelers are now the 'fourth or fifth' largest tourist market for Vuitton, and the company is working to install Mandarin-speaking sales in its key stores ... prices for Vuitton are roughly ten percent less in Hong Kong and twenty-five percent less in Europe than in Mainland China due to luxury taxes," reported *Women's Wear Daily* on December 29, 2005. In December 2007, the United States and China signed an agreement to bring in Chinese tourists to the United States, hoping to boost consumption through the lavish spending of Chinese tourists.[39]

Unlike in the rest of the world, where women make up the key customer base for luxury goods, in China luxury clients in the 1990s were mostly middle-aged men. They accounted for 90 percent of sales when male-oriented brands like Hugo Boss, Zegna, and Dunhill thrived.[40] Early luxury consumers sought out Pierre Cardin suits, Rolex watches, and Louis Vuitton briefcases. As Bernard Arnault, Louis Vuitton's chairman and chief executive officer, commented at the reopening of the China World store in 2005, "Our customer at first was the entrepreneur, who had to have the Louis Vuitton briefcase and the Rolex watch. A few years ago, we started to cater to his wife. Today, the customer is already a very sophisticated buyer, similar to internationally."[41] The broadening luxury customer base opened up more opportunities in women's fashion and other product areas such as household furnishings, fragrances, and cosmetics.

China's luxury consumer base is mainly made up of entrepreneurs of state-owned and private-owned enterprises, business executives, bankers, real estate moguls, mine owners, expatriates, and governmental officials. Over the last two decades, movie stars and athletes also arose as prominent luxury patrons, with many of them frequently attending promotional events for luxury brands. They have also appeared in ad campaigns. Another growing luxury consumption market is constituted by the so-called *haigui* (sea turtles)—Chinese who have studied or worked in the West and have returned to China with their PhDs and MBAs, along with their high-paying executive or management positions. Furthermore, the number of expats living in China from all over the world has also exploded, while twenty years ago expats in China mainly hailed from Hong Kong and Taiwan.

A rapidly expanding middle class that aspires to live a luxury lifestyle has also become an important market for luxury products. Hong Huang, a media mogul and publisher of the glossy magazine *iLook,* contended that maintaining "the status quo and doing well materially is probably the number one priority for the Chinese middle class."[42] It is not uncommon for middle-class women holding office jobs to save up for months for a Louis Vuitton handbag. According to *National Geographic,* the Chinese middle class numbered between 100 million and 150 million people in 2008. "Though definitions vary—household income of at least $10,000 a year is one standard—middle-class families tend to own an apartment and a car, to eat out and take vacations, and to be familiar with foreign brands and ideas."[43]

In middle-class urban families, the generation born during the reform era in the 1980s and 1990s has adjusted to a new lifestyle characterized by the regular consumption of foreign brands. They grew up in a less frugal environment and are more in tune with international fashion than the previous generation. Their childhood memories are associated with KFC, Coca-Cola, Häagen-Dazs, and the internet. They like brands from iPod to Izod. Thus, they tend to be more susceptible to brand-name marketing. Most of them still live with and are financially supported by their parents. In most cases, due to China's one-child policy, they are only children who have been pampered since birth. They wear Versace jeans and Nike shoes while their parents may still cling to their own habits of frugality born of hardship. This new generation buys luxury goods mainly for themselves while their parents buy or use luxury goods mainly for or through gift giving.

According to Andrew Wu, LVMH's Group Director for China, luxury consumption in China has been influenced by the herd mentality that was prevalent during the Cultural Revolution.[44] As a considerable portion of the population came to view luxury products as an affordable necessity, the drive to conform spurs the rich as well as the middle class to become luxury consumers. And the consumption of global brands makes the younger generation more confident when global jobs put them at the same table with Western competitors.

Growing up amid China's growing prosperity and increasing prominence on the world stage, this new generation also exhibit greater confidence in their own nation and rally quickly to the defense of their national pride. This newfound confidence and sensitivity has not escaped the notice of big brands. For instance, to avoid upsetting Chinese consumers, especially the young cyber generation, the LVMH Group dropped Sharon Stone from Dior ads in China in 2008 shortly after she "suggested the May 12 earthquake that killed more than 68,000 may have been 'karma' for the nation's treatment of Tibet."[45] This incident occurred only one month after the Chinese internet community called for boycotts of French retailers such as Carrefour and luxury brands like Louis Vuitton after Paris protests disrupted the Olympic torch relay in April 2008. Boycotts were soon expanded to other Western businesses such as McDonald's and KFC. This anti-Western backlash was seen as justified by the Chinese mainstream, including MIT graduate Charles Zhang, who runs Sohu.com, one of China's biggest Web sites. "That was the first time Chinese people as a whole stood up to the world," he says. "It's good for Chinese people ... That incident proves that when Chinese are upset, they can find their voice."[46]

Under the influence of nationalism promoted by the media, this slightly self-conscious but confident young generation is seeking outlets to express their own aesthetic, one that is no longer entirely identified with Western standards and values. This generation is also attempting to differentiate itself from their parents' generation, who opted for Western aesthetics. This may partially explain the Japan and Korean crazes in urban youth fashion in China. Vivienne Tam, a New York–based designer who was born on the mainland but moved to Hong Kong at the age of three, said that she looks forward to the day when "Chinese people have enough self-confidence to support their own luxury brands and stop buying stuff just because it comes from somewhere else."[47] As a well-established designer in the West known for her use of Asian design elements, Tam "insisted on stocking her new Shanghai boutique with items featuring the same Asian design elements she uses outside China and keeping labels identifying her clothing as 'Made in China.'"[48] This day that Tam looks forward to may not be far off—and once it arrives Armani will perhaps need to change the doors of his Chinese stores again.

But at present the luxury market is entirely dominated by global brands. Domestic designers Zhang Da, Wang Yiyang, and Wang Wei all agreed that Chinese brands should target the midrange market niche. It has taken decades for luxury brands to establish their global fame, and Chinese brands all lack a history, an essential ingredient of a luxury brand. Meanwhile, at the lower end of branded fashion, global chain stores are extremely competitive because of their huge investments in expansion. Stressing fast fashion, Spanish brand Zara quickly hit in Beijing, Shanghai, Hangzhou, Harbin, Nanjing, Shenzhen, and Tianjin within two years of its initial opening in 2006 in

**Figure 8.9**   On July 25, 2005, a Chinese employee of Walmart adjusts his gear as the forty-eighth Walmart store in China opens. Courtesy of Yong He, photographer.

China. Swedish H&M stores also attract China's brand-conscious and price-sensitive urban youngsters. Big-box discount retailers such as Walmart, Carrefour, and Lotus have also made their way into the low-end fashion market (Fig. 8.9).

Despite the exclusivity foreign luxury brands enjoy in the Chinese market vis-à-vis domestic brands, the Chinese market is still full of traps and pitfalls. Piracy is a global issue luxury brands face, and markets selling fake luxury brands have been thriving in China for years. Fake luxury brands, copying Gucci, Chanel, Burberry, Louis Vuitton, and Dior, are readily available all over the county. Bruno Sälzer, chairman and CEO of Hugo Boss, told *China International Business* (November 8, 2007), "If you go into the fake market and your brand is not there, but all the others—Gucci, Louis Vuitton—are there, then something is wrong."

The fast-growing economy and the correspondingly vast changes in society, such as the direction of development, also present a challenge, according to Bruno Sälzer. "Take Fifth Avenue in New York: it is always Fifth Avenue," he said; it is a fixed area where the economy and city are more mature. But the high growth rate in Shanghai and Beijing leads to a situation in which "you may have today a very perfect area, and it could be that in two years' [time] there is a new area coming up, a new place where it makes sense for us to be. This makes it very challenging, to always be in the hotspots of such cities."

# Epilogue

As China unofficially abandoned communism in the reform era, it also discarded the looks, styles, and aesthetics of communism. Despite China's efforts to select economic reform à la carte from the West, capitalism came to China packaged with Western consumer culture, Western fashions, and Western aesthetics. However, the process of fashioning China was not without its hesitations, struggles, negotiations, and pains. The separation of fashion from morality and political ideology finally legitimized the expression of individuality—in opposition to both communist collectivism and traditional conformist values.

However, the same tension between modernization and Westernization that the Chinese experienced at the beginning of the twentieth century was once again intensified during the reform era. Did modernization mean Westernization? In fashion, the answer seemed to be yes. In the span of a decade, ordinary Chinese exchanged their Mao suits for Western suits. And subsequently Chinese fashion designers abandoned Chinese-style designs for those geared toward international standards. It seemed that five thousand years of splendid sartorial culture got lost somewhere on the road to modernization.

Consequently, a new tension arose between the Chinese desire to leave the isolation of the past behind to become citizens of world and the desire to remain Chinese. The search for a sartorial symbol to mark Chinese identity coincided with the rediscovery of Chinese aesthetics in fashion design. Ultimately, Chinese aesthetics—not made-in-China garments—will define Chineseness in fashion and authenticate Chinese designs. The quest for this new aesthetic that melds Chineseness with Western culture led the younger generation to turn to Japanese and Korean fashions and pop cultures.

The revival of China's own pop culture, which the West and China's neighbors influenced in multiple ways, provided rich inspirations for Chinese fashion throughout the reform era. Mass fashions were more closely tied to the music industry, television, cinema, and print media than the apparel industry, especially in the 1980s and 1990s. Chinese fashion designers have yet to acquire the kind of influence in China that Western designers such as Charles Worth, Chanel, Yves Saint Laurent, Mary Quant, or Ralph Lauren have had on fashion in the West. Instead, pop idols, who served as both fashion icons and cultural ideals, influenced the ways young Chinese dressed and expressed their own individuality—with Chinese characteristics.

Chinese women in particular found greater freedom to express and define themselves through personal adornment as they continued their century-long journey from an exquisite but confined imperial femininity to an "iron" asexuality to sexually liberated independence. The female body, masked and draped and concealed for millennia in China—even after the so-called liberation of 1949 and through the Mao era—has finally been publicly unmasked in both art and fashion, giving women more space in which to define their physical and spiritual femininity.

But as the pursuit of material wealth took precedence over the "spiritual civilization" that socialist China once took as its goal, China moved from a supposedly classless, equitable poverty to an increasingly stratified, class-conscious society. Class differences proved harder to erase than Mao Zedong could have ever imagined. But the great disparity in economic and social standing between urban centers and rural villages has made fashion itself a luxury for the majority of Chinese, and Chinese fashion is still in many ways Chinese urban fashion.

Deeply influenced by Confucianism, China remains prone to hierarchical order. This order was reestablished in the post-Mao era based upon material wealth and consumption in place of family background and heritage. In search of high social status, the newly rich embraced Western luxury brands. But intense feelings of patriotism and nationalism, along with the potential for instability and social strife, bring uncertainty to the future of luxury global brands in China. As prominent symbols of the West in China, global brands are easy targets of patriotic and nationalist sentiment—sentiments that may also eventually lead to the cultivation of China's own luxury brands.

Many see the worldwide economic downturn in 2008 as China's opportunity to switch from an export-oriented economy to one driven by satisfying internal needs. Although it will inevitably be affected by this economic storm, China's vast markets (both actual and potential) along with the wealth China has accumulated over the past thirty years of high-speed development still mean big business, in fashion as well as in other fields.

The history of the reform era, and of modern China itself, is still being written in, and partially by, the clothes people design, wear, and consume. As post-Mao China continues its rise, the issues of national identity, gender, modernization, and globalization will continue to intersect with fashion, creating new meanings, new controversies, and new fashions.

# Notes

## Preface

1. Alix Browne, "It Is Always Inspiring to See Dior through Someone Else's Eyes," *New York Times Magazine,* December 7, 2008.

## 1. The Post-Mao Fashion Revival

1. Roderick Macfarquhar and Michael Schoenhals, *Mao's Last Revolution* (Cambridge, MA: Belknap Press of Harvard University Press, 2006), 116.

2. Paulette Flahavin, "Chinese Fashion Blossoms," *Christian Science Monitor,* July 23, 1987.

3. Feng Weiguo, "Qingshen yigao—fang Beijing hong du shizhuang gongsi gaoji fuzhuang shi Tian Atong" [Deep Feelings and High Skills—Interview with Master Clothing Maker at the Beijing Hong Du Clothing Company], *China Garment* 1 (1986), 40.

4. Xue Yan, ed., *Shishang bainian: 20 shiji zhongguo fuzhuang* [A Century of Fashion: Chinese Dress in the 20th Century] (Hangzhou: Zhongguo Meishu Xueyuan Chubanshe, 2004), 108.

5. Zhang Jingqiong, *Xifu dongjian—20 shiji zhongwai fushi jiaoliu shi* [Western Dress Migrates to the East—Exchange of Chinese and Foreign Dress in the 20th Century] (Hehui: Anhui Meishu Chubanshe, 2002), 63.

6. *Wenhua yu shenghuo* [Culture and Life] 1 (1979), 51.

7. Joan Lebold Cohen and Jerome Alan Cohen, *China Today,* 2nd ed. (New York: Harry N. Abrams, 1980), 325–27.

8. Valerie Steele and John Major, *China Chic: East Meets West* (New Haven: Yale University Press, 1999), 64–65.

9. Wang Weiming, "Shizhuang: Yige shidai de xinhao" [Fashion: Sign of the Times], *Shanghai Style* 1 (1994), 10–11.

10. Yu Qiuyu, "Dui sige zhongda wenti de jinji huida" [Urgent Answers to Four Important Questions], Yu Qiuyu's Blog, posted March 26, 2007, http://blog.sina.com.cn/u/46e94efe010008ti (accessed July 16, 2007).

11. Ibid.

12. Liu Qing, "1983 nian shui zai fanzui" [Who Was Committing Crimes in 1983], *Zhongguo sixing guancha* [China Death Penalty Watch], http://www.china monitor.org/news/yanda/83sfz.htm (accessed July 8, 2007).

13. Ma Licheng and Ling Zhijun, *Jiaofeng: dangdai zhongguo sanci sixiang jiefang shilu* [Crossed Swords: Record of the Three Mind Emancipations in Contemporary China] (Beijing: Jinri Zhongguo Chubanshe, 1998), http://www.guangzhou.gov.cn/files/zjyc/jf/004.htm (accessed September 1, 2008).

14. Zhang, *Xifu dongjian—20 shiji zhongwai fushi jiaoliu shi,* 68.

15. Guan Deliang, "Ershisan ming qinggong jiandiao chang toufa" [Twenty-Three Young Workers Have Their Long Hair Cut Off], *Xinmin Evening News,* February 26, 1982.

16. Ibid.

17. Zhang Zhiming, "Duo yidian ziran mei" [A Little More Natural Beauty], *Xinmin Evening News,* March 12, 1982.

18. Ibid.

19. See *Xinmin Evening News,* January 23, 1982, and *Xinmin Evening News,* January 25, 1982.

20. Wang Guorong, "Xiaojie shan, shenshi xue zhilei" [Miss Shirt, Gentlemen Boots, etc.], *Xinmin Evening News,* October 16, 1982.

21. Ma and Ling, *Jiaofeng: dangdai zhongguo sanci sixiang jiefang shilu.*

22. Guo Siwen, "Tan yindao—cong qingnianren de fashi he kujiao tanqi" [Discussing Guidance—Starting from Youth Hairstyle and Trouser Legs]," *China Youth* 6 (1979): 20–21.

23. Ibid.

24. Ibid.

25. Yang Fan, "Kan wo zhongguoren bian bian bian: 25 nian liuxing quan jilu" [Witness the Changes in Chinese: A Complete Record of Fashion over 25 years], *Wenhui Weekly* 9 (2003).

26. Ibid.

27. Pan Xiao, "Rensheng de lu a, zenme yue zou yue zhai ..." [The Road of Life Ah, How It Got Narrower and Narrower ...], *China Youth* 5 (1980).

28. Tan Fuyun, "Wei Shanghai fushi shiye tuibo zhulan" [Add Fuel to the Fire of Shanghai's Apparel Industry], *Shanghai fuzhuang nianjian* [Shanghai Apparel Yearbook] (1985), 5–7.

## 2. The Spread of Fashion through Mass Media

1. Jonathan D. Spence, *The Search for Modern China* (New York: Norton, 1991), 672.

2. Yi Hong, "Yiyi, shengchan, xiaofei: dianshiju de lishi yu xianshi" [Meaning, Production, and Consumption: The History and Current Situation of TV Dramas],

*China Broadcast and Television Yearbook,* posted January 8, 2007, http://media.people.com.cn/GB/22100/76588/76590/5258957.html (accessed July 13, 2007).

3. Pan Xinhua, "Shisi yingcun mingpai dianshiji weihe nanmai" [Why Is It Difficult to Buy a 14" Brand Name Television Set?], *Xinmin Evening News,* July 8, 1983.

4. Jiang Hua and Juanjuan Wu, "Fengshang shisan dian—Shanghai 1970–1999" [Fashion in the Past—Shanghai 1970–1999], *Metropolis* 6 (2000), 72–75.

5. Yue Xiao, "'Gaozi shan' yu 'lao fan xin'" ['Gaozi Shirt' and 'Revamping the Old'], *Beautifying Life* 1 (1983), 36–37.

6. Shanghai fuzhuang yanjiu suo [Shanghai Garment Research Institution], ed., *Shanghai Apparel Yearbook* (Shanghai: Zhishi Chubanshe, 1985), 35.

7. Yang Fan, "Kan wo zhongguoren bian bian bian: 25 nian liuxing quan jilu" [Witness the Changes in Chinese: A Complete Record of Fashion over 25 Years], *Wenhui Weekly* 9 (2003).

8. *Shanghai dianshi* [Shanghai TV] 1 (1982), 21.

9. Guangzhou Television Web site, http://news.gztv.com/commend/node_1004/node_1027/2007/08/15/118720521482328.shtml (accessed April 25, 2008).

10. Ibid.

11. Ba Jin, "Tan 'wangxiang'" [Discussion of Sandakan Brothel No. 8], in *Suixiang lu* [Whimsy Collection] (Beijing: Zuojia Chubanshe, 2005), http://book.sina.com.cn/nzt/his/suixianglu/6.shtml (accessed September 6, 2008).

### 3. From Asexual to Unisex

1. Su Su, *Qianshi jinsheng* [Life Then, Life Now] (Shanghai: Shanghai Yuandong Chubanshe, 1996), 43.

2. Lei Shi, "Jindai shanghai fushi yanjiu ji shanghai shi danan guan de xiangguan ziliao" [Study Of Shanghai Clothing and Accessories in Modern Times and Related Materials from the Shanghai Municipal Archives], *Danan yu shixue* [Archives and History] 1 (2001): 74–78.

3. Martha Huang, "A Woman Has So Many Parts to Her Body, Life Is Very Hard Indeed," in *China Chic: East Meets West,* ed. Valerie Steele and John S. Major (New Haven: Yale University Press, 1999), 133.

4. Su, *Qianshi jinsheng,* 46.

5. W. T. Tsien, "Chinese Women and Dresses," *Shanghai Puck* 1, no. 4 (1918): 21.

6. Eileen Chang, "A Chronicle of Changing Clothes," trans. Andrew F. Jones, *Positions* 11, no. 2 (2003): 425–41.

7. Ibid.

8. Huang, "A Woman Has So Many Parts to Her Body, Life Is Very Hard Indeed," 139.

9. Antonia Finnane, "What Should Chinese Women Wear?: A National Problem," *Modern China* 22, no. 2 (April 1996): 112.

10. Huang "A Woman Has So Many Parts to Her Body, Life Is Very Hard Indeed," 139.

11. Finnane, "What Should Chinese Women Wear?: A National Problem," 114.

12. Louise Edwards, "Policing the Modern Woman in Republic China," *Modern China* 26, no. 2 (April 2000): 115–47.

13. Ibid.

14. Jonathan D. Spence, *The Search for Modern China* (New York: Norton, 1990), 415–16.

15. Ibid.

16. Emily Honig, *Personal Voices: Chinese Women in the 1980's* (Stanford University Press, 1988), 4.

17. Elisabeth Croll, *Changing Identities of Chinese Women: Rhetoric, Experience and Self-Perception in Twentieth-Century China* (London: Zed Books, 1995), 153.

18. Zha Jianying, *Bashi niandai fangtan lu* [Interviews: The 1980s] (Beijing: Sanlian Shudian, 2006), 452.

19. James P. Sterba, "Peking's Women in Fashions, Men in Undershirts," *New York Times,* July 29, 1981.

20. Michael Weisskopf, "Shanghai Chic: China Discovers Fashion; More Ruffles and Frills, Fewer Mao Uniforms," *Washington Post,* February 9, 1984.

21. *Women of China* 6, 1980, p. 32.

22. *Women of China* 10, 1991, p. 12.

23. Li Yan, "20 shiji 80 niandai Shanghai funv fushi liuxing" [Shanghai Women's Fashion in the 1980s], (master's thesis, Donghua University, 2002), 61.

24. Ibid., 65.

25. Ibid., 61.

26. Mai Tong, "Ganga de shishang" [Embarrassing Fashion], *Shanghai Style* 2 (1994), 10.

27. Acang, "Yonggan de 'ta' xiaqu" [Courageously Step Onward], *Shanghai Fashion Times,* June 1, 1992, section 1.

28. Croll, *Changing Identities of Chinese Women,* 73.

29. James P. Sterba, "Peking's Women in Fashions, Men in Undershirts," *New York Times,* July 29, 1981.

30. Zha Jianying, *China Pop* (New York: New Press, 1995), 158.

31. Ibid.

32. *Shanghai Apparel Yearbook* (1985), image plate no. 36–37.

33. Elizabeth Wilson, *Adorned in Dreams: Fashion and Modernity* (New Jersey: Rutgers University Press, 2003), 162.

34. Ibid., 165.

35. Lin Shengqing, "Meiguo dianying cheng—haolaiwu" [American City of Film—Hollywood], *Wenhua yu shenghuo* [Culture and Life] 3 (1979), 24–25.

36. *Xinmin Evening News,* February 25, 1982, 4.

37. Shi Lei, "Jindai shanghai fushi yanjiu ji shanghai shi danan guan de xiangguan ziliao" [Study of Shanghai Clothing and Accessories in Modern Times and

Related Materials from the Shanghai Municipal Archives], *Danan yu shixue* [Archives and History] 1 (2001): 74–78.

38. *The Economist,* April 14, 1984, World Politics and Current Affairs section, U.S. edition, 50.

39. "Lingdao tongzhi tan fuzhuang" [Leader Cadres Talk about Dress], in *Shanghai Apparel Yearbook* (1985), 1.

40. R. Zachary, "As Business Rolls In, the Western Suit Makes a Comeback in China," *International Herald Tribune,* March 5, 2005.

41. *The Economist,* April 14, 1984, World Politics and Current Affairs section, U.S. edition, 50.

42. Zhang, *Xifu dongjian—20 shiji zhongwai fushi jiaoliu shi,* 67.

43. Zhang, N., "Xiongmao chenshan" [Panda Shirts], *Southern Metropolitan Daily,* 156 (2004).

44. Wang Li, "Yanguan qunfang, yizhong quan qiu—qianjin zhong de beijing chenshan chang" [The Prettiest of All, Fame around the Globe—the Growing Beijing Shirt Factory], *Fashion* 4 (1985), 6.

45. *China Textile News* 4 (1986), 4.

46. Valerie Steele, *Paris Fashion,* 2nd ed. (Oxford: Berg, 1998), 283.

47. Nicholas Kristof, "Beijing Journal: Even Gloomy T-Shirts Fall Under Censorship," *New York Times,* July 29, 1991, World section.

48. Ibid.

49. Ibid.

50. Bao Mingxin and Wu Juanjuan, *Shimao cidian* [Fashion Dictionary] (Shanghai: Shanghai Wenhua Chubanshe, 1999), 140.

51. *The Economist,* April 14, 1984.

52. Zhuang Shan and Yao Dongmei, "Huaxue shan: Cong dansheng dao liuxing" [Ski Jacket: From Birth to Popularity], *Xinmin Evening News,* December 12, 1981.

53. Shen Zhong and Lu Jinhong, "Wuxi jietou yi dongjing: Wuzhi guitai heyi jita? Zhiwei zhenggou yurong yishan" [A Winter Scene on a Street of Wuxi: Why Were Five Counters Smashed? Just to Rush to Buy Down Jackets], *China Textile News,* February 1, 1988, section 2.

54. Nan Ni, "Meiyou dongtian" [There Is No Winter], *Shanghai Style* 1 (1995), 33.

55. Joan Lebold Cohen and Jerome Alan Cohen, *China Today,* 2nd ed. (New York: Harry N. Abrams, 1980), 335.

56. Zha Jianying, *China Pop,* 105.

57. Ibid., 129.

## 4. Fashion in Print

1. See *China Youth* 2 (1979), 46; *China Youth* 5 (1979), 20; *China Youth* 6 (1980), 20–21; *China Youth* 5 (1980), 36; *China Youth* 12 (1984), 58; *China Youth* 4 (1989), 42.

2. *Women of China* 5 (1979), 48.

3. Bao Mingxin and Ma Ni, *Shizhuang pinglun* [Fashion Criticism] (Chongqing: Xinan Shifan Daxue Chubanshe, 2002), 43.

4. Wang Jing, "Chinese Popular Cultural Studies: A Luce Project, 1997–2001," The Faculty Forum at Duke University 10, no. 1 (September 1998), http://www.duke.edu/web/FacultyForum/vol10/ffsept98.htm (accessed April 15, 2008).

5. Wang Jing, "Chinese Popular Cultural Studies: A Luce Project, 1997–2001," The Faculty Forum at Duke University 10.1 September 1998, http://www.duke.edu/web/FacultyForum/vol10/ffsept98.htm (accessed April 15, 2008).

6. Wang Jing and Leo Ching, "China and the Ideology of Asianism," The Faculty Forum at Duke University 10.1 (1998), http://www.duke.edu/web/Faculty Forum/vol10/ffsept98.htm (accessed April 15, 2008).

7. Bao and Ma, *Shizhuang pinglun,* 44.

8. See *Shizhuang L'OFFICIEL,* http://women.sohu.com/20060621/n243860309.shtml (accessed September 6, 2008).

9. Editorial, *Fashion* 1 (1980).

10. Valerie Steele and John Major, *China Chic: East Meets West* (New Haven: Yale University Press, 1999), 63.

11. Tan Fuyun, "Fa kan ci" [Foreword], *Shanghai Style* 1 (1985), 1.

12. Yi, F., "Clothing—Mirror of Era," *Modern Dress and Dress Making* 1 (1985), 10.

13. Bao Mingxin and Ma Ni, *Shizhuang pinglun* [Fashion Criticism] (Chongqing: Xinan Shifan Daxue Chubanshe, 2002), 8.

14. Wu Juanjuan, ed., *Bao Mingxing jiedu shizhuang* [Bao Mingxin Decoding Fashion] (Shanghai: Xuelin Chubanshe, 1999), 181.

15. See *Shizhuang* (Fashion) 2 (1988), p.14.

16. Hong Huang, *Wo de fei zhengchang shenghuo* [My Abnormal Life], Sina's Reading Channel, posted August 7, 2003, http://book.sina.com.cn/myabnormallife/2003-08-07/3/13900.shtml (accessed May 17, 2009).

17. Hong Huang's blog, "Di yi kou bingqilin" [The First Bite of Ice Cream], posted July 10, 2008, http://blog.sina.com.cn/s/blog_476bdd0a01009x5i.html (accessed September 14, 2008).

18. See the cover of *Shanghai Style* 9 (2001).

19. See the cover of *Shishang* [Cosmopolitan] 1 (2007).

20. See the cover of *How* 3 (2001).

21. Yu Lei, "Wuo dongle yule quan—yige yuji qinli de yule shijian" [I Touched the Entertainment Circle—Incidents in the Entertainment Industry Experienced by an Entertainment Journalist] (Nanchang: 21 Shiji Chubanshe, 2004), http://book.sina.com.cn/longbook/1079504063_wodongleyulequan/30.shtml (accessed September 30, 2008).

22. Bao Mingxin and Wu Juanjuan, *Shimao cidian* [Fashion dictionary] (Shanghai: Shanghai Wenhua Chubanshe, 1999), 49.

23. Chen Jian, "Shuo bu jin de xingxiang sheji huati" [Endless Issues on Image Design], *Shanghai Style* 1 (2000), 47.

24. Bao and Ma, *Shizhuang pinglun,* 59.

25. Ibid., 59.

26. Xie Geng, "Xin linian xia de baozhi banshi" [Newspaper Layout], http://www.my9w.com/baozhibanmian/banmianxinshang/index.htm (accessed April 2, 2008).

27. Hou Hongbin, "Vogue jinru zhongguo, zhongguo shishang zazhi chongxin xipai?" [Vogue Entering China Reshuffles Chinese Fashion Magazines?], *Southern Metropolitan Daily,* August 29, 2005.

28. Ibid.

29. Seth Faison, "A Chinese Edition of Elle Draws Ads and Readers," *New York Times,* January 1, 1996.

30. Ibid.

31. Ibid.

32. Ibid.

33. Claire Wilson, "Elle's Foreign Forays Open Door in China," *Advertising Age,* March 14, 1988.

34. Sarah Woodall, "Elle's Belle—China Gets Its First Glossy: Whether This Will Be a Fine Romance or Merely a Doomed Affair," *Campaign,* July 29, 1988.

35. Wilson, "Elle's Foreign Forays Open Door in China."

36. Woodall, "Elle's Belle."

37. Interview with the director and editor-in-chief of *Fashion,* August 14, 2003, http://eladies.sina.com.cn/2003–08–14/72588.html (accessed May 6, 2008).

38. Zhang Wenhe, "Chinese Magazine Industry: Clothes Horse for Global Fashion Brands," *Rising East Online,* http://www.uel.ac.uk/risingeast/archive04/essays/wenhe.htm (accessed August 3, 2007).

39. Hou, "Vogue jinru zhongguo, zhongguo shishang zazhi chongxin xipai?"

40. Hua Shaojun, "Ruili: Bansui nvren de mei yige jieduan" [Rayli: Accompanying Women at Every Stage of Life], *China Today* 53, 8 (2004), 34–35.

41. According to the exchange rate at as of May 7, 2008, 1 USD = 6.99 CNY, http://www.xe.com/ucc (accessed May 7, 2008).

42. *ELLE* 1 (2008), p. 44.

43. Su Mang, "Yige zazhi yu yige jieceng de dangsheng" [The Birth of a Magazine and a Class], Su Mang's Blog, posted on February 12, 2008, http://blog.sina.com.cn/s/blog_476bf06001008hiy.html (accessed May 7, 2008).

44. Ibid.

45. James Borton, "Magazine Licensing Red-Hot in China," *Asia Times Online,* December 16, 2004, http://www.atimes.com/atimes/China/FL16Ad01.html (accessed August 3, 2007).

46. Hou, "Vogue jinru zhongguo, zhongguo shishang zazhi chongxin xipai?"

47. Ibid.

48. Dai Jingting, "Shishang de yuwang: *Vogue*" [The Desire for Fashion: *Vogue*], *Zhongguo xinwen zhoukan* [China News Weekly], September 12, 2005, http://www.chinanewsweek.com.cn/2005–09–19/1/6350.html (accessed April 24, 2008).

49. *Chuanmei shixian* [Media Vision], January 18, 2007, http://media.people.com.cn/GB/40699/5302599.html (accessed May 7, 2008).

50. "China Becomes Biggest Net Nation," BBC, July 28, 2008, http://news.bbc.co.uk/2/hi/technology/7528396.stm (accessed August 6, 2008).


## 5. Importing Fashion Icons

1. Song Xiangrui, "Zhongyang dianshitai yu gangtai gexing" [CCTV and Star Singers from Hong Kong and Taiwan], *Journal of the Wuhan Conservatory of Music* 4 (2007): 21.

2. Ibid., 22.

3. Wu Yongyi, ed., *Zenyang jianbie huangse gequ* [How to Distinguish Yellow Songs], Editorial Department of People's Music (Beijing: People's Music Publishing House, 1982), 1.

4. Ibid., 20–24.

5. Ibid., 9.

6. Song Xiangrui, "Zhongyang dianshitai yu gangtai gexing," 103.

7. Ibid., 15.

8. Ibid., 107.

9. Bai Liping, "Xin shiqi woguo liuxing yinyue de fazhan gaikuang" [An Overview of the Development of Pop Music in Our Country in the New Era], *Yishu yanjiu* [Art Research] 1 (2008): 64–65.

10. Zha Jianying, *Bashi niandai fangtan lu* [Interviews: The 1980s] (Beijing: Sanlian Shudian, 2006), 148.

11. Ibid., 150.

12. Wu Yongyi, ed., *Zenyang jianbie huangse gequ,* 58.

13. Charles Foran, "Red Scare," *GQ,* June 2000, 123.

14. Huang Liaoyuan, ed., *Shinian—1986–1996 zhongguo liuxing yinyue jishi* [Ten Years—1986–1996 a Chronic of Chinese Pop Music] (Beijing: Zhongguo Dianying Chubanshe, 1997), 119.

15. Tie Cheng, "Dalu gexing, ni zenme le?" [Mainland Star Singers, What Happened to You?] *Yinxiang shijie* [Audio and Video World] 8 (1990), cited in Huang Liaoyuan et al., *Shinian—1986–1996 zhongguo liuxing yinyue jishi* [Ten Years—1986–1996 a Record of Chinese Pop Music] (Beijing: Zhongguo Dianying Chubanshe, 1997), 36–37.

16. Jin Zhaojun, "1994—zhongguo liuxing yinyue de jushi he youhuan" [1994—The Situation and Obstacles of Chinese Pop Music], *Zhongyang yinyue xueyuan xuebao* [Journal of the Central Conservatory of Music] 4 (1994): 82–87.

17. Huang et al., *Shinian—1986–1996 zhongguo liuxing yinyue jishi,* 402, 407.

18. Xiaoquan, "Mingxing zhi yi xi hua duanchang" [Pros and Cons of the Star System], *Yinxiang shijie* [Audio and Video World] 4 (1992), cited in Huang

Liaoyuan et al., *Shinian—1986–1996 zhongguo liuxing yinyue jishi* [Ten Years—1986–1996 a Record of Chinese Pop Music] (Beijing: Zhongguo Dianying Chubanshe, 1997), 100.

19. Yang Lin, "Nanhai tuanti hong sannian shi guilv" [Boy Bands Being Popular for Three Years Is Law], *Beifang yinyue* [Northern Music] 6 (2007): 60.

20. Ibid.

21. Richard Corliss, "Cantopop Kingdom," *Time,* September 15, 2001, http://www.time.com/time/magazine/article/0,9171,1000778–1,00.html (accessed June 30, 2008).

22. Guinness World Records, March 2000, http://web.archive.org/web/20021023184715/http://www.guinnessworldrecords.com/content_pages/record.asp?recordid=54458 (accessed June 23, 2008).

23. Pan Wei, " 'Linglei' de Wang Fei" [Strange Faye Wong], *Tianya* [Frontiers] 1 (2002), 180–86.

24. Ibid.

25. *Next Magazine,* October 25, 2001, 607.

26. Kate Drake, "The Elvis Factor: Big King, Little King," *Time,* March 3, 2003, http://www.time.com/time/asia/covers/501030303/elvis.html (accessed July 1, 2008).

27. Ibid.

28. Susan Jakes, "Li Yunchun Loved for Being Herself," *Time,* October 10, 2005, http://www.time.com/time/asia/2005/heroes/li_yuchun.html (accessed July 1, 2008).

29. Ibid.

30. Xu Liangen, "Ha ri tanyuan" [A Study of the Origin of the Japan Craze], *Yuwen zhishi* [Language and Literature] 12 (2003): 22.

31. Yang Fan, "Kan wo zhongguoren bian bian bian: 25 nian liuxing quan jilu" [Witness the Changes in Chinese: A Complete Record of Fashion over 25 Years], *Wenhui Weekly,* posted July 23, 2004, http://www.xici.net/b329546/d21189861.htm (accessed May 17, 2009).

32. Sun Zhongmin, "Ha han ha ri daodi ha shenme?" [What Are the Korea and Japan Crazes About?], *Zhiye jishu jiaoyu* [Professional Technology Education] 5 (2005): 28–31.

33. Ibid.

34. Li Minzi, "Hanliu: Dazhong wenhua de qiangjin zhi feng" [Korean Wave: A Strong Wind in Pop Culture], *Baike zhishi* [Encyclopedic Knowledge] 12 (2004): 48–49.

35. Ibid.

36. Sun Zhongmin, "Ha han ha ri daodi ha shenme?" [What Are the Korea and Japan Crazes About?]

37. Ibid.

38. Ibid.

39. Xinhuanet.com, December 6, 2005, http://news.xinhuanet.com/video/2005–12/06/content_3884433.htm (accessed July 6, 2008).

## 6. Reinvented Identity

1. William C. Kirby, foreword to *Chinese Nationalism in Perspective: Historical and Recent Cases* (Westport, CT: Greenwood Press, 2001), foreword.

2. Ibid.

3. Bao Mingxin et al., *Zhongguo qipao* [Chinese *Qipao*] (Shanghai: Shanghai Wenhua Chubanshe, 1998), 2.

4. Chiung-fang Chang, "After a Fashion: The Search for Modern Chinese Clothing," *Taiwan Panorama* 8 (1997): 52.

5. Jennifer Craik expressed similar views on clothes as a weapon in the struggle between colonizers and colonized. See *The Face of Fashion: Cultural Studies in Fashion* (London: Routledge, 1994), 27.

6. Lei Shi, "Jindai Shanghai fushi yanjiu ji Shanghai shi danan guan de xiangguan ziliao" [Study of Shanghai Clothing and Accessories in Modern Times and Related Materials from the Shanghai Municipal Archives], *Danan yu shixue* [Archives and History] 01 (2001): 74–78.

7. Huaibai Huang, "Tan ouhua" [Discussing Westernization], *Shenbao,* August 11, 1934, 20.

8. Lei Shi, "Jindai shanghai fushi yanjiu."

9. Antonia Finnane, "What Should Chinese Women Wear?: A National Problem," *Modern China* 22, no. 2 (1996): 99–131.

10. Zhaohui Cai, "Qian yi guanggao de shiliao jiazhi—yi shenbao guanggao wei li" [Brief Discussion of the Historical Value of Advertisements—an Example From Shenbao], *Xinjiang shehui kexue* [Xinjiang Sociology] 2 (2006): 104–9.

11. Shupeng Jing, "25 nian lai zhongguo ge da duhui zhuangshi tan" [25 Years of Discussions of Adornment in Large Chinese Cities] in *Xianshi gongsi 25 zhounian jinian ce* [The 25-Year Album of the Xianshi Firm], ed. Yingbao Ma (Xianshi Firm, 1924). *Shanghai Puck* also discussed three types of fashionably dressed women. See *Shanghai Puck* 1, no. 4 (Dec. 1918): 22.

12. Ellen Johnston Laing, "Visual Evidence for the Evolution of 'Politically Correct' Dress for Women in Early Twentieth Century Shanghai," *Nan nv* 5, no. 1 (2003): 69–114.

13. Bian Xiangyang, "Shanghai's Fashion during the Late Qing Dynasty Period," *Journal of Dong Hua University* 27, no. 5 (October 2001): 26–32.

14. John Vollmer, *Ruling from the Dragon Throne: Costume of the Qing Dynasty (1644–1911)* (Berkeley: Ten Speed Press, 2002), 132.

15. Ellen Johnston Laing, "Visual Evidence."

16. See similar views in Bao Mingxin et al., *Zhongguo qipao,* 2.

17. Bao Mingxin et al., *Zhongguo qipao,* 5. Also, Yan Xue, ed., *Shishang bainian: 20 shiji zhongguo fuzhuang* [A Century of Fashion: Chinese Dress in the Twentieth Century] (Hangzhou: Zhongguo Meishu Xueyue Chubanshe, 2004), 35.

18. Eileen Chang, "A Chronicle of Changing Clothes," trans. Andrew F. Jones, *Positions* 11, no. 2 (2003): 435; Finnane, "What Should Chinese Women Wear?," 109.

19. Bao Mingxin, *Jindai zhongguo nvzhuang shilu* [A Record of Chinese Women's Wear in Modern Times] (Shanghai: Dong Hua Daxue Chubanshe, 2004), 196.

20. Eileen Chang, "A Chronicle of Changing Clothes," trans. Andrew F. Jones, *Positions* 11, no. 2 (2003): 427–41.

21. Bao Mingxin et al., *Zhongguo qipao,* 39.

22. Ibid., 46.

23. Hazel Clark, *The Cheongsam* (New York: Oxford University Press, 2000), 24–25.

24. Finnane, "What Should Chinese Women Wear?"

25. Z. Li, "Funv ai chuan qipao, hebi xincunyuji" [Women Like to Wear the *Qipao:* There Is No Need to Fear], *Xinmin Evening News,* July 11, 1983.

26. Clark, *The Cheongsam,* 57.

27. Valerie Steele and John Major, *China Chic: East Meets West* (New Haven: Yale University Press, 1999), 69.

28. Vivienne Tam and Martha Huang, *China Chic* (New York: HarperCollins, 2000), 274.

29. See *Shanghai Style* 5 (1996), 13.

30. Wu Juanjuan, "Han Bridal Dress," in *The Berg Encyclopedia of World Dress and Fashion,* ed. Joanne B. Eicher, Vol. 6, *East Asia,* ed. John E. Vollmer (Oxford: Berg, forthcoming).

31. Kai Robert Worrell, "Branding from the Product Out: How to Connect with Chinese Consumers" (lecture, Minnesota Chapter of the American Marketing Association, Minneapolis, July 17, 2008).

32. Acosta, "Wo zancheng dizhi jilefu" [I Support Boycotting Carrefour], *Jidi yangguang* blog, posted April 16, 2008, http://blog.sina.com.cn/s/blog_56cca78401009eir.html (accessed July 19, 2008).

33. *Shanghai fuzhuang fushi hangye nianjian* [Shanghai Apparel and Accessories Industry Yearbook] (Shanghai: Dong Hua Daxue Chubanshe, 2003), 38.

34. Ibid.

35. Hu Yue, "Tangzhuang de ganga" [Embarrassed Status of the Tang-Style Jacket], *Art Observation* 6 (2003), 87.

36. Zhou Xing, "Xin tangzhuang, hanfu, he hanfu yundong" [New Tang-Style Jacket, Han Chinese Dress and Its Movement], *Kaifang shidai* [Open Times] 3 (2008): 125–40.

37. Hu Yue, "Tangzhuang de ganga," 37.

38. Steele and Major, *China Chic: East Meets West,* 55.

## 7. The Evolution of the Fashion Industry

1. Scribes of the Orient, "Wang Wei: China's First Fashion Design Star?" http://www.scribesoftheorient.com/soto/library/2008/march/article_04_032008.html (accessed August 6, 2008).

2. Xinhuanet, October 15, 2007, http://news.xinhuanet.com/newscenter/2007–10/15/content_6883381.htm (accessed July 25, 2008).

3. Hu Zongxiao and Lu Lu, "Fuzhuang hangye de gaikuang" [A Survey of the Apparel Industry], in *Zhongguo fuzhuang dadian* [Chinese Clothing Encyclopaedia] (Shanghai: Wenhui Chubanshe, 1999), 26–33.

4. "Overcoming the Challenge of Clothing Eight Hundred Million People," *People's Daily,* May 25, 1978.

5. *Shanghai Fashion Times,* September 16, 1989, section 2.

6. Leng Yun, *Duihua zhongguo sandai shizhuang sheji shi* [Conversations with Three Generations of Chinese Fashion Designers] (Shanghai: Shanghai Shudian Chubanshe, 2005), 4–32.

7. Ibid.

8. Ibid.

9. Wang Zengjing, foreword to *20 shiji zhongguo fuzhuang sheji shi ziji* [The Footprint of Chinese Fashion Designers in the Twentieth Century], by Yuan Jieying (Shenyang: Liaoning Chubanshe, 1999).

10. Ibid.

11. Bao Mingxin, Jiang Zhiwei, and Cheng Rong, *Zhongguo mingshi shizhuang jianshang cidian* [Dictionary of Famous Chinese Fashion Designers] (Shanghai: Shanghai Jiaotong Daxue Chubanshe, 1993), 189–90.

12. Ibid.

13. Bao et al., *Zhongguo mingshi shizhuang jianshang cidian,* 118–19.

14. *Shanghai Style* 6 (2005), 46.

15. Yin Yan, "Women yu guoji hua jiaoyu, guoji ji sheji shi jiegui de juli you duoyuan" [How Far Are We from International Education and World-Class Designers], *Shanghai Style* 12 (2003), 102–3.

16. Scribes of the Orient, "Wang Wei: China's First Fashion Design Star?"

17. Yin, "Women yu guoji hua jiaoyu, guoji ji sheji shi jiegui de juli you duoyuan," 102–3.

18. Leng Yun, *Duihua zhongguo sandai shizhuang sheji shi,* 4–32.

19. Lise Skov, "Fashion-Nation: A Japanese Globalization Experience and a Hong Kong Dilemma," in *Re-Orienting Fashion,* ed. Sandra Niessen, Ann Marie Leshkowich, and Carla Jones (Oxford: Berg, 2003), 215.

20. Wang Wei, conversation with the author, January 2007, Shanghai.

21. Bao et al., *Zhongguo mingshi shizhuang jianshang cidian,* 17–18.

22. Ibid., 113–14.

23. Ibid., 50–51.

24. Donghua University Web site, http://zs.dhu.edu.cn/latestNews_one.aspx?newid=235 (accessed July 30, 2008).

25. Donghua University Website, http://zs.dhu.edu.cn/latestNews_one.aspx?newid=235 and http://zs.dhu.edu.cn/latestNews_one.aspx?newid=482 (accessed July 30, 2008).

26. Shanghai daxue—bali guoji shizhuang yishu xueyuan [Shanghai University—Paris International Institute of Fashion and Art] Web site, http://modart.cn/article.php?r_id=299 (accessed August 2, 2008).

27. IFA Paris Shanghai Web site, http://www.025edu.com/ifa/ (accessed August 2, 2008).

28. Bao Mingxin, "Fushi wenhua de fanrong shi fuzhuang ye tengda de zhongyao beijing" [A Thriving Apparel Culture Is an Important Foundation of the Prosperity of the Apparel Industry], *Shanghai Style* 2 (1990), 6.

29. Yuniya Kawamura, *Fashion-ology* (Oxford: Berg, 2005), 52, 60.

30. Cited in David Gilbert, "From Paris to Shanghai," in *Fashion's World Cities,* ed. Christopher Breward and David Gilbert (Oxford: Berg, 2006), 3.

31. *Shanghai Apparel Yearbook* (1985): 17.

32. Ibid., 19.

33. Ibid., 6. See also Li, *20 Shiji 80 Niandai Shanghai Funv Fushi Liuxing,* 63.

34. Li, *20 Shiji 80 Niandai Shanghai Funv Fushi Liuxing,* 63.

35. *China Textile News* 49 (1986).

36. *Fashion* 4 (1993), 34.

37. Hu Zongxiao, Wu Jiangping, and Lu Lu, "Guoji guonei zhongda fuzhuang hangye huodong ji fuzhuang hangye xiehui jianjie" [A Brief Review of International and National Major Events and Associations in the Apparel Industry] in *Zhongguo fuzhuang dadian* [Chinese Clothing Encyclopaedia] (Shanghai: Wenhui Chubanshe, 1999), 36–42.

38. See the official Web site, http://www.cnga.org.cn/fzxh3/1xhjs_1xhjj.asp (accessed August 2, 2008).

39. Sheryl Wudunn, "Out There: Beijing; The Great Leap on the Runway," *New York Times,* May 23, 1993.

40. Suzy Menkes, "In Beijing, a Sleeping Dragon of Fashion Awakens," *International Herald Tribune,* May 18, 1993.

41. See the official Web site, http://www.chiconline.com.cn/profile/intro.aspx (accessed August 2, 2008).

42. Liu Ruipu, "The End of Brother Cup," *Shizhuang guancha* [Fashion Observation] 7 (2002): 6.

43. Wu Jianping, "Guoji guonei fuzhuang zhuming shejishi jianjie" [A Brief Introduction to International and Domestic Famous Fashion Designers] in *Zhongguo fuzhuang dadian* [Chinese Clothing Encyclopaedia] (Wenhui Chubanshe, 1999), 70.

44. Chen Jian, "Sheji dasai de taiqian muhou" [Ins and Outs of Design Competitions], *Shanghai Style* 1 (1999), 38–39.

45. Valery M. Garrett, *Chinese Clothing: An Illustrated Guide* (New York: Oxford University Press, 1994), 107.

46. See "Liu Yang" in *Design China* by the China Fashion Designers Association (Beijing: Zhongguo Fangzhi Chubanshe, 2007), 13.

47. Ibid.

48. Bao Mingxin, "Zuihou de jianke" [The Last Swordsman], *Fashion* 6 (1998), 54.

49. Sun Xinghua, "Shejishi de charisma" [Fashion Designer's Charisma], *Shanghai Style* 5 (2003), 18–19.

50. Bao et al., *Zhongguo mingshi shizhuang jianshang cidian,* 77.

51. Liu Yang, in a written interview with the author, January 27, 2007.

52. Bao et al., *Zhongguo mingshi shizhuang jianshang cidian,* 86–97.

53. *Renmin wang* [People's Web Site], http://chinese.people.com.cn/GB/42314/4813625.html, (accessed August 12, 2008).

54. *Shanghai Style* 6 (2005), 45.

55. *Zhongguo fuzhuag wang* [China Garment Web Site], http://www.efu.com.cn/data/2005/2005–07–08/111137.shtml (accessed August 12, 2008).

56. Ibid.

57. *Fashion* 5 (2000), 86.

58. Wang Xinyuan, conversation with the author, January 11, 2007, Shanghai.

59. Bian Xiangyang, "Dang shejijie ye you waiyuan de shihou," *Shanghai Style* 6 (1997), 30–31.

60. David Barboza, "Chen Yifei, 59, Painter and Entrepreneur, Dies," *New York Times,* April 14, 2005.

61. Wu Juanjuan, "Chen Yifei pukai shizhuang juan" [Chen Yifei and His Fashion Business], *Mode* 1 (1998).

62. Wang Wei, conversation with the author, January, 2007, Shanghai.

63. Wang Yiyang, conversation with the author, January 9, 2007, Shanghai.

64. Ying Ye, "Wang Yiyang: Sheji shi xianshi de jingzi" [Wang Yiyang: Design Mirrors Reality], *Economic Observer,* March 19, 2007, http://www.eeo.com.cn/Business_lifes/lifestyle/2007/03/19/49971.html (accessed August 13, 2008).

65. Zhang Da, conversation with the author, August 14, 2008.

66. Ibid., June 28, 2007.

67. Ibid., December 1, 2007.

68. Bao et al., *Zhongguo mingshi shizhuang jianshang cidian,* 3–4.

69. Quoted in Xiaoping Li, "Fashioning the Body in Post-Mao China," in *Consuming Fashion: Adorning the Transnational Body,* ed. Anne Brydon and Sandra Niessen (Oxford: Berg, 1998), 78.

70. China Radio International, "Ji Wenbo—First Chinese Designer to Shine Milan Fashion Week," http://english.cri.cn/4026/2007/10/12/167@283233.htm (accessed August 15, 2008).

71. Ibid.

72. Valerie Steele and John Major, *China Chic: East Meets West* (New Haven: Yale University Press, 1999), 96.

73. Victoria and Albert Museum Web site, http://www.vam.ac.uk/collections/fashion/fashion_motion/ma_ke/index.html (accessed August 15, 2008).

74. Fashion Trend Digest Web site, http://www.fashiontrenddigest.com/digest_fn.asp?ID=983&s=remarks (accessed August 16, 2008).

75. See "Ma Ke," in *Design China,* China Fashion Designers Association (Zhongguo Fangzhi Chubanshe, 2007), 169.

76. Xu Wenyuan, "Shizhuang biaoyan dui de kailuren—tiesheng laoren" [Fashion Modeling Team Pioneer—Elder Tiesheng], *Shanghai yishujia* [Shanghai Artists] 3 (1998): 62–64.

77. *Xinmin Evening News,* August 8, 1982, section 4.

78. Wu Juanjuan, ed., *Bao Mingxin jiedu shizhuang* [Bao Mingxin Decoding Fashion] (Shanghai: Xuelin Chubanshe, 1999), 28.

79. Bian Xiangyang, ed., *Shanghai jin xiandai fuzhuang yishu shi* [History of Dress and Art in Modern Shanghai] (Donghua Daxue Chubanshe, forthcoming, 2009).

80. Xu, "Shizhuang biaoyan dui de kailuren—tiesheng laoren," 62–64.

81. Ibid.

82. *Xinmin Evening News,* August 8, 1982, section 4.

83. Wu, *Bao Mingxin jiedu shizhuang,* 17.

84. *Fashion* 3 (1992), 8.

85. Donghua University's 2008 catalogue, http://zs.dhu.edu.cn/upload/00428–001.doc (accessed August 19, 2008).

86. James Sterngold, "China in High Heels, a Wobbly School for Models," *New York Times,* August 8, 1990.

87. Bruce Shu, "Chinese Teens Train to Conquer Fashion World," *Agence France-Presse,* November 1, 1991.

88. Wu, *Bao Mingxin jiedu shizhuang,* 19.

89. Song Wenwen, "Zhang Jian—zai 'mei de shijie li' benzou" [Zhang Jian—Walking in the World of Beauty], *Fashion* 3 (1999), 10–11.

90. Chen Jian, "Guanyu Shanghai mote ye de yousi" [Worries about the Modeling Profession in Shanghai], *Shanghai Style* 6 (1998), 40–41.

91. Wu, *Bao Mingxin jiedu shizhuang,* 24–25.

92. See *Fashion* 8 (2001), 144–45.

93. Sun Xinghua and Shen Mu, "Zhonngguo zuijia zhiye mote quanbu chuzi xinsilu, 17 jia mote jingji gongsi jiti tuichu pingxuan yishi kangyi" [All of China's Best Professional Models Were from the New Silk Road, 17 Models Agencies Dropped Out of the Competition in Protest], *Shanghai Fashion Times,* December 30, 2000.

94. Ibid.

95. *Fashion* 8 (2001), 144–45.

96. Sheryl WuDunn, "Out There: Beijing; the Great Leap on the Runway," *New York Times,* May 23, 1993.

97. *Fashion* 8 (2001), 144–45.

98. Coe Chiang, "Shishang tianshi zai niuyue" [Fashion Angle in New York], *Fashion* 1 (2001), 62.

99. Zhu Guoliang, "Shijie mingmo Li Xin jiang yu guicai daoyan kunding hezuo zhongguo gongfu" [World Famous Model Li Xin Will Work with Maverick Director Quentin], *Popular Cinema* 9 (2005), 58–59.

100. Cheng Hong, "Li Fang: John Galliano zui xihuan de zhongguo mote" [Li Fang: John Galliano's Favorite Chinese Model], *Fashion* 11 (2001), 18–19.

101. Ibid.

102. Shao Hui, "Lv Yan yinxiang" [Impressions of Lv Yan], *Fashion* 6 (2002), 56–59.

103. Ibid.

104. *Fashion* 2 (2002), 62–63.

105. Du Juan's Bio, IMG Models Web site, http://portfoliopad.com/images/9121/40653/bio/Du%20Juan%20bio.pdf (accessed September 9, 2008).

106. Ibid.

## 8. Importing Dreams of Luxury

1. Dana Thomas, *Deluxe: How Luxury Lost Its Luster* (New York: Penguin Press, 2007), 300.

2. *China Daily* Web site, "China to Be Top Luxury Goods Consumer," posted December 12, 2005, http://www.chinadaily.com.cn/english/doc/2005–12/12/content_502708.htm (accessed September 25, 2008).

3. Su Mang's Blog, "Yiben zahi yu yige jieceng de dangsheng" [The Birth of a Magazine and a Class], posted February 12, 2008, http://blog.sina.com.cn/s/blog_476bf06001008hiy.html (accessed September 16, 2008).

4. Joan Lebold Cohen and Jerome Alan Cohen, *China Today*, 2nd ed. (New York: Abrams, 1980), 24.

5. Zha Jianying, *Bashi niandai fangtan lu* [Interviews: The 1980s] (Beijing: Sanlian Shudian, 2006), 440.

6. Pierre Cardin Website, http://www.pierrecardin.com/DInternational/chinagb.htm (accessed September 13, 2008).

7. Wang Weiming, "Shizhuang: Yige shidai de xinhao" [Fashion: A Sign of the Times], *Shanghai Style* 1 (1994), 10–11.

8. Huang Ai Dongxin, "Mingpai" [Famous Brands], *Shanghai Style* 5 (1998), 40.

9. Ben Jacklet, "Nike's Great Leap," *Oregon Business*, August 2008, http://www.oregonbusiness.com/.docs/_sid/271e6074496c2c8afdb1f0c62bb8a8fa/action/detail/rid/33660/pg/10516 (accessed September 16, 2008).

10. Ibid.

11. Fondation Pierre Berge and Yves Saint Laurent Web site, "Palace of Fine Arts, Beijing," http://www.fondation-pb-ysl.net/site/Art-314.html (accessed September 16, 2008).

12. Nien Cheng, *Life and Death in Shanghai* (New York: Grove Press, 1986), 524–25.

13. Lisa Movius, "Armani's China Tour: New Shanghai Flagship Ignites Expansion Drive," *Women's Wear Daily,* April 21, 2004, http://www.movius.us/articles/wwd-armani.html (accessed September 13, 2008).

14. Wang Weiming, "Jingshen queshi, shui neng gei chengshi wenhua zhuru xin de huoli" [Lacking Spirit: Who Could Give City Culture New Energy?], *Shanghai Style* 2 (1995), 12–13.

15. Lisa Movius, "Armani's China Tour."

16. Fan Bing, "Yige nvren gai bei ji shuang xie" [How Many Pairs of Shoes Should a Woman Prepare], *Shanghai Style* 1 (1999), 46–47.

17. Thomas, *Deluxe,* 304.

18. Jiang Yifeng, "Yuanzheng, yizuo chengshi yu yilei pinpai" [Expedition, a City and a Type of Brand], *Shanghai Style,* 3 (1996), 8–9.

19. Ibid.

20. Josephine Bow, "In Huge China Market, Early Arrivals Zegna and Hugo Boss Make Gains," *DNR* 29, January 4, 1999, 24.

21. Lisa Movius, "Zegna Continues China Push," *DNR,* February 14, 2005, 36.

22. Movius, "Armani's China Tour."

23. Thomas, *Deluxe,* 301.

24. Movius, "Armani's China Tour."

25. Ibid.

26. Jiang Feng, "Wan fuzhuang de" [Playing at Fashion], *Shanghai Style* 1 (1994), 12–13.

27. Zhao Xia, "Zou jin Beijing fuhao julebu" [A Close Look at Beijing's Rich Man Clubs], *China Business Times,* November 1, 2006.

28. Bing, "Yige nvren gai bei ji shuang xie," 46–47.

29. Clay Chandler, Annie Wang, and Dahong Zhang, "China Deluxe Armani, Mercedes, Dior, Cartier—Luxury Brands Are Rushing into China's Red-Hot Market," *Fortune,* July 26, 2004.

30. Ibid.

31. Ka Fei, "Mingpai" [Famous Brands], *Shanghai Style* 5 (1998), 40.

32. The Auto Channel, "Bentley Sales in China Rose 93 Percent in 2007," http://www.theautochannel.com/news/2008/02/18/077930.html (accessed January 26, 2009).

33. People's Web site, "China Becomes Rolls-Royce's Largest Asian market," posted December 15, 2006, http://english.peopledaily.com.cn/200612/15/eng2006 1215_332651.html (accessed January 26, 2009).

34. *China Daily,* posted October 12, 2006, http://www.chinadaily.com.cn/city life/2006–10/12/content_707041.htm (accessed October 15, 2008).

35. Yvonne Kong, "Seeking to Understand China Market for Luxury Consumption," Beijing International MBA at Peking University, Lecture and Forum section, posted November 20, 2007, http://en.bimba.edu.cn/article.asp?articleid=2740 (accessed September 23, 2008).

36. Jess Cartner-Morley, "From Florence to Shanghai, Ferragamo Eyes a Make-over," *The Guardian,* March 29, 2008, http://www.guardian.co.uk/lifeandstyle/2008/mar/29/fashion.italy (accessed September 23, 2008).

37. Alexandra Seno, "Shoppers from the Mainland Get Red Carpet in Hong Kong: Buying Luxury: 'An Exceptional Moment,'" *International Herald Tribune,* December 5, 2002, http://www.iht.com/articles/2002/12/05/rchine_ed2_.php (accessed September 25, 2008).

38. Shu-Ching Jean Chen, "U.S. Opens Its Arms to Chinese Tourists," *Forbes,* December 12, 2007, http://www.forbes.com/markets/2007/12/12/china-us-tourism-markets-econ-cx_jc_1212markets01.html (accessed September 25, 2008).

39. Ibid.

40. Thomas, *Deluxe,* 300.

41. Lisa Movius, "China's Luxury Rush: Expanding Vuitton Shows Market's Growth," *Women's Wear Daily,* December 29, 2005, http://www.movius.us/articles/WWD-LVBJ.html (accessed September 23, 2008).

42. Everyzing Web site, "On Point with Tom Ashbrook Podcast—City Life with Hong Huang," April 23, 2008, http://search.everyzing.com/viewMedia.jsp?res=0&dedupe=1&index=73&col=en-all-public-ep&sort=rel&e=19717988&channelTitle=Oprah+&num=16&start=64&ci=39&expand=true&match=none&channel=127&bc=45&filter=1 (accessed August 2, 2008).

43. Leslie T. Chang, "China's Middle Class," *National Geographic,* May 2008, http://ngm.nationalgeographic.com/2008/05/china/middle-class/leslie-chang-text/1 (accessed September 24, 2008).

44. Kong, "Seeking to Understand China Market for Luxury Consumption."

45. "LVMH Drops Sharon Stone from Chinese Dior Ads on Quake Remark," *Los Angeles Times,* May 30, 2008.

46. Melinda Liu and Duncan Hewitt, "Rise of the Sea Turtles," *Newsweek,* August 9, 2008, http://www.newsweek.com/id/151730 (accessed September 25, 2008).

47. Chandler, Wang, and Zhang, "China Deluxe Armani, Mercedes, Dior, Cartier."

48. Ibid.

# Selected Bibliography

Ba, Jin. *Suixiang lu* [Whimsy Collection]. Beijing: Zuojia Chubanshe, 2005.

Bao, Mingxin. *Jindai zhongguo nvzhuang shilu* [A Record of Chinese Women's Wear in Modern Times]. Shanghai: Dong Hua Daxue Chubanshe, 2004.

Bao, Mingxin, Jiang Zhiwei, and Cheng Rong. *Zhongguo mingshi shizhuang jianshang cidian* [Dictionary of Famous Chinese Fashion Designers]. Shanghai: Shanghai Jiaotong Daxue Chubanshe, 1993.

Bao, Mingxin, and Ma Ni. *Shizhuang pinglun* [Fashion Criticism]. Chongqing: Xinan Shifan Daxue Chubanshe, 2002.

Bao, Mingxin, and Wu Juanjuan. *Shimao cidian* [Fashion Dictionary]. Shanghai: Shanghai Wenhua Chubanshe, 1999.

Bao, Mingxin, Wu Juanjuan, Ma Li, Yang Shu, and Wu Di. *Zhongguo qipao* [Chinese *Qipao*]. Shanghai: Shanghai Wenhua Chubanshe, 1998.

Breward, Christopher, and David Gilbert, eds. *Fashion's World Cities*. Oxford: Berg, 2006.

Brydon, Anne, and Sandra Niessen, eds. *Consuming Fashion: Adorning the Transnational Body*. Oxford: Berg, 1998.

Cheng, Nien. *Life and Death in Shanghai*. New York: Grove Press, 1986.

China Fashion Designers Association. *Design China*. Beijing: Zhongguo Fangzhi Chubanshe, 2007.

Chinese Clothing Encyclopedia Editorial Committee. *Zhongguo fuzhuang dadian* [Chinese Clothing Encyclopedia]. Shanghai: Wenhui Chubanshe, 1999.

Clark, Hazel. *The Cheongsam*. New York: Oxford University Press, 2000.

Cohen, Joan Lebold, and Jerome Alan Cohen, *China Today*. 2nd ed. New York: Harry N. Abrams, 1980.

Craik, Jennifer. *The Face of Fashion: Cultural Studies in Fashion*. London: Routledge, 1994.

Croll, Elisabeth. *Changing Identities of Chinese Women: Rhetoric, Experience and Self-Perception in Twentieth-Century China*. Hong Kong: Hong Kong University Press, 1995.

Finnane, Antonia. *Changing Clothes in China: Fashion, History, Nation*. New York: Columbia University Press, 2008.

Garrett, Valery M. *Chinese Clothing: An Illustrated Guide*. New York: Oxford University Press, 1994.

Hong, Huang. *Wo de fei zhengchang shenghuo* [My Abnormal Life]. Beijing: Zhong-guo Youyi Chuban Gongsi, 2007.

Honig, Emily. *Personal Voices: Chinese Women in the 1980's.* Stanford, CA: Stanford University Press, 1988.

Hu, Zongxiao, and Lu Lu. "Fuzhuang hangye de gaikuang" [A Survey of the Apparel Industry]. In *Zhongguo fuzhuang dadian* [Chinese Clothing Encyclopedia]. Shanghai: Wenhui Chubanshe, 1999.

Kawamura, Yuniya. *Fashion-ology.* Oxford: Berg, 2005.

Leng, Yun. *Duihua zhongguo sandai shizhuang sheji shi* [Conversations with Three Generations of Chinese Fashion Designers]. Shanghai: Shanghai Shudian Chubanshe, 2005.

Link, Perry, Richard P. Madsen, and Paul G. Pickowicz, eds. *Popular China: Unofficial Culture in a Globalizing Society.* Lanham, MD: Rowman & Littlefield, 2002.

Ma, Licheng, and Ling Zhijun. *Jiaofeng: Dangdai zhongguo sanci sixiang jiefang shilu* [Crossed Swords: Record of the Three Mind Emancipations in Contemporary China]. Beijing: Jinri Zhongguo Chubanshe, 1998.

MacFarquhar, Roderick, and Michael Schoenhals. *Mao's Last Revolution.* Cambridge, MA: Belknap/Harvard University Press, 2006.

Niessen, Sandra, Ann Marie Leshkowich, and Carla Jones, eds. *Re-Orienting Fashion.* Oxford: Berg, 2003.

Spence, Jonathan D. *The Search for Modern China.* New York: Norton, 1991.

Steele, Valerie. *Paris Fashion.* 2nd ed. Oxford: Berg, 1998.

Steele, Valerie, and John Major. *China Chic: East Meets West.* New Haven: Yale University Press, 1999.

Su Su, *Qianshi jinsheng* [Life Then, Life Now]. Shanghai: Shanghai Yuandong Chubanshe, 1996.

Tam, Vivienne, and Martha Huang. *China Chic.* New York: HarperCollins, 2000.

Thomas, Dana. *Deluxe: How Luxury Lost Its Luster.* New York: Penguin Press, 2007.

Vollmer, John. *Ruling from the Dragon Throne: Costume of the Qing Dynasty (1644–1911).* Berkeley: Ten Speed Press, 2002.

Wei, C. X. George, and Liu Xiaoyuan, eds. *Chinese Nationalism in Perspective: Historical and Recent Cases.* Westport, CT: Greenwood Press, 2001.

Wilson, Elizabeth. *Adorned in Dreams: Fashion and Modernity.* New Jersey: Rutgers University Press, 2003.

Wu, Juanjuan, ed. *Bao Mingxin jiedu shizhuang* [Bao Mingxin Decoding Fashion]. Shanghai: Xuelin Chubanshe, 1999.

Wu, Yongyi, ed. *Zenyang jianbie huangse gequ* [How to Distinguish Yellow Songs]. Editorial Department of People's Music. Beijing: People's Music Publishing House, 1982.

Xue, Yan, ed. *Shishang bainian: 20 shiji zhongguo fuzhuang* [A Century of Fashion: Chinese Dress in the Twentieth Century]. Hangzhou: Zhongguo Meishu Xueyuan Chubanshe, 2004.

Yu, Lei. *Wuo dongle yule quan—yige yuji qinli de yule shijian* [I Touched the Entertainment Circle—Incidents in the Entertainment Industry Experienced by an Entertainment Journalist]. Nanchang: 21 Shiji Chubanshe, 2004.

Yuan, Jieying. *20 shiji zhongguo fuzhuang sheji shi ziji* [The Footprint of Chinese Fashion Designers in the Twentieth Century]. Shenyang: Liaoning Chubanshe, 1999.

Zha, Jianying. *Bashi niandai fangtan lu* [Interviews: The 1980s]. Beijing: Sanlian Shudian, 2006.

Zha, Jianying. *China Pop: How Soap Operas, Tabloids, and Bestsellers Are Transforming a Culture.* New York: New Press, 1995.

Zhang, Jingqiong. *Xifu dongjian—20 shiji zhongwai fushi jiaoliu shi* [Western Dress Migrates to the East—Exchange of Chinese and Foreign Dress in the Twentieth Century]. Hehui: Anhui Meishu Chubanshe, 2002.

# Index